The Book
of Legal
Anecdotes

Peter Hay

Facts On File®
New York · Oxford

The Book of Legal Anecdotes

Copyright © 1989 by Peter Hay

Library of Congress Cataloging-in-Publication Data

Hay, Peter
    The book of legal anecdotes / Peter Hay.
       p. cm.
    Bibliography: p.
    Includes index.
    ISBN 0-8160-1523-6
    1. Law—Anecdotes. I. Title.
K183.H39 1989
340—dc19 88-19925

British CIP data available on request

Printed in the United States of America

10 9 8 7 6 5 4 3 2 1

For John Hogarth —
visionary, pragmatist,
and teacher of the law —
in memory of the days
when we were developing
justice together,
and with present friendship,
affection, and admiration.

Books by Peter Hay

Contents

ACKNOWLEDGMENTS

My interest in the law and association with the legal profession dates back to the mid-1970s, when I worked two years as director of public programs for the Justice Development Commission in British Columbia. I learned a great deal of respect for the law by working with many fine and caring professionals in the Canadian justice system, in particular with David Vickers, then the deputy attorney general of B.C., and my friend John Hogarth, then chairman of the B.C. Police Commission, and now professor of law at the University of British Columbia. I also recall with special warmth many of my coworkers, Loy Leland, Marilyn Johnson, and Anna Terrana among many others.

I am indebted to my friend Herbert Shore for drawing to my attention the Twentieth Festival of American Folklife (1986), which presented a joint program by the American Trial Lawyers and the Folklife Programs of the Smithsonian Institution on lawyers as storytellers. I am grateful for tapes provided by Marion Goetz, media director of the Association of American Trial Lawyers, for advice from Diane Parker at the Smithsonian, and of course to the participants whose stories appear in this book.

I very much appreciate advice from Robert Berring of Bault Hall, at the Law School of the University of California at Berkeley, who is editor of *Legal Reference Services Quarterly* and an expert on legal humor; from librarian Jill Sidford of the Los Angeles firm of O'Melveny and Myers; from Dallas attorney and novelist, Paul E. Coggins (including Judge Jerry Buchmeyer's book); from John Rendell of Dallas and Ned Mead in Pasadena.

Jordan D. Luttrell of Meyer Boswell Books in San Francisco, specializing in rare and scholarly books on the law, helped both personally and with his annotated catalogs. I found the catalogs from Frognal Books in London also useful.

I am grateful to many libraries: the reference staff and collections of the University of California at Los Angeles, of the University of Southern California, and especially the superb holdings of the Los Angeles County Law Library, where Basil Wilson was particularly helpful.

I have been fortunate during the past twenty years in meeting and being represented by many fine lawyers who uphold the high standards of their profession: Peter F. Buxton, Michael Donaldson, Gary Lauk, Tamara Murányi, Sidney B. Simons, and Ron Stern.

Among my friends, I wish to thank David Ambrose, Anthony Anderson, Dr. János Bak, Dr. William Cutter, Hermine Fuerst-Garcia, Paul Jarrico, Dr. Gerard Kahan, Richard Kahlenberg, Joshua Karton, Alan Mandell, Hilda Mortimer and Michael Szász.

I am indebted to my editor, Gerard Helferich, for many good suggestions, his assistant, Laurie Muchnick, and copy editor Michael Laraque for their patient help.

Finally, as always, my mother, Eva Hay, and my wife, Dorthea Atwater, have provided unfailing encouragement and concrete assistance way beyond the legal definitions of their roles.

PREFACE

The other day I was reading an article in *Newsweek* about Tom Clancy, the best-selling novelist, in which he gives birth to the casual simile that "a lawyer is just like an attack dog, only without a conscience." One of the popular jokes making the rounds recently asks why using lawyers makes for better laboratory experiments than using rats. And almost everybody knows the one about professional courtesy preferred by a shark to the overboard lawyer. This book begins by tracing back this last one to its origins as a genuine anecdote from eighteenth-century England.

The proliferation of tasteless anti-lawyer jokes has roused the concern of many in the profession. For example, P. Terry Anderlini, president of the California State Bar Association, has been on a campaign against jokes that he believes contribute to the poor public image of lawyers, reinforcing undesirable stereotypes about the profession. Other attorneys are urging their colleagues to stop spreading such jokes or walk out of the room where they are told.

There is nothing new about that poor image. Shakespeare's Jack Cade rallies his rebellious mob with the cry "The first thing we do, let's kill all the lawyers!" (*Henry VI*, Part II). And Hamlet, holding up poor Yorick's skull asks: "Why may not that be the skull of a lawyer? Where be his quiddities now, his quillets, his cases, his tenures, and his tricks?" Master Peter Pathelin, in the French medieval farce of the same title, is shown as a thief and a cheat who is treated to a dose of his own medicine. He is hired by a simple shepherd accused of sheep-stealing, whom he instructs to act dumb—literally—in the courtroom. When questioned by the judge, the shepherd replies only with "baaaa!" After winning the case, Pathelin tries to collect his fee, but the client continues to bleat. Presumably the audience enjoyed the tricking of the trickster, one of the common themes in mythology.

I hasten to point out that anecdotes have little in common with myth or jokes. They tend to be about historical figures or real people alive today, and even when their provenance is suspect, they remain true in essence. The stories may have been recorded originally because of an eccentric character or incident thought to be noteworthy at the time, but they are passed on through the centuries because of their universal application to people and situations in subsequent ages. Because of this process of distillation and conservation, the anecdotal form is particularly well matched with legal process, another of the great conservative forces providing continuity and stability to society. Common law uses precedent fundamentally in an anecdotal fashion: a specific instance, no matter how peculiar, gains authority and legal status by the simple fact that it has happened once before.

Lawyers live by the word and are constantly called on to perform acts of verbal virtuosity in order to win over a jury or judge. A trial is not only of the accused but also of the lawyer's dramatic skills. Anecdotes are essential weapons in waging their battles, as folklorist Samuel Shrager, curator of the American Trial Lawyers Program, remarked in the Smithsonian's booklet for its 1986 Festival of American Folklife:

When trial lawyers exchange stories and lore with each other, the focus is usually on their trial experiences. No part of the trial is as hedged by superstitions as jury selection, where lawyers must make snap judgments based on initial impressions and fragmentary information. They have rules-of-thumb about the attributes of the jurors they want and those they fear in a given case, and tales of disasters that resulted when someone picked for the jury turned out to be the wrong choice. Judges are a prominent conversational topic, their actions and idiosyncracies catalogued in humorous stories that also serve as practical guides for dealing with them to best advantage. Lawyers keep "book" on other lawyers, too, as athletes do on other themes. Many like to "scout" the strength and vulnerabilities of upcoming opponents by watching them in court, getting colleagues' opinions, or reviewing transcripts of their past trials, and in the competitive heat of the trial they may exploit perceived weaknesses however they can. The trials and circumstances surrounding them provide unlimited grist for "war stories," as lawyers dub accounts of their battles. Most often these are singular incidents, memorable because they distill something of the character of the vocation. They can also become full-blown chronicles that draw listeners far into the complexities of a case and the paradoxes of human conduct.

Many such singular and memorable incidents are to be found in this book. Many more are not, simply because the selection is subjective, the well is inexhaustible, and the compiler quickly runs into limits set by time, the publisher, and his own resources. It is usually at the point when I have to stop that I wish I could begin all over again. There are some important names missing, to my regret, because I could not find suitable anecdotes attached to them. More importantly, I was not compiling an alphabetical encyclopedia about famous lawyers, but more a book about the law itself. This is in line with Isaac D'Israeli's definition in his *Dissertation on Anecdotes* (1793). The father of the future prime minister criticized Dr. Johnson's dictionary definition for following the French in confining anecdote "merely to biography . . . We give anecdotes of the art as well as of the Artist; of the war as well as the General; of the nation as well as the Monarch." What I have tried to do in this volume—as in my other anecdotal books about theater and the business world—is to give an overview of a venerable and proud profession in vignettes and stories from many periods and sources. I have attempted to counterbalance the sick jokes and the negative image of lawyers by providing the best examples of classic legal humor, which is usually distinguished by verbal elegance and subtle repartee. Although it is easier to be witty at somebody's expense, in my selections cruelty is usually reserved for hanging judges or bad attorneys, while the struggles and foibles of both great and small are treated with sympathy.

I have traced the origins of colorful traditions, described quaint customs, and investigated legendary lore with the express purpose of restoring to the professions within the criminal justice system some of the rich heritage that is rightly theirs. At the same time I hope I have managed to retain the perspective of the nonspecialist reader (to whose ranks I belong), often mystified and overawed by the majestic mumbo jumbo of the law. Understanding our legal heritage is fundamental to maintaining a free society. If lawyer-bashing is on the increase, this partly reflects the anti-intellectual bias of the age: history, literacy, and persuasion by rhetoric or logic, once considered crowning accomplishments of the human mind, are in decline. In an overspecialized world, where only experts understand each other, lawyers are among the few generalists. They are perceived as needed everywhere, and consequently with their nimble minds, competitive training, and professional competence, they keep conquering ever new territories—in business, politics, and the arts. From surrogate babies, through marriage contracts, divorce settlements, transfer of property, real injury and perceived discrimination, to death and taxes, lawyers attend every significant phase of our complex life. And as surrogate warriors fighting our battles in a litigious, overregulated and consumer-conscious society, they provide convenient, if not always fair, targets when they lose for us—as they do statistically in fifty percent of all cases.

We lick our wounds, resent the costs, and forget the many fights lawyers have helped us all win in the great march toward greater equity and justice: by the drafting and passing of good legislation, the successful prosecution of criminals, by winning acquittal for the unjustly accused. The great corporations, the nonprofit organizations that lobby for change and to enhance the quality of life, modern government itself—these are all inconceivable without lawyers, many of whom are working at low salary for the public good. As Adlai Stevenson quipped once to President Kennedy, who kept raiding his Chicago law office to staff his administration: "I regret that I have but one law firm to give to my country."

Lawyers and the law are commonly criticized for being dry, cold, and inhuman. The legal process seems designed to reduce passion and compassion to an intricate game played by puppets and puppeteers. Yet much blood has been shed to win the political, civil, and human rights that we enjoy in countries governed by the rule of law. And each time a murderer is convicted, or an innocent person is acquitted by a jury of ordinary citizens, our souls are stirred. Even fighting an unjust fine in traffic court successfully can arouse our emotions, reminding us that the social contract works as it is supposed to. Behind the constantly evolving laws, drawn up and revised to suit different societies and changing times, there are also higher, much less mutable, tenets held by the vast majority of our species. We call it morality, the unwritten or higher law, and more simply—justice. More than anything, a sense of justice defines human society, whether it is called primitive or civilized, as much in the breach as in the observance. The trials of Socrates, Jesus, Galileo, and Dreyfus resonate down the ages, and continue to be dramatized on stage and screen; the principals may have turned to dust, but their principles have not.

Each time the United States Senate debates the nomination of a judge to the Supreme Court, we hear the fundamental concerns about social justice not as intellectual abstractions, but as they may be understood and resolved inside one fallible human being. Great judges interpret law and tradition using what they know in their minds, and also in their hearts. Justice is not a fact, but a quality, of which Portia spoke, when she cautioned Shylock that "earthly power doth then show likest God's/ When mercy seasons justice." We may depict justice symbolically as blind, but we do not want her to turn a blind eye to injustice. Human judgment over human mistakes and foibles is what matters, so that humanity becomes the essence of the justice dispensed. It is also, I hope, the essence of this book.

Peter Hay
Los Angeles
November 1, 1988

NOTE ON ORTHOGRAPHY
AND NOMENCLATURE

Since many of the following anecdotes are directly quoted from British, American, Canadian, and Australian sources, there are inconsistencies of English spelling and style throughout the book. In passages other than quotes the editors and I generally have followed *The Chicago Manual of Style*. Legal sources are also uncharacteristically imprecise in identifying judges beyond their surname. The matter is further complicated when British jurists are raised to the peerage and assume yet another name. For example, both Lord Eldon and Lord Clonmell were called John Scott when they practiced at the Bar. I have identified either in the text or in the index many of Their Honours, but I might as well confess that neither my methods nor the results would stand up to close examination in a court of law.

P.H.

· 1 ·
THE NATURE
OF THE BEAST

DEFINITIONS

Professional Discourtesy

Comparisons between sharks and lawyers surface frequently in jokes. The following story from eighteenth-century England might be the ancestor of them all:

Alderman Watson was in his youth a midshipman, and while bathing in the West Indies had the misfortune to lose his leg by the bite of a shark. Some years afterwards, when he and John Wilkes were both in the House of Commons, a tax was proposed to be levied on attorneys. Alderman Watson spoke strongly in favor of the tax, and inveighed warmly against lawyers in general. Somebody asked Wilkes what made his brother alderman so severe upon the attorneys? "Why," replied Wilkes (who was fond of repeating that lawyer was just another name for scoundrel), "my brother alderman was bit by a shark when he was young, and he has never forgiven it."

Of Lawyers

"The law is sort of a hocus-pocus science that smiles in yer face while it picks yer pocket, and the glorious uncertainty of it is of mair use to the professors than the justice of it." So wrote the eighteenth-century Irish actor Charles Macklin in *Love à la Mode*. And in our century, Oscar Levant once defined a lawyer as "a man who helps you get what's coming to him."

George Ade, a well-known humorist in the early part of the century, had just finished a speech and sat down. Then one of the organizers, a well-known lawyer, got to his feet, shoved his hands deep into his

1

trouser's pockets, as was his habit, and asked the company:

"Doesn't it strike anyone as a little unusual that a professional humorist should be funny?"

When the laughter subsided, Ade rose and drawled out:

"Doesn't it strike the company as a little unusual that a lawyer should have his hand in his own pockets?"

And of Judges

Judge Charles E. Clark (1889-1963), of the U.S. Court of Appeals for the Second Circuit, once remarked that a judge is merely a lawyer who has been benched.

A nameless wag defined the perfect judge: "He should be about sixty, clean shaven, with white hair, China-blue eyes, and hemorrhoids so that he will have that concerned look."

Judge Herbert Goodrich (1889-1962) of the Third Circuit said a judge should be completely impartial—"with no axe to feather, no nest to grind."

What Is Law?

From a book of miscellanies titled Salad for the Social, *which was published anonymously in New York in 1856:*

Law is law—and, as in such, and so forth, and hereby, and aforesaid, provided always, nevertheless, notwithstanding. Law is like a blistering plaster—it is a great irritator and only to be used in cases of great extremity. Law, again, is compared to a country dance: people are led up and down in it 'till they are thoroughly tired. Law is like a book of surgery: there are a great many terrible cases in it. It is also like a physic: they that take the least of it are best off. It is like a scolding wife; very bad when it follows us. It is like bad weather: people are glad when they get out of it.

Take again the following lucid definition of legal science: "Law always expresses itself with true grammatical precision, never confounding moods, tenses, cases, or genders, except, indeed, when a *woman* happens accidentally to be slain, then the verdict brought in is *man*slaughter. The essence of law is altercation, for the law can altercate, fulminate, deprecate, irritate, and go on at any rate. Now the quintessence of the law has, according to its name, five points—the first is the beginning or *incipiendum*, the second its uncertainty, or *dubitandum*, the third delay, or *puzzliendum*, the fourth replication without *endum*, and fifth *monstrum* and *horrendum*." (Quoted from the famous eighteenth-century monologue *Lecture on Heads*, by the English actor George Alexander Stevens.)

On the Legal Mind

"Law sharpens a man's mind by narrowing it," wrote Edmund Burke. Somewhat earlier, across the Channel, Louis XII of France said: "Lawyers use the law as shoemakers use leather: rubbing it, pressing it, and stretching it with their teeth, all to the end of making it fit for their purposes."

And Professor Thomas Reed Powell of Harvard (b. 1880) offered this: "If you can think of something which is connected with something without thinking of the something it is connected to, you have a 'legal mind.'"

Take Your Suits to the Laundromat

Justice Logan E. Bleckley of Georgia wrote during the last century, "Some people think that a lawyer's business is to make white black; but his real business is to make white white in spite of the stained and soiled condition which renders its true color questionable. He is simply an intellectual washing-machine."

From the Cynic's Corner

Ambrose Bierce published his definitions in various newspapers throughout the United States between 1881 and 1906, when they appeared in book form as The Cynic's Word Book. *The following selections pertain to the subject at hand:*

COURT FOOL—The plaintiff.
DEFAME—To lie about another. To tell the truth about another.
DELIBERATION—The act of examining one's bread to determine which side it is buttered on.
FELON—A person of greater enterprise than discretion, who in embracing an opportunity has formed an unfortunate attachment.
GALLOWS—A stage for the performance of miracle plays, in which the leading actor is translated into heaven. In this country the gallows is chiefly remarkable for the number of persons who escape it.
HANGMAN—An officer of the law charged with duties of the highest dignity and utmost gravity, and held in hereditary disesteem by a populace having a criminal ancestry. In some of the American States his

functions are now performed by an electrician, as in New Jersey, where executions by electricity have recently been ordered—the first instance known to this lexicographer of anybody questioning the expediency of hanging Jerseymen.

HOMICIDE—The slaying of one human being by another. There are four kinds of homicide: felonious, excusable, justifiable and praiseworthy, but it makes no great difference to the person slain whether he fell by one kind or another—the classification is for the advantage of the lawyers.

HONORABLE—Afflicted with an impediment in one's reach. In legislative bodies it is customary to mention all members as honorable; as, "the honorable gentleman is a scurvy cur."

JUSTICE—A commodity which in a more or less adulterated condition the State sells to the citizen as a reward for his allegiance, taxes and personal service.

LAWYER—One skilled in the circumvention of the law.

LIAR—A lawyer with a roving commission.

LITIGATION—A machine which you go into as a pig and come out as a sausage.

MISDEMEANOR—An infraction of the law having less dignity than a felony and constituting no claim to admittance into the best criminal society.

PARDON—To remit a penalty and restore to a life of crime. To add to the lure of crime the temptation of ingratitude.

PRECEDENT—In Law, a previous decision, rule or practice which, in the absence of a definite statute, has whatever force and authority a Judge may choose to give it, thereby greatly simplifying his task of doing as he pleases. As there are precedents for everything, he has only to ignore those that make against his interest and accentuate those in the line of his desire. Invention of the precedent elevates the trial-at-law from the low estate of a fortuitous ordeal to the noble attitude of a dirigible arbitrament.

PROOF—Evidence having a shade more of plausibility than of unlikelihood. The testimony of two credible witnesses as opposed to that of only one.

RETALIATION—The natural rock upon which is reared the Temple of Law.

SELF-EVIDENT—Evident to one's self and to nobody else.

TECHNICALITY—In an English court a man named Home was tried for slander in having accused a neighbor of murder. His exact words were: "Sir Thomas Holt hath taken a cleaver and stricken his cook upon the head, so that one side of the head fell upon one shoulder and the other side upon the other shoulder." The defendant was acquitted by instruction of the court, the learned judges holding that the words did not charge murder, for they did not affirm the death of the cook, that being only an inference.

TRIAL—A formal inquiry designed to prove and put upon record the blameless characters of judges, advocates and jurors. In order to effect this purpose it is necessary to supply a contrast in the person of one who is called the defendant, the prisoner or the accused. If the contrast is made sufficiently clear this person is made to undergo such an affliction as will give the virtuous gentlemen a comfortable sense of their immunity, added to that of their worth.

More Cynical Definitions
The nineteenth-century British judge, Lord Brougham, defined a lawyer as "a learned gentleman who rescues your estate from your enemies and keeps it himself." Some other, anonymous definitions in the vast literature on the subject:

A lawyer is the shrewdest distance between two points.
A person who is summoned when the felon needs a friend.
A fellow who is willing to give all and spend your last cent to prove it.

Definition of a jury: Twelve men who are chosen to decide which of the parties has the better attorney.

It's Better Not to Kiss Them
A man asked Dr. Johnson why he so hated lawyers. "I don't hate them, sir; neither do I hate frogs; but I don't like to have either hopping about my chamber." And his friend Mrs. Piozzi tells when a gentleman was leaving the company, somebody who sat next to Dr. Johnson asked him who he was. "I cannot exactly tell you, Sir (replied he), and I would be loath to speak ill of any person who I do not know deserves it, but I am afraid he is an attorney."

But Johnson had respect for the law: "Law is the science in which the greatest powers of understanding are applied to the greatest number of facts." On another occasion when a superficial critic reflected upon the law and lawyers, Dr. Johnson brusquely said: "Let us have no general abuse. The law is the last result of human understanding acting upon human experience for the benefit of the public."

The Devil's Due

An indictment for libel was once tried before Sir William Maule (1788-1858). The learned counsel for the defense told the jury: "This, gentlemen, is a shameful, and infamous, I may say, a diabolical prosecution." When the time came for summing up, Maule said: "Gentlemen of the jury, you are told that this is a diabolical prosecution; but gentlemen, you must give the devil his due, and find the defendant guilty."

The Devil's Troops

There has been a long tradition of identifying the lawyer with the devil. When it looked as though Napoleon might be planning an invasion of England, all classes and professions of Englishmen sprang to arms, and among others the lawyers of the Temple organized a regiment. The king came to review this unit. At the conclusion His Majesty sent for its honorary colonel, Lord Erskine, and asked him what he called his regiment. Erskine replied that it had no name as yet, to which the king replied, "Call it the Devil's Own."

The Road to Hell

Retired law professor Milton Green cites in his book, It's Legal To Laugh, *the case of a man against whom a judgment had been rendered by default. His defense was that he had intended to hire a lawyer, and believed that he had hired a lawyer to look after the case. A Judge Houser, in disallowing the defense, used the following language:*

Defendant's mistaken belief that he had retained counsel, under the circumstances, is not sufficient to excuse him. Good intentions are not enough. "Hell is paved with good intentions."—Dr Johnson, Boswell's *Life of Johnson*, Annus 1775.

This original opinion came back to Judge Houser from the St. Louis Court of Appeals, after making the rounds of the judges, with the following notes appended to it:

I am unaware that Hell is paved, not having visited the place. I have been asked to go many times, but have refused the invitation.

E.M.R.

You are forthwith assigned to Springfield Court of Appeals.

M.C.M.

I concur in the conclusions reached by Judge Houser except for the statement that "Hell is paved with good intentions." This is a matter about which there has been a great conflict of opinion.

"Hell is paved with infants' skulls," says Baxter.

"Hell is paved with priests' skulls," says Saint Chrysostom.

"Hell is paved with the skulls of great scholars and paled in with the bones of great men," says Oiles Firmin in *The Real Christian*.

There is, as Judge Ruddy suggests, some doubt about Hell being paved at all. This view is supported by Milton who wrote in *Paradise Lost*: "All Hell broke loose."

If, however, we should conclude that hell is paved, the great weight of authority is that skulls of some sort are the materials used. This seems more logical, for good intentions may be of many forms but skulls are appropriately rounded and durable.

I dissent for the further reason that the opinion places this court on record against good intentions. This has been rebuked by Southey who, in his *Colloquies on Society*, states, "It has been more wittily than charitably said that Hell is paved with good intentions; they have their place in Heaven also."

John J. Wolfe

Lord Malaprop

Lord Kenyon was famous in the eighteenth century for his imperfect knowledge of Latin tags and historical allusions. Once he told the jury in a blasphemy case that the Emperor Julian was "so celebrated for the practice of every Christian virtue that he was called *Julian the Apostle*." (He meant "Julian the Apostate.")

On another occasion, in dismissing a grand jury, he finished a complex peroration this way: "Having thus discharged your consciences, gentlemen, you may return to your homes in peace, with the delightful consciousness of having performed your duties well, and may lay your heads on your pillows, saying to yourselves, *Aut Caesar, aut nullus.*" (He meant *Aut Caesar, aut nihil*: "Caesar or nothing" or "all or nothing.")

Detecting an attorney's attempt to delay a trial, Lord Kenyon once delivered himself of this mixed metaphor: "This is the last hair in the tail of procrastination, and it must be plucked out."

Law Latin

The motives of lawyers in employing a dead or foreign language for so long a period have been questioned frequently. According to Sir John Davies (1569-1626), attorney general to James I, it was objected "to the professors of our law, that, forsooth, they write their reports and books of the law in a strange, unknown tongue, which no one can understand but themselves, to the end that the people, being kept in ignorance of the law, may the more admire their skill and knowledge, and value it at a higher price." This was merely echoing a charge reported by Cicero against the earliest Roman lawyers. And Julius Caesar mentioned that the Druids, who were judges and interpreters of the laws among the ancient Britons, were unintelligible, though they spent twenty years in acquiring knowledge of those laws.

Law French

After Latin began to fall into disuse, in order to remain obscure and unintelligible, English lawyers fell back on their Norman traditions and employed a bastard language known as Law French, here described by a delightfully lucid English attorney, Reginald Hine (1883-1949):

Most of all, I liked to dip into *Coke upon Littleton*, marvelling at the misguided talent of that young poet who, doomed to take up law, turned this very learned and laborious treatise into rhyming couplets. One marvelled, too, at the bastard Law French in which most of the early black-letter reports were written, and that it should have continued for so long. Cromwell, that master of Vernacular English, had his dictatorial way. But no sooner was he dead than the customary language was revived. "The Law," said Roger North, "is scarce expressible in English." With that acid comment the lawyers of England heaved a sigh of relief at the Restoration, and once again, in reporting, it was possible to concoct sentences like the famous one of 1631, so dearly beloved of our profession: *Il ject un brickbat à le dit Justice que narrowly mist.*

Terms of Abuse

Reginald Hine also found some antique pearls one could cast at members of the legal profession:

Lawyers and attorneys have possessed such a bad reputation from the beginning that you may revile them at your pleasure. Here are a few phrases of abuse that the judges have allowed: "He is the falsest knave in England and by God's blood I will cut his throat," and this: "Thou art a common maintainer of suits and a Champerter. I will have thee throwne over the Barre next term." And magistrates, too, have had to put up with some rough usage in the exercise of the king's commission. Of one it was said: "He is a vermin in the commonwealth, and a hypocrite and a dissembler in the Church of God." Of another: "He is a blood-sucker and thirsteth after blood; but if any man will give him a couple of capons and a score of wethers he will take them and be his friend." A much more exalted personage, the Lord Keeper, Francis North, of whom it was disrespectfully alleged, in that fourth figure of rhetoric called *sauce malapert*, that "he had been seen riding on the back of a rhinoceros." This "most impudent buffoon lie," with "the brazen affirmations of truth to it," are said to have "roiled him extreamly."

Green Bag

"Green Bag" occurs in old English plays as an unfriendly nickname for attorneys because they carried their clients' deeds in a green bag. From the time of Charles II (1660-1685) and for a century afterward clients were accustomed to revile their attorneys as green bag carriers. For example, in Wycherley's *Plain Dealer*, Widow Blackacre upbraids the barrister who refused to argue for her:

"You puny upstart in the law, you green bag carrier, you murderer of unfortunate cases, the clerk's ink is scarce off your fingers."

One old comedy calls a lawyer, "an odd sort of fruit: first rotten, then green, then ripe."

In the nineteenth century, *Green Bag* was a humorous magazine for the legal profession.

Terms of Distinction

A barrister is simply the name for one who has been called or admitted to plead at the Bar. In England there used to be two degrees: the 'outer' or 'utter' barristers, and the higher King's (or Queen's) Counsel, usually designated as K.C. (or Q.C). When raised to the senior position, a barrister is said to "take silk," enjoying the privilege to wear a silk gown and on special occasions a full-bottomed wig. Junior counsel, on the other hand, wear plain gown and a short wig.

Serjeants-at-laws were the highest rank of British lawyers, until their order was abolished in 1880.

An attorney (from the French *atourner*, to turn over to another) means one who is legally qualified to manage matters in law for others. This original sense is preserved in the legal phrases "power of attorney" and "warrant of attorney."

Solicitors

A solicitor, in British jurisprudence, is one who solicits or petitions in Courts of Equity on behalf of his clients. This branch of legal practitioners is thought to have their origin in petitioning suits in the Star-Chamber, the monarch's judicial council, which dealt with crimes against the state under the direct supervision of the Lord Chancellor. (It was abolished in 1641.) Until 1873 solicitors belonged to Courts of Equity, and attorneys to the other courts.

For a long time, solicitors were unpopular among the rest of the profession. A barrister of Gray's Inn named Hudson railed, in the reign of Charles I, against these upstarts:

"In our age, here are stepped up a new sort of people called Solicitors, unknown to the records of the law, who, like the grasshoppers in Egypt, devour the whole land . . . I mean not where a lord or gentleman employed a servant to solicit his cause—for he may justify his doing thereof; but I mean those which are common solicitors of causes, and set up a new profession, not being allowed in any court, or at least not in the court where they follow causes; and these are the retainers of causes, and devourers of men's estates by contention, and prolonging suits to make them without end."

By the eighteenth century, attorneys were rushing to assume the title of solicitor. To such, Lord Chancellor Tenterden (1762-1832) extended neither courtesy nor forbearance.

"What are you, sir? Who are you?" he inquired of an attorney who was pushing through the crowded Court of King's Bench.

"I am the plaintiff's solicitor, my lord," answered the unwary practitioner.

"The plaintiff's solicitor!" the judge responded with a contemptuous accent on the title. "We know nothing of solicitors here, sir; had you been in the respectable rank of an attorney, I should have ordered room to be made for you."

A Thorough Understanding

William St. Julian Arabin (1775-1841), Serjeant and Commissioner at the Old Bailey, collected some of the unintentional absurdities that are spoken in court. A collection of Arabiniana was first published in 1843 and republished in the 1960s. One of Arabin's citations is from the 1834 case of Regina v. Harris, *where the Court addressed counsel:*

The Court: Mr. Phillips, you must distinctly understand that I know nothing of this arrangement.

Phillips: Yes, my lord; it is thoroughly understood that your lordship knows nothing.

The Court: Certainly.

Try It Sometime

In the early eighteenth century, Sir Richard Steele suggested in one of his essays in the *Tattler* the following penal cure for the busy work of lawyers: "If any lawyer is above two days in drawing a marriage settlement or uses more words in it than one skin of parchment will contain or takes above five pounds for drawing it, let him be thrown over the bar."

A World Without Lawyers

Lady Chatterton, in her Rambles in the South of Ireland in the Year 1838, *describes the ways of justice among the simple people of Dingle, a small town in the southwest of Ireland:*

"Law, sir," repeated the man of Dingle, with a look of astonishment and affright, "law, sir! We never mind the law in our court. We judge by the honesty of the case that comes before us. And let me tell you, sir, that if every court were so conducted there would be but few attorneys, and the country would be quiet and happy."

"But what would you do if any person brought an attorney these twenty-two long miles, and hilly roads, from Tralee, and introduced him into your courts; and if he started some points of law, which required professional skill to reply to?"

"I'll tell you what I did myself," was the reply to this apparently perplexing question. "When I was deputy-sovereign, two fools in this town employed each of them an attorney, whom they brought in at great expense from Tralee. When the attorneys went into court and settled themselves, with their bags and papers all done up with bits of red tape, and one of them was getting up to speak, 'Crier,' said I, 'command silence.' 'Silence in court!' says he. So I stood up, and looking first at one attorney, and then at the other, I said with a solemn voice, 'I adjourn this court for a month.' 'God save the king!' said the crier; and then I left them all. And I assure you," he added, "that from that day to this no attorney ever appeared in our court; and, please God, we never will mind law in it, but go on judging by the honor and honesty of the cases that come before us."

Quotable Justice
Jurists like to quote Justice Oliver Wendell Holmes more than any other American judge. Here are a few favorites:

Orthodoxy is my doxy, heterodoxy is your doxy.

No generalization is wholly true, not even this one.

The highest courage is to stake everything on a premise that you know tomorrow's evidence may disprove.

Constitutional Law
At a Washington reception in the 1930s, the Brazilian ambassador Oswaldo Aranha, who also wrote a new constitution for his country, found himself in conversation with Chief Justice Charles Evans Hughes. They were discussing a strict interpretation the Supreme Court had recently made of the Constitution and against Franklin Roosevelt's New Deal legislation.

"If the law does not solve a difficult problem," the ambassador ventured, "it should not be applied."

"On the contrary," the chief justice argued, "it prevents us from going off on tangents. The Constitution has been our cornerstone."

"Constitutional law," replied Aranha, "is like a virgin. It must be violated to reach its fullest flower."

Extreme Penalty

Sir Charles Russell (1832-1900), later Lord Chief Justice, in the early part of his career was in court one day, during the trial of a case of bigamy. One of the counsel, whom he knew, asked: "Russell, what's the extreme penalty for bigamy?" Without a beat, Russell replied: "Two mothers-in-law."

THE PROFESSION

How To Be Professional

Rufus Choate, the founder of the dynasty of distinguished nineteenth-century American lawyers, was said to have instructed his office not to accept any piece of legal business without a minimum retainer of a hundred dollars—in cash. Returning from court one day, his clerk showed him a brief that a prospective client had left during his absence.

"William, did Mr.———leave the customary retainer?" inquired the lawyer.

"Well, Mr. Choate," said the clerk, "he left only seventy-five dollars."

"That, you know, is very unprofessional and against the rules of the office."

"But I took all the man had," the clerk explained.

"Ah, William, that entirely alters the case—to take all a man has is quite professional."

The Crux of the Matter

In a conversation with Dr. Samuel Johnson, his biographer James Boswell grapples with the perennial ethical problems of the legal profession:

Boswell: I asked him whether, as a moralist, he did not think that the practice of the law, in some degree, hurt the nice feeling of honesty.

Johnson: Why no, sir, if you act properly. You are not to deceive your clients with false representations of your opinion; you are not to tell lies to a judge.

Boswell: But what do you think of supporting a cause which you know to be bad?

Johnson: Sir, you do not know it to be good or bad till the judge determines it. I have said that you are to state facts fairly, so that your thinking, or what you call knowing, a cause to be bad, must be from reasoning, must be from your supposing your arguments to be weak and inconclusive. But, sir, that is not enough. An argument which does not convince yourself, may convince the judge to whom you urge it: and if it does convince him, why, then, sir, you are wrong, and he is right. It is his business to judge, and you are not to be confident in your own opinion that a cause is bad, but to say all you can for your client, and then hear the judge's opinion.

Boswell: But, sir, does not affecting a warmth when you have no warmth, and appearing to be clearly of one opinion when you are in reality of another opinion, does not such dissimulation impair one's honesty? Is there not some danger that a lawyer may put on the same mask in common life, in the intercourse with his friends?

Johnson: Why no, sir. Everybody knows you are paid for affecting warmth for your client, and it is, therefore, properly no dissimulation; the moment you come from the Bar you resume your usual behavior. Sir, a man will no more carry the artifice of the Bar into the common intercourse of society, than a man who is paid for tumbling upon his hands will continue to tumble upon his hands when he should walk on his feet.

Already Then

We tend to think that overcrowding in the legal profession is a recent phenomenon, or a problem confined to countries like the United States. In fact, Thomas Heywood, writing in mid-sixteenth-century London, recalled a conversation in which someone said that the increasing number of lawyers would mar the occupation. "No," Heywood replied, "for always the more spaniels in the field, the more game."

In fifteenth-century England there was a petition from the Commons of two counties, showing that "the number of attornies had lately increased from six or eight to fourteen, whereby the peace of those counties had been greatly interrupted by suits. The Commons, therefore, petition that it may be ordained that there shall be no more than six attornies for Norfolk, six for Suffolk, and two for the city of Norwich." The Crown granted the petition.

And I found the following in an English book of *Legal Facetiae* (1887) about my native Hungary, which was then a backward, agricultural country.

"It is the ambition of the Hungarian peasant to make one of his sons an advocate, as it is the ambition of the Breton and the Irish peasant to make one son a priest. It is related of the son of a small farmer near Budapest who was sent to the law school of that town but was plucked in the qualifying examination, that not daring to return home empty-handed after all the money that had been spent upon his education, he forged a legal diploma. The father was not, however, so ignorant as not to be aware that such diplomas are always written on dogskin parchment in Hungary.

"'Why is your certificate not made out on dogskin?' asked the old man.

"'The fact is,' replied the youth, 'there are more barristers than dogs in Hungary, and so there is not enough dogskin to make diplomas for us all.'"

Occupation for Gentlemen

Thomas Leaming, a lawyer from Philadelphia, wrote a book (in 1911) about the British system of justice:

Traditionally, the sons of gentlemen and the younger sons of peers were restricted, when seeking an occupation, to the Army, the Navy, the Church, and the Bar. They never became solicitors, for that branch, like the profession of medicine, was somewhat arbitrarily excluded from possible callings, but this tradition, as is the case with many others, has been gradually losing its force of late years. It must always have been a little hazy in its application, owing to the difficulty of ascertaining accurately the status of the parent, if not a peer; and Sir Thomas Smith, who, more than three centuries ago, after describing the various higher titles, attempted a definition of the word "gentleman," could formulate nothing more definite than the following: "As for gentlemen they be made good cheap in this kingdom; for whosoever studieth the laws of the realm, who studieth in the universities, who professeth the liberal sciences, and to be short, who can live idly and without manual labor, and will bear the port, charge and countenance of a gentleman, he shall be called master and shall be taken for a gentleman." The ancient books, too, afford, a glimpse of a struggle on the part of the bar to demand a certain aristocratic deference, for an old case is reported where the court refused to hear an affidavit because a barrister named in it was not called an "esquire."

That the struggle was not in vain is evidenced by the reply of an old-time Lord Chancellor, who, when asked how he made his selection from the ranks of the barristers when obliged to name a new judge, answered: "I always appoint a gentleman, and if he knows a little law, so much the better."

Patron Saint

Lawyers have not been popular, especially with the populace, and they are usually depicted in medieval literature as conniving, unethical and too clever for their own good. The hero of the fifteenth-century French farce of *Master Peter Pathelin*, which is still revived on occasion, is shown as lazy, ignorant, always broke, a cheat and a thief. Yet the patron saint of lawyers is also French: a thirteenth-century advocate who devoted all his practice to helping the poor. He was remembered by them in the ditty:

> Saint Yves is from Brittany,
> A lawyer but not a thief,
> Such a thing is beyond belief!

Precious Lawyer

Ben Jonson, the seventeenth-century English playwright, was going through a churchyard in Surrey, when he saw some poor people crying over a grave. He asked one of the women why they were weeping. "Oh!" said she, "we have lost our precious lawyer, Justice Randall. He kept us all in peace, and was always so good as to keep us from going to law; the best man that ever lived."

True Knights

In France, Italy, and Germany, a forensic order of knighthood was frequently conferred on the successful practitioner at the bar. Bartoli, the oracle of the law in the fourteenth century, asserted that at the end of the tenth year of successful professional exertion, the *avocat* belonging to the denomination of *l'Ordre des Avocats* became *ipso facto* a knight.

When the distinction was applied for, the king commissioned some ancient Knight of the Forensic Order to admit the postulant into it. The *avocat* knelt before the knight-commissary and said: "I pray you, my lord and protector, to dress me with the sword, belt and golden spurs, golden collar, golden ring, and all the other ornaments of a true knight. I will not use the advantages of knighthood for profane purposes; I will use them only for the purposes of religion, for the Church, and the holy Christian faith, in the warfare of the science to which I am devoted." The postulant then rose, and being fully equipped, and girded with the sword, he became, for all purposes, a member of the order of knighthood.

In 1795 *l'Ordre des Avocats* was suppressed in France, after 427 years of brilliant existence.

Stay Away from the Bar

Dr. Thomas Arnold, the famous English educator in the early nineteenth century, considered the profession of an advocate "as of necessity immoral," and he looked upon the study of law, "which is as wholesome to the human mind as the practice of it is injurious." In writing to a friend, the Master of Rugby School asked whether there is no way by which a man can hope to reach the position of a judge without exposing himself to the injurious influences of the Bar.

Consultation

The constitution of the State of Indiana (Section 21, Article VII) adopted in 1851, allowed that "every person of good moral character, being a voter, shall be entitled to practice law in all courts of justice."

Although we take it for granted that all judges were lawyers first, this has not always been the case. Just as there are lay preachers, there used to be lay judges. For example, New Jersey's high courts used to have one so-called law judge, and two lay judges until the latter were abolished in 1887. To mark the retirement of the last of the lay judges, the Bar Association of Burlington County decided to hold what bar associations tend to do best—a dinner.

After the toasts and speeches, the lay judge thanked the assembled lawyers and said:

"It has been a memorable forty years. I would not exchange one day of it for all the wealth in the world. I've seen many of you, now grown grey in the law, enter my courtroom as fledglings. Today you are honored members of a great profession. Your toastmaster asked me a few minutes ago if my relations during these years with my associates on the bench were harmonious. Well, candidly, I can tell you that the only time in forty years that the law judge ever consulted me was three weeks ago when he leaned over and said: 'Doesn't your ass ever get tired from sitting on these hard boards?'"

Worse than Disbarment

Abraham Lincoln, respected and admired by all the young lawyers of the Illinois Bar who knew him, was assigned one day the unpleasant task of reprimanding a youthful barrister against whom disbarment proceedings had been brought.

As a law student serving his apprenticeship in the office of a member of the Bloomington Bar, this young man had learned some valuable information concerning the business of a client of his preceptor. Shortly after the student's admission to the bar, his preceptor filed a suit in the circuit court at Bloomington on behalf of this client, the litigation being based on the very information that had passed through the hands of the young man.

When the case came up for trial, to the great surprise of the older lawyer, his former apprentice appeared as counsel for the defendant. It soon became apparent that the student had disclosed to his client the confidential information he had learned in his preceptor's office.

At the disbarment proceedings which followed, the young lawyer regretfully admitted his indiscretion and beseeched Judge Davis to show leniency and spare him from the impending disgrace. He would voluntarily leave the bar and the country, he pleaded, and with tears in his eyes he begged for the dismissal of the disbarment proceedings so he could start anew in some other state.

Judge Davis was inclined to grant the request, but he was determined that this young lawyer who had disgraced his profession should not leave without first receiving a severe and open reproof for his offense. Seeing Abraham Lincoln in the crowded courtroom, Judge Davis called him to the bench and urged him to convey to the young man the censure and indignation of the bar. In a low voice, which expressed the sorrow he felt, Lincoln addressed the fallen lawyer.

"Sir," he said, "you have polluted the ermine of this court of justice, that should be as pure and spotless as the driven snow or the light of the brightest stars in the firmament. Justice is not a fiction; and though it is often held to be a sentiment only, or a remote ideal, it is real, and it is founded and guarded on all sides by the strongest powers of Divine and human law. The court will not pronounce your disbarment; you have done that yourself. The people will trust no one, without sincere reformation, who has been wrong and reckless, as you admit, in one of the most confiding relations that ever exists between men.

"A client appears in court by his lawyer so often and the custom so generally prevails that if he is not represented by honorable and trustworthy counsel, the right is of little value and he is virtually denied the justice to which our law entitles him . . . A lawyer who becomes by his admission to the Bar of any of our courts part of the judicial establishment of the land should have integrity beyond question or reproach. Courts of law as of equity can sustain no other without themselves becoming venal and corrupt. A tarnished lawyer is a homeless man. Therefore seek until you find a real reformation in honest work, and the court will approve."

When Abraham Lincoln finished these impromptu remarks, the deep silence which prevailed in the courtroom was broken only by the soft sobbing of the contrite youth. The impressive words so firm with reproof yet filled with genuine sympathy had accomplished their purpose. The older lawyer slowly walked over to the young man, took hold of his hand and said:

"We bid thee Godspeed in a work that will make you a better man."

In sorrowful silence Lincoln then returned to his seat.

Standards

Judge Joseph A. Wapner is probably the best known judge in America through his popular television series, The People's Court. *I was recently sharing the dais with Judge Wapner at an author's luncheon in Los Angeles, and he seemed a fatherly, kind, and compassionate man. He also deeply cares about standards in the legal profession, as I learned from his book,* A View from the Bench:

Mr. Cleveland, Esquire and Gentleman, practiced criminal law in Los Angeles. When I had been on the bench for two years in Superior Court, his face had become quite familiar to me. He handled many different cases simultaneously, and he always gave the impression of a juggler tossing case jackets into the air and hoping that he could somehow keep them from falling.

He couldn't do it.

Even though he was a former deputy attorney general and a lawyer of ten years' experience, he was chronically late for cases. Often he simply did not appear, or appeared so late that he made it impossible to address his case that day. Throughout the Criminal Department of Superior Court, he was notorious for his habitual lateness, and that is not a good reason to be known.

One day in April of 1964, Vernon Cleveland had two cases pending before me in Department 100 of the Superior Court. As it happened, Mr. Cleveland had been so incautious as to have two other cases pending in other departments of the Superior Court. One of them was a jury return-ing to give a verdict on a criminal case in which his client was the defendant.

Cleveland completed his attention to one of the cases before me. Then, during a brief recess, he was told that he had to go to another room to hear the jury's verdict. Therefore, when I resumed court, handling a very busy Master Calendar, where all criminal cases are assigned, Mr. Cleveland was gone. I had already suffered for two years with his relent-less lateness. I was annoyed for myself and for the rest of the people in court. Because he was absent, the judge, the bailiffs, the other lawyers—even Mr. Cleveland's client—had to twiddle their thumbs while we wondered where he was. After a few minutes, I sent my bailiff out into the hallway to find Mr. Cleveland and bring him back.

Incredibly, Mr. Cleveland did not return to my courtroom. Later, he told the schoolboy's story that he thought my bailiff was from another courtroom and he got lost going to that courtroom! (It reminded me very much of students claiming that they actually completed their homework but somehow it had inexplicably gotten lost on the school bus. Or perhaps their dogs had chewed it up! Interestingly enough, even though Mr. Cleveland "thought" he was supposed to go to another courtroom and not mine, he somehow never showed up in that courtroom either.)

When the bailiff came back and told me that Mr. Cleveland refused to return to the courtroom where his client was sitting accused of a felony, I was deeply concerned. Here was a lawyer, sworn to the highest duty of care for his clients, simply refusing the order of a judge, empowered by the laws of California, to return to defend his client.

In a very swift hurry, I sent my bailiff back out to the court to fetch Mr. Cleveland and to arrest him if necessary. This time, the bailiff could not even find Mr. Cleveland.

I was steaming. Now, in my public as well as my private life, I do not ask for any special treatment. I do not make headwaiters give me special tables in restaurants, and I always wait in line with everybody else. Without my robes on, I am just the same as any other Joe. But in my court, I represent the law.

I saw incredibly fine men, with families and children waiting for them back home, men with the fullest possible measure of decency and courage, get blown to pieces by Japanese artillery to preserve our system of law. When I came back from Cebu, I had to call wives and mothers and tell them that their sons were not coming back alive, and I knew then they had died to keep us all under a system of law. When I sat in Department 100 and thought of a *lawyer* thumbing his nose at the law, I became truly determined to set an example.

I immediately cited Mr. Cleveland for contempt. Now, it pains me to say that this lawyer's record for contemptuous behavior was so bad that I had already been forced to cite him for contempt and impose a small fine once before. Now, I was done with fines. I ordered Mr. Cleveland found and put in County Jail for two days.

You can probably imagine that lawyers are all too accustomed to seeing anybody but themselves in jail. When Mr. Cleveland learned that he, a member of the bar, was going to be put in jail, like the men and women he represented, he was hysterically upset. In fact, he at first thought I was joking. I was not.

Mr. Cleveland was not lazy. He appealed his jail term immediately, and he raised some ingenious defenses. Mainly, he said that he could not be summarily sentenced for contempt because he had not been there in person! To me, this was the precise equivalent of a child who murders his parents then pleads for mercy from the court because he is an orphan.

The Supreme Court of California heard Mr. Cleveland's arguments and weighed them carefully. Then the high court of California affirmed my sentence of contempt. Their reasoning was beautiful. The opinion by Justice Stanley Mosk was so clearly set out, and makes the problems of running a court so clear, that I would like to quote a few lines from it:

"When an attorney fails to appear in court with his client, particularly in a criminal matter, the wheels of justice must temporarily grind to a halt. The client cannot be penalized, nor can the court proceed in the absence of counsel. Having allocated time for this case, the court is seldom able to substitute other matters. Thus the entire administration of justice falters. . . .

"In the case before us, we cannot find [Cleveland's] conduct to have been excusable. While it may be true that he could not avoid the conflict, he did little to mitigate the effects of the proceedings before Judge Wapner. His client was left unrepresented and the court lost precious time that vanished forever. . . ."

It is rare that a reader gets to see poetry in an appellate court opinion. Appreciation is in order, especially by the judge whose opinion was upheld.

Bankers and Lawyers

Justice Louis D. Brandeis told Ferdinand Pecora, who was conducting a Senate investigation of the banking industry in the 1930s: "You should be kind to the bankers. Bankers are not men of ingenuity. It's always the lawyers who develop the chicanery."

But when it was proposed that lawyers should be investigated, Brandeis threw up his hands: "That would be useless. Who would do the cross-examining?"

Straight Talk

During the preparations for the trial of Black Panthers Bobby Seale and Ericka Huggins in 1971, Judge Mulvey had issued a gag order. But Charles Garry, Seale's defense attorney, traveled around giving speeches, trying to raise money. He writes about one invitation that had come from the New London Bar Association, about a hundred miles from New Haven, where the trial was held:

The meeting was held in a beautiful old resort that was covered in snow. We arrived to find a big fire going in the old stone fireplace and the banquet room full. The dais was filled with dignitaries from all over Connecticut—judges of every kind and description, including a former chief justice of the Connecticut Supreme Court. After dinner I leaned over to ask the president of the bar association what he wanted me to talk about. He said, "Well, Garry, I'll tell you this. If you don't tell it like it is, if you don't raise hell with the judicial system, then I personally will be very disappointed. You can talk about anything. But lay it on the line. Don't pull punches. This group has been in need of some straight talk for many years."

I stood up and looked around and began by saying:

"I don't in this entire crowd here tonight see one black face. I guess that tells the story, doesn't it? It says to me that there is not one black lawyer in your group or, if there is, he or she wasn't interested enough to be here. Judging from the people I'm sitting next to, I would have to say that there are hardly any women lawyers amongst you. Perhaps that tells the story of the American judicial system."

I ended up talking about the difficulties of a fair trial under the system.

"A fair trial implies that both sides are equal in strength, equal in the money and resources at their disposal, and equal in their ability to handle themselves in and out of court. When you have the all-powerful state on one side and Joe Blow on the other, Joe Blow is always in trouble."

I got a standing ovation. I had a little trouble understanding this because if this all-white, mostly male body had agreed with me and put its beliefs into practice, I wouldn't have been in New Haven defending Bobby Seale and Ericka Huggins. After I sat down again a superior court judge next to me offered me an explanation. Pointing down the dais, he said:

"The man over there is the former chief justice of our supreme court. He didn't know what the hell you were saying, I'm sure, because he's very hard of hearing. But when everybody else stands up, he stands, too. The reason some of the others stood up was probably to relieve the pressure on their balls."

PLACES IN TIME

Courts

The word *court* takes us back to a remote period, for a court was originally a sheepfold, and people who possessed the district called Latium before it became Rome used to establish enclosures with hurdles in which to place their sheep, which they called *cors*. A collection of these *cors* was called a *cohors*, and then a further group became the center of a hamlet or a town, and later on, of a fortified place, gradually of a royal residence, and eventually, of a legal establishment of which the king was the head, so the court.

Inns of Court

The poet Edmund Spenser spoke of the inner sanctum of English legal life, the maze of quads and chambers in the heart of London, already venerable in the age of the first Elizabeth:

> Those bricky towers,
> Where now the studious lawyers have their bowers.
> There whilom wont the Temple Knights to bide
> Till they decayed through pride.

According to Thomas Leaming's 1911 book about the London courts:

An Inn of Court may be defined as an unincorporated society of barristers, which, originating about the end of the thirteenth century, possesses by immemorial custom the exclusive privilege of calling candidates to the Bar, and of disciplining, or when necessary, of disbarring barristers.

Physically, an Inn of Court is not a single edifice, nor even an enclosure. It is rather an ill-defined district in which graceful but dingy buildings of diverse pattern and of various degrees of antiquity are closely grouped together and through which wind crooked lanes, mostly closed to traffic, but available for pedestrians. Unexpected open squares, refreshed by fountains, delight the eye, the whole affording the most peaceful quietude, despite the nearness of the roar of surrounding London. The four Inns of Court (as distinguished from the Inns of Chancery and Serjeant's Inn, all of which are now obsolete) are, the Middle Temple, the Inner Temple, Lincoln's Inn and Gray's Inn, but the last is of minor importance in these modern days [i.e., in 1911], having fallen out of fashion.

The Middle Temple and the Inner Temple acquired by lease in the fourteenth century, and by actual purchase in 1609, the lands of the Knights Templar, consisting of many broad acres situated on the south side of the Strand and Fleet Street, opposite the present Law Courts Building, and the whole space is now occupied by an intricate mass of structures—the great Halls, the Libraries, the quaint barristers' chambers—and by the beautiful Temple Gardens, sloping to the Thames, adorned with bright flowers and shaded by fine trees.

The wonderful Hall of the Middle Temple, where the benchers, barristers and students still eat their stated dinners, was built about 1572, and is celebrated for its interior, especially for the open-work ceiling of ancient oak. Shakespeare's comedy, *Twelfth Night*, was performed in the Hall in 1601, and it is believed that one of the actors was the author himself.

Lincoln's Inn became possessed about 1312 of what was once the country seat of the Earl of Lincoln, which, running along Chancery Lane, adjoins the modern Law Courts Building on the north and consists of two large, open squares surrounded by rows of ancient dwellings, long since converted into barristers' chambers.

Leaming, himself a Philadelphia lawyer, explains the origins of this practical term:

Gray's Inn, which probably took its name from the Grays of Wilton who formerly owned its site, has long ceased to be of much importance, although the old Hall and the classic architecture of some of the chambers still attracts the eye. It happens, however, that a Philadelphia student, who attended this ancient Inn nearly two hundred years ago, was responsible for the phrase still proverbial on both sides of the Atlantic: "that's a case for a Philadelphia lawyer." The unpopular royal judges of the province of New York had, in 1734, indicted a newspaper publisher for libel in criticising the court and they threatened to disbar any lawyer of the province who might venture to defend him. But, from the then distant little town of Delaware, the former student of Gray's Inn, although an old man at the time, journeyed to Albany and, by his skill and vehemence, actually procured a verdict of acquittal from the jury under the very noses of the obnoxious court; the fame of which achievement spread throughout not only the colonies but the mother country itself.

I Said I Was Sorry

The nineteenth-century antiquarian John Timbs in his Romance of London *tells the story of an incident long remembered.*

The celebrated Sir John Davies, who was of the Middle Temple, on February 12, 1597-8, while masters of the bench and the other members of the Society were sitting quietly at dinner, came into the hall with his hat on his head, and attended by two persons armed with swords, and going up to the barristers' table, where Richard Martin was sitting, he pulled out from under his gown a cudgel, and struck him over the head repeatedly, and with so much violence that the bastinado was shivered into many pieces. Then retiring to the bottom of the hall, Davies drew one of his attendants' swords and flourished it over his head, turning his face towards Martin, and then hurrying away down the water-steps of the Temple, threw himself into a boat.

For this outrageous act Sir John Davies was immediately disbarred and expelled the house, and deprived forever of all authority to speak or consult in law. After nearly four years' retirement, he petitioned the bench for his restoration, which they, knowing his merits and believing in his penitence, accorded on October 30, 1601, upon his making a public submission in the hall, and asking pardon of Mr. Martin, who at once generously forgave him.

Martin went on to become Recorder of London and member of Parliament, while Davies rose to be Speaker of the Irish Parliament and Attorney-General for Ireland; he was appointed Lord Chief Justice of England on the very day that he died.

Lost His Head

Some other gentlemen of the Inns of Court were not let off so easily. In 1757, Henry Justice, of the Middle Temple, was sentenced to death for stealing books from the library of Trinity College, Cambridge.

Peter Burchet of the Middle Temple was hanged for "barbarously murdering his gaoler, 12th November, 1573—his right hand being first stricken off, and nailed to the gibbet."

John Ayloff of the Inner Temple, convicted of high treason, was hanged opposite the Temple Gate, 1685.

Christopher Layer, also of the Inner Temple, was executed at Tyburn for attempted murder, March 15th, 1723. His head was placed in Temple Bar, where it remained, we are told, "upwards of thirty years, when a storm at last blew it down. The pieces were picked up by Mr. John Pearce, Attorney-at-Law."

Boy's Eye View

Benjamin F. Butler, law partner of Martin Van Buren, was appointed Attorney General of the United States by Andrew Jackson in 1833. Upon arriving in Washington, he took his eight-year-old son to show him the Supreme Court. William, who became also a prominent lawyer, recalled the event in later life:

My boyish attention was fastened upon the seven judges as they entered the room—seven being the number then composing the Court. It was a procession of old men—for so they seemed to me—who halted on their way to the bench, each of them taking from a peg hanging on the side of the wall near the entrance a black robe and donning it in full view of the assembled lawyers and other spectators. This somewhat extra-judicial act impressed me more than any subsequent proceeding of the Court, and left a vivid picture in my memory.

Long afterward when I went to Washington to argue cases before the highest tribunal, contrasting the dignified formalities which attended the opening of the Court at every session with the robing method which I have described, I began to think I must have been mistaken and that I could not have seen Chief Justice Marshall, Judge Story and their associates doing so informal a thing as putting on their robes after entering the courtroom.

One day after the adjournment of the Court, Chief Justice Taney stopped, as was oftentimes the habit, to exchange a word with me. I seized the opportunity to ask him whether my recollection in this matter of the robing of the Justices was correct or at fault. He said that I was quite right in my remembrance and that until the Court was moved upstairs, the Judges always put on their robes in the courtroom.

Justice in the Afternoon

The atmosphere of the United States Supreme Court in the post Civil War period is captured by journalist Mary Clemmer Ames:

One of the few rooms in the Capitol wherein harmony and beauty meet and mingle, is the Old Senate Chamber, now the Supreme Court Room of the United States. Defiance and defeat, battle and triumph, argument and oratory, wisdom and folly once held here their court. It is now the chamber of peace. Tangled questions concerning life, liberty and the pursuit of personal happiness are still argued within these walls, but never in tones which would drown the sound of a dropping pin. Every thought is weighed, every word measured that is uttered here. The judges, who sit in silence to listen and decide, have outlived the tumult of youth and the summer of manhood's fiercer battles. They have earned fruition, they have won their gowns—which, while life lasts, can never be worn by others. Theirs is the mellow afternoon of wise judgment and wine-dinners.

In the Court room itself we seem to have reached an atmosphere where it is always afternoon. The door swings to and fro noiselessly, at the pull of the usher's string. The spectators move over a velvet carpet, which sends back no echo, to their velvet cushioned seats ranged against the outer walls. A single lawyer, arguing some constitutional question, drones on within the railed inclosure of the Court; or a single judge in measured tones mumbles over the pages of his learned decision in some case long drawn out. Unless you are deeply interested in it you will not stay long. The atmosphere is too soporific, you soon weary of absolute silence and decorum and depart.

In the Law Library

Veteran journalist Benjamin Perley Poore recalled some of the lore associated with the old Law Library in his Reminiscences of Sixty Years *(1886):*

In December 1860, the Law Library was removed into the basement room of the Capitol, just vacated by the Supreme Court. This unique room is supported by pillars in clusters of stalks of maize, with capitals of bursting ears of corn, the design of Mr. Latrobe. The chamber itself is of semicircular form seventy-five feet in length. The arches of the ceiling rest upon immense Doric columns. The spandrels of the arches are filled in with solid masonry—blocks of sandstone, strong enough to support the whole Capitol. Their tragic strength springs from the fact that the arch above fell once, burying and killing beneath it its designer, Mr. Lenthall. The plan of his arch in proportion to its height was pronounced unsafe by all who examined the drawing, except himself. To prove his own faith in his theory he tore away the scaffolding before the ceiling was dry. It fell, and he was taken out hours later, dead and mangled, from its fallen ruins. It will never fall again. The tremendous masonry which now supports a very light burden makes it impossible. The Doric columns diverge from the center to the circumference like the radii of a circle. Form this center diverge the alcoves lined with books in the regulation binding, likened by Dickens to "underdone pie-crust." On the western wall near the ceiling is a group in plaster, representing Justice holding the scales, and Fame crowned with the rising sun, pointing to the Constitution of the United States, the work of Franzoni, the sculptor of the History-winged clock, in old Hall of Representatives. In this room, Daniel Webster made his great speech in the Dartmouth College case, and Horace Binney his argument in the case of the Girard will. The Librarian's semicircular mahogany desk, with its faded brocade draperies, once stood in the old Senate Chamber and re-echoed the gavel of every vice president who reigned in the Senate from 1825 to 1860.

It was in the earlier Law Library that Chief Justice Marshall one day fell from a step-ladder, bruising himself severely and scattering an armful of books in all directions. When an alarmed attendant ran to his assistance, his Honor dryly remarked, "That time I was completely floored."

As Long as They Are White

When today's Supreme Court building opened in Washington in 1935, Justice Harlan Stone contemplated the vast plaza, the massive Greek columns, the huge bronze doors, and the brow and beard of Chief Justice Hughes carved in Dorsett marble above. "Whenever I look at that building," he remarked, "I feel that the justices should ride to work on elephants."

Ye Olde Lawe Office

Law, by definition, is full of tradition, customs, and historical association. Reginald Hine joined the English firm of solicitors, Messrs. Hawkins and Co. of Hitchin, Hertfordshire, at the turn of the century. It had occupied the same building since 1591, a fact that young Hine found reflected by his surroundings:

It would not be correct to describe the interior as comely. Like most lawyers' offices (but why, why, why!) the rooms—littered with files, the dust of ages upon them—looked dishevelled and untidy. The wall-papers were of the mock varnished and grained pine in favor a century before, though if you explored with a penknife you might light upon five or six other specimens, each more attractive than the one above. The windows were made to open, but a ponderous legalistic atmosphere hung about the chambers: a curious conglomerate of parchment, sealing wax, corroding ink, calf bindings, stale tobacco, escaping gas, and myriad decaying matters. But very soon one became 'part and parcel' of all this; one accepted, one even liked one's surroundings; they were all of a piece with the antiquity of the firm; one was proud to be able to smell one's way back to Elizabethan times.

Then there were other attractions. One's fancy was caught by the double doors of some of the principal rooms, an inner door of baize, warranted to muffle the guiltiest of intimate confessions. The room I occupied possessed a secret chamber, opened by a hidden spring in the wall, large enough to conceal a confidential clerk if earshot evidence of a ticklish interview were needful. Everywhere one came upon cupboards, some of them undisturbed for centuries, filled with family skeletons and other surprising things. One of the first I opened contained the reports and account books of the celebrated Macadam (1756-1836), whom the firm, as clerks to the local Turnpike Trusts, had called in to macadamize and improve the Hitchin-to-Welwyn and Hitchin-to-Bedford roads. In another cupboard I came upon a marked catalogue of the sale of Byron's furniture and books, and I remembered that on 13th July 1824 his funeral cortege passed through Hitchin, with a black slave and a Greek attendant, and that some of Hawkins & Co.'s clients had been privileged, for one memorable moment, to take up the precious casket enshrining the poet's heart, and hold it in their hands, and that one of the women Friends was 'scandalously reported to have kissed it.' Tied up with a bundle of title-deeds in another cupboard I found two letters from the Cromwellian and Restoration poet, Andrew Marvell, written when member for Hull in 1670, and complaining that no one could expect promotions, spiritual or temporal, unless he made his court to the king's mistress, the Duchess of Cleveland.

On a shelf in that same cupboard, deep in dust, reposed the draft of a Bill introduced into the House of Commons in 1770, forbidding any woman 'to impose upon, seduce, or betray into Matrimony any of His Majesty's subjects by means of scent, paints, cosmetic washes, artificial teeth, Spanish wool, iron stays, hoops, high-heeled shoes, or bolstered hips.' Any marriage so contrived was to be null and void.

The Bar Building

By the early 1940s, Fanny Holtzmann's legal practice stretched from Europe's royal circles to Hollywood's self-made royalty. She ran her empire from offices in New York,

. . . a light-green, dusty suite of rooms in the Bar Building at 36 West Forty-fourth Street, furnished with the same carpets, tables, and chairs that she bought when she opened it in 1923. Pictures of Daniel Webster and John Marshall lend an Old World tone to the entrance hall, but the walls of Fanny's private office are lined with signed photographs of more spirited people, all friends or clients—Ina Claire, Clifton Webb, Noel Coward, Lady Astor, Lord Haldane, Justice Cardozo, Fred Astaire, Mme. Wellington Koo, and thirty or forty others.

Margaret Case Harriman in the same profile in the New Yorker *mentions the difficulties Miss Holtzmann had originally encountered from other lawyers in the then newly completed Bar Building:*

There had been some hostility toward admitting her as a tenant; she was female, young—barely twenty-one—and Jewish. She lived in Brooklyn and commuted on the subway, and her clients seemed, to the startled eyes of the other tenants, to be chiefly actors and actresses and wild-haired authors, all pretty spectacular. The New York Bar had admitted its first woman member only five years before, and was still inclined to look upon women lawyers as unnecessary. Fanny, however, was firm about establishing herself in the Bar Building. Woodrow Wilson and Bainbridge Colby had had offices there; Justice Cardozo, then Associate Justice of the Court of Appeals, had the office directly above the one Fanny wanted for herself. She liked to think of walking the same corridors as these distinguished men, and she felt, too, that a little dignity would add to her own success as a lawyer. The Character Committee of the Building finally admitted her, chiefly through the influence of her older brother, Jacob L. Holtzmann, a prominent lawyer in New York and Brooklyn. Justice Cardozo was the first of the older tenants to speak to her graciously in the elevator. "Well, are you coming or going this time?" he would say when he found that her rapidly growing clientele was tak-ing her frequently to Hollywood and to London; and one day he talked to her for quite a long time in the hall, and said that she was realizing his own youthful ambition, which had been connected not with being a Chief Justice but with rushing around all over the world on behalf of his clients. Fanny never brought a case before him after he was appointed to the Supreme Court, but whenever he saw her in Washington, he always remembered her and made a point of saying, "How do you do?"

No Joy

When he was appointed to the Supreme Court, Justice Cardozo missed the warm congenial atmosphere he left behind at the Court of Appeals in Albany. He found the Supreme Court stiff and remote and the only time he could establish real human contact with his colleagues was when they adjourned to the washroom next to the old Court chamber in the Capitol Building. But such opportunities for informal gossip came to an abrupt end with the new building in 1935: "Now that we have private washrooms," the mild-mannered Justice Cardozo complained, "there is no pleasure even in urination any more."

Another Roadside Attraction

Chief Justice William Rehnquist recalls the first glimpse he had of the U.S. Supreme Court on his first day of clerking for Justice Jackson:

It was essentially a square, flanked on each of its sides by four pairs of Ionic columns, which looked to me to be at least thirty feet high. Between the pediments atop the columns and the intricately inlaid ceiling were four bas-relief friezes, showing what I assumed must be great moments in the history of the law. Stretching across the front of the courtroom and covering the entire side of the room was the bench at which the nine justices sat. When the justices eventually came on the bench, they, like every other human being in the room, seemed dwarfed by the architecture. No wonder that former Chief Justice Stone was said to have remarked, when the justices first moved into the new building in 1935, that he felt like a beetle entering the temple of Karnak!

The courtroom itself was divided by the traditional "bar"—this one of ornate brass—separating the part of the room reserved for lawyers admitted to practice before the Court from that to which the general public was admitted. Men who were obviously attorneys were seated at two sets of counsel tables within the bar. Several of the attorneys were dressed in morning coats, and I later learned that all lawyers representing the United States before the Supreme Court, and some private attorneys as well, made their arguments in formal morning wear.

Thirty or forty spectators were seated on the upholstered benches provided for the general public. They looked as if they were impressed, as I was, by the magnificence of their surroundings. There couldn't be very many public buildings like this in the United States, I thought to myself. Above the spectators at the rear of the courtroom was a large clock, hanging by a thick metal cord from the pediment.

Just then the marshal of the Court, who was sitting at a desk to the right of the bench, rose, pounded his gavel, and called out, "All rise!" Simultaneously, three groups of three justices each came on the bench—three through an opening in the middle of the red velvet curtain behind the bench, three from around the left end of the curtain, and three from around the right end of the curtain. When each was standing by his chair, the marshal intoned his familiar words:

"Oyez, oyez, oyez. The Honorable, the Chief Justice and the Associate Justices of the Supreme Court of the United States. All persons having business before this honorable Court are admonished to draw nigh and give their attention, for the Court is now sitting. God save the United States and this honorable Court."

This ceremony moved me deeply. It was a ritual that had been used to open Anglo-Saxon courts for many centuries. A year and a half's exposure to it on a regular basis as a law clerk, and now fifteen years' exposure to it as a member of the Court, have convinced me that it is not only a stirring ceremony with which to open the Court, but that it is also one of the best tourist sights in Washington.

It is recorded that on one occasion, after these solemn words had been uttered, Justice Oliver Wendell Holmes was overheard to whisper playfully to one of his associates: "Christ, what dignity."

· 2 ·

PEOPLE OF THE LAW

LAWYERS AND JUDGES

Lying

Lord Hatton was hearing a case about land boundaries during the reign of Queen Elizabeth I. One counsel had stated with emphasis, "We lie, on this side, my lord," and the opposing counsel with equal vehemence asserted, "And we lie on this side, my lord." The Lord Chancellor asked them both, "If you lie on both sides, whom am I to believe?"

Lord Thomas Erskine (1750-1823) was much addicted to puns, and he tells of one example himself:

A case being laid before me by my veteran friend, the Duke of Queensberry—better known as 'old Q'—as to whether he could sue a tradesman for breach of contract about the painting of his house. The evidence being totally insufficient to support the case, I wrote thus: "I am of the opinion that this action will not lie unless the witnesses do."

Not a Medical Problem

More than fifty years ago, a plaintiff brought suit against the City of New York. He had been injured by a fall into a "corporation hole" (a manhole in modern parlance). During his trial, Dr. Willard Parker was appearing as expert witness on the plaintiff's behalf. In the process of cross-examining him, the associate counsel of the city elicited the statement that the plaintiff had been so gravely injured that he could lie only on one side. No sooner had the medical witness given his answer, the counsel said: "I suppose, doctor, you mean he would make a very poor lawyer?"

Inveterate Punster

Lord Norbury (1745-1831), Chief Justice of Ireland, was, perhaps, the most inveterate punster that ever sat on the bench, according to a contemporary admirer. When William Cobbett brought over the remains of Tom Paine's bones in 1817, Lord Norbury, on being asked what could be meant by such an importation of bones, is said to have answered that he supposed that Cobbett "wanted to make a broil."

A counsel thought he could overcome the punster on the bench. So one day when Lord Norbury was charging a jury, and the address was interrupted by the braying of a donkey, "What noise is that?" cried Lord Norbury. "It is only the echo of the Court, my lord," answered the lawyer. Nothing disconcerted, the judge resumed his address, but soon the barrister had to interpose with technical objections. While he was stating them, again the donkey brayed. "One at a time, if you please," said the judge.

Not Lame Where It Counts

John Clerk (1757-1832), later Lord Eldin, was about as plain-looking a man as could be well imagined. His inattention to dress was proverbial. In walking he had a considerable halt, one of his legs being shorter than the other. As he was proceeding down the high street one day, from the Court of Session, two young ladies passed him, one of whom said in an audible tone, "There goes Johnny Clerk, the lame lawyer." He immediately replied, "Johnny Clerk may be a lame man, but he's no lame lawyer."

Manners

Kindly old Justice Sir James Willes (1814-72) was hearing an application in chambers and found himself being badgered by a very persistent counsel. Trying to resist the pressure, he remarked mildly:

"I'm one of the most obstinate men in the world."

"God forbid that I should be so rude as to contradict your lordship," the barrister replied.

A Change of Mind

The speculation about nominees to the Supreme Court often revolves around how much past judgments and opinions can predict the future. Many great judges mature and change their minds, as Josiah Quincy recalls in his Journals:

In the beginning of the year 1826, Judge Story invited me to accompany him to Washington, whither he was going to discharge his duties upon the Supreme Bench. My acquaintance with this distinguished man began when, as an undergraduate, I dined with him in

Salem, during a visit to that town. As a boy I was fascinated by the brilliancy of his conversation, and now that I was at the base of the profession which he adorned I regarded him with peculiar reverence. I remember my father's graphic account of the rage of the Federalists when "Joe Story, that country pettifogger, aged thirty-two," was made a judge of our highest court. He was a bitter Democrat in those days, and had written a Fourth of July oration which was as a red rag to the Federal bull. It was understood that years and responsibilities had greatly modified his opinions, and I happened to be present upon an occasion when the Judge alluded to this early production in a characteristic way. We were dining at Professor Ticknor's, and Mr. Webster was of the party. In a pause of the conversation, Story broke out:

"I was looking over some old papers this morning, and found my Fourth of July oration. So I read it through from beginning to end."

"Well, sir," said Webster, in his deep and impressive bass, "now tell us honestly what you thought of it."

"I thought the text very pretty, sir," replied the Judge; "but I looked in vain for the notes. No authorities were stated in the margin."

The Young Lion

A certain N. P. Rogers of New Hampshire wrote to the New York Tribune *about the legends of Daniel Webster's earliest career in Grafton County in that state:*

The court-house was a little one-story building that stood on a hill. Daniel made his first speech, they tell me, in that house, and tried his first case there. It was a small case, and the only one he had. He wanted to get it put by. The lawyer on the other side was opposed to it, and Daniel got up and made a speech to the court that made the little old house ring again. They all said—lawyers and judges and people—that they never heard such a speech, or any thing like it. They said he talked like a different creature from any of the rest of them, great or small—and there were men there that were not small. There was a man tried for his life in that court, or one soon after, and the judges chose Webster to plead for him; and, from what I can learn, he never has spoken better since than he did there when he first began.

He was a black-raven-haired fellow, with an eye as black as death, and as heavy as a lion's—and no lion in Africa ever had a voice like him; and his look was like a lion's—that same heavy look, not sleepy, but as if he didn't care about anything that was going on about him or any thing anywhere else. He didn't look as if he was thinking about anything; but as if he would think like a hurricane if he once got waked up to it. They say the lion looks so when he is quiet. It wasn't an empty look, this of Webster's, but one that didn't seem to see anything going on worth his while.

Drama

Stephen J. Field was appointed to the Supreme Court by Abraham Lincoln in the middle of the Civil War. He stayed there for thirty-five years, until he became so eccentric and senile that his fellow justices asked him to resign. Before that, one of his opinions caused such a furor that in 1889 he was assaulted in a California railroad station by Judge David S. Terry, who was shot and killed by a deputy marshall appointed to defend Field.

Legal Prayer

A British Divorce Court judge at the turn of this century, Lord St. Helier, was a handsome man who did great play with his monocle, now plucking at his beard with his long, white fingers, now making brief notes with a scratchy quill, and anon sipping hot water from a steaming glass. Many a fair lady, blushing in the witness box, had fallen straightway in love with the kind eyes and sympathetic voice of the man.

Although he saw so much of the seamy side of life, Lord St. Helier always retained high spirits. He was something of a wit. He was once reproached by a legal friend for joining in prayers at the Archbishop's Court, when they had gone there to impugn its competency in a certain case. "But I prayed without prejudice," was his retort.

A Theatrical Judge

The architect of modern divorce laws in England was Sir James (later Lord) Hannen, who presided over the Divorce Court (after it was established in 1857) for more than twenty years. Henry Fenn was Senior Reporter in his court:

His habitual frown, affected cough, and theatrical air were studies in themselves. And so he played his part, no counsel daring to take a liberty with him. His facility and power of expression seemed to grow with his position, and no judge delivered more finished judgments.

One of his sayings was: "Every good judge must be something of an actor." It was in no conventional sense that he used the phrase, "This court is not a theatre," and would immediately suppress the slightest attempt at a demonstration in Court, or any indication of frivolity on the part of counsel only too eager to excite the risible faculties of those present, always an easy matter if not sternly checked by a strong judge. His reproachful glance at such persons was quite enough, and while he presided the Court was a model of propriety, far different to what has too often occurred at a later date.

He was a most interesting personality. His courtesy and kindness to the junior branch of the Bar was well known. On an occasion of a "call night," referring to what he did with his first brief, he told the newly fledged barristers to act as he did when he first got briefed. "Read it carefully. Then forget all about it as quickly as you can, for it's sure to be all wrong. Tell the Court a plain, straightforward story, and when you've lost your case, go back to your client, and tell him it was all the fault of that old fool."

On one occasion, replying at a banquet at Trinity House, he observed that, in his threefold capacity as President of the Probate, Divorce and Admiralty Division, it was a "hard matter to do justice between man and man; harder still between ship and ship; and hardest of all between man and woman."

Like Patience on a Monument

Oddly enough for a lawyer, Sir William Grant (1752-1832), Master of the Rolls (chief assistant to the Lord Chancellor), was a very silent man; he was the most patient of judges. Once, listening for two days to an elaborate argument based on the meaning of an Act of Parliament, after learned counsel had finished, Sir William said simply, "Gentlemen, the Act on which the pleading has been founded is repealed."

On one of his visits to Banff, he rode out a few miles into the country, accompanied by some friends. The only observation that escaped his lips was in passing a field of peas: "Very fine peas." Next day he rode out with the same friends, and said nothing, until passing the same spot: "And very finely podded, too," he muttered.

Beliefs

Lord Chelmsford (Frederick Thesiger, 1794-1878), was walking down St. James's Street one day when he was accosted by a stranger, who exclaimed: "Mr. Birch, I believe." "If you believe that, sir, you'll believe anything," his lordship pronounced and passed on.

Courtroom Genius

Francis X. Busch, court reporter and author, knew Clarence Darrow for fifty years and delighted in the company of this American original:

Darrow was not so well-rounded or profound a lawyer as many of his contemporaries. His love was not for such humdrum matters as the study of the current decisions. Rather, in the language of Pope, whom he liked to quote, Darrow believed that "the proper study of mankind is man," and his quest for knowledge of man's history and philosophies was a continuing one. He sought out men's religions, their psychology and their adjustments or maladjustments to continually changing social conditions. His mind was perceptive, alert and imaginative, his memory prodigious. It was his background of knowledge, the attributes of his mind and that indefinable quality found in all exceptional men that made him the courtroom genius that he was. As court reporter and lawyer I had the valued privilege of witnessing repeatedly the triumphs of his genius in the cross-examination of witnesses and in the assembling and persuasive argument of facts. In these departments he was without a peer.

Though without pretense, Darrow was a picturesque and arresting figure. A distinctive manner and appearance are of special value to the criminal lawyer.

Picture the man! Nearly six feet tall, broad-shouldered but slightly stooped, he had a massive, well-shaped head and thin, stringy, unruly hair. His brows projected over a rugged, leathery, lined face, and his kindly blue-green eyes twinkled. His voice was low-pitched, musical, drawling. This was Darrow the man. Dress him in a suit of clothes, well-made but never pressed, and see him then as he stood to address a court of jury, a hand hooked through one of his suspenders, pulling it through the armhole of his vest. This was Darrow the advocate.

The Fly-Catcher

The last hurrah of William Jennings Bryan, the once brilliant lawyer, then failed presidential candidate and demagogue, is portrayed by his antagonist, Clarence Darrow, on the opening day of the fundamentalist "Monkey Trial" in Tennessee:

Down below, at a long table, near the judge's bench, sat William Jennings Bryan, wearing as few clothes as possible. So few, indeed, that had he seen some girl so arrayed he would have considered her a bad sort, and straightway turned his head the other way. His short sleeves were rolled up as high as they would go, and his soft collar and shirt front were turned away from his neck and breast about as far as any one less modest would venture; not for the fray, but because of the weather. In his hand was the largest palmleaf fan that could be found, apparently, with which he fought off the heat waves—and flies . . . He slapped away at them with the big fan, constantly and industriously. Somehow he did not look like a hero. Or even a Commoner. He looked like a commonplace fly-catcher. It is this picture of Bryan that abides with me. Of course, hair, or the lack of it, has nothing to do with intellect, and much less learning; but then, the day was hot and sticky, and one cannot look like a hero unless he dresses and poses for the part. And, even then, he should be engaged in something more heroic than swishing flies.

The Country Lawyer in Washington

Toward the end of his life, Senator Sam Ervin, Jr. published a charming little book called *Humor of a Country Lawyer*. As chairman of the Senate Select Committee investigating the Watergate scandal, Sam Ervin became a national figure. During his cross-examination of Maurice Stans, the finance chairman of President Nixon's re-election campaign, Senator Edward J. Gurney, objected to Ervin's style of questioning.

"I have asked the witness," the chairman replied, "questions to find out what the truth is. I am sorry my distinguished friend from Florida does not approve of my method of examining the witness. I am an old country lawyer, and I don't know the finer ways to do it. I just have to do it my way."

Senator Irvin was in fact a graduate of the Harvard Law School, but he liked the way he had been once introduced in his native North Carolina: "I understand our speaker is a graduate of the Harvard Law School, but, thank God, no one would ever suspect it."

Sam Ervin also liked to tell of his exchange with Lyndon Johnson, who once said to him:

"When I see a country lawyer approaching, I grab my pocketbook, and run." To which Sam Ervin replied:

"That's not surprising. Country lawyers often compel evil-doers to disgorge their ill-gotten gains."

Economy Drive

The following letter was sent by an exasperated U.S. circuit court judge to his employer in the early part of our century:

To the Honorable
   The First Comptroller of the Treasury.

Sir:

The following items paid by the Marshal of the United States for the Southern District of New York, which were ordered by me, have been disallowed in his account, namely:

One box linen paper $1.00
Six packages water-closet paper......... .90
500 Envelopes, printed in two colors. 5.50

$7.40

I certify that all the foregoing articles were for official use, unless the water-closet paper does not fall within that category. Whether it should be treated as for official use is a mixed question of law and fact. Water-closet paper was ordered not solely for my own use, but for the use of the several judges who have occasion to resort to the water closet appurtenant to some of the court rooms.

Water closet is undoubtedly applied to private use, and is not ordinarily used officially. In former times, as appears from Campbell's *Lives of the Chief Justices*, (see *Life of Lord Kenyon*), the judges were accustomed to urinate in the court room, turning their backs to the spectators, and using a vessel provided for the purpose. Such a vessel would seem to be officially used when used in that way.

By analogy, water-closet paper, although not used in the Court room, may be used *sub modo* in the discharge of judicial duty.

The judges might undoubtedly use legal cap when they retire to the water closet. Their act in so doing would hardly be tortious, certainly not larcenous, as could be demonstrated if time permitted. They probably would do this rather than not clean themselves. It may be readily seen that such a practice would cost the government more, annually, than the inexpensive water-closet paper.

The Government of the United States seems to have recognized the theory that its judicial officers should keep themselves clean. It provides wash basins and soap for this purpose, and I understand has uniformly paid for the soap which has been used by the judges in their rooms. Does it make any material difference whether the article is used to clean the judge's hands or his backside?

These considerations are respectfully submitted to the First Comptroller of the Treasury.

Very respectfully,
William J. Wallace,
U.S. Circuit Judge

FRIENDS AND ENEMIES

Out of Town, Out of Mind

After some years of absence as proconsul to one of the Roman provinces, Cicero was returning to Rome. He landed at the seashore resort of Baiea, and as soon as he disembarked he ran into a fellow lawyer. Cicero asked him, with that mixture of vanity and curiosity not uncommon among the profession:

"What do they say in Rome of my return?"

"Oh, Cicero," replied his friend, "they have not yet commenced to talk of your departure."

Quick on the Draw

Sir Fletcher Norton, the eighteenth-century British barrister, was noted for his want of courtesy. When pleading before Lord Mansfield on some question of manorial right, he chanced to say, "My lord, I can illustrate the point in an instance in my own person; I myself have two little manors . . ." The judge immediately interposed with one of his blandest smiles, "We all know it, Sir Fletcher."

Lord Sandwich said of Mansfield that "his talents were more for common use, and more at his fingers' ends, than those of any other person he had known."

Egomaniac

Henry Erskine (1746-1817), later Lord Advocate of Scotland, was so fond of the first person singular that he was nicknamed Counsellor Ego. Flattered by his friends as the champion of the trial by jury, on his promotion to the bench he chose those words for his motto. Garrow told him that he might have chosen a more classical and just as appropriate motto from Virgil: *Ille ego qui quondam* ("I am who I was before," i.e., unchanged).

Colleagues

When at the Bar, Erskine was always encouraged by the appreciation of his brother barristers. On one occasion, when making an unusual exertion on behalf of a client, he turned to Mr. Garrow, who was his colleague, and not perceiving any sign of approbation on his countenance, he whispered to him, "Who do you think can get on with that damned wet blanket of yours before him?"

One nervous old barrister named Lamb, who usually prefaced his pleadings with an apology, said to Erskine one day that he felt more timid as he grew older. "No wonder," replied Erskine, "the older the lamb the more sheepish he grows."

On the Receiving End

Lord Norbury was a notorious hanging judge, as well as a wit. Once he got as good as he liked to give. Riding along with a man named Parsons, a commissioner of the Irish Insolvency Court, they passed a gibbet. "Where would you be, Parsons," the judge chuckled, "if the gallows had its due?" "Riding alone, Norbury," was the commissioner's instant reply.

Origins

In the early part of his professional career, Charles Abbott, later Lord Chief Justice Tenterden, had a quarrel with a fellow barrister who had the bad taste to taunt him with his lowly social origins. "Yes, sir," Abbott replied, "I am the son of a barber. You would have been a barber yourself."

Unkosher Remark

Judah P. Benjamin, Secretary of State for the Confederacy during the American Civil War, was smeared by a political opponent with an anti-Semitic remark. "It is true that I am a Jew," Benjamin shot back, "and when my ancestors were receiving their Ten Commandments from the immediate hand of Deity, amidst the thunderings and lightenings of Sinai, the ancestors of the distinguished gentleman, who is opposed to me, were herding swine in the forests of Scandinavia."

Some of His Best Friends Were Not Jewish

Associate Justice William McReynolds was so strongly anti-Semitic that when Louis Brandeis was appointed to the High Court, he did not speak to his new colleague for three years. In 1924 he refused to sit next to Brandeis for the traditional annual photograph of the Supreme Court, so no picture was taken that year. McReynolds explained his behavior to Chief Justice Taft in a letter that includes the sentence: "As you know I am not always to be found when there is a Hebrew aboard."

Solidarity

Despite Justice McReynolds's anti-Semitic stance, Justice Brandeis would not

*tolerate any criticism of his colleague, as recalled by journalists Drew Pearson
and Robert S. Allen:*

Once, while visiting in the Brandeis home, professor Walton H.
Hamilton of Yale told this story to a group of guests, including the Justice.
A lawyer from Wyoming, with the picturesqueness of a cowboy and an
even more picturesque method of speech, was arguing a case before the
Supreme Court while Justice Holmes was still on the bench, and despite
a most impassioned appeal to the Court, full of the language of the
frontier, he lost. As he concluded, Holmes, who sat on the right of
Hughes, leaned over and in one of his loud, hoarse whispers said:
    "Can we hear that old bird again?"
The clerk of the Court heard the remark and afterward advised the
cowboy lawyer that, if he applied for a rehearing, it might be granted.
This was done. In the rehearing, the lawyer opened his appeal to the
Court with these words:
    "I come to you as John the Baptist saying, 'Repent ye, repent ye.'"
Whereupon Justice McReynolds, who was enjoying the performance
almost as much as Justice Holmes, leaned forward and said:
    "But are you not aware of what happened to John the Baptist?"
    "Yes, I am quite aware," was the immediate response. "He lost his
head through the influence of a harlot. But I know the Supreme Court
would not be so influenced."
At this point in Professor Hamilton's narration of the story, Justice
Brandeis, who had been listening, came to the defense of his colleague.
    "I do not believe that Justice McReynolds made such a remark," he
said. And, turning on his heel, he walked out.

Mutual Admiration

Daniel Webster's association with Jeremiah Mason, some sixteen years
his senior, was based on mutual admiration. Of Mason's legal abilities he
had the highest opinion. He regarded him as superior to any other lawyer
who he ever met. "I should rather," Webster eulogized him, "with my
own experience (and I have had some pretty tough experience with
him), meet them all combined in a case, than to meet him alone and
single-handed." And Jeremiah Mason once said to a friend: "If there is
any greater man than Webster in our country, it has not been my fortune
to meet him or read of him."
A friend and admirer of both told a story about them:
    "I happened one day to enter the courtroom at Portsmouth, where I

often went to hear Webster and Mason, who were always opposed to each other in important cases. I accidentally overheard the following dialogue between them, when a new case was called, and the clerk of the court asked who the counsel were on each side:

"'Which side are you on in this case?' asked Mason of Webster. The other replied: 'I don't know, take your choice.'"

One Lawyer About Another

Rufus Choate said about John Quincy Adams: "He had an instinct for the jugular and the carotid artery as unerring as that of any carnivorous animal."

Abraham Lincoln remarked about a fellow lawyer: "He can compress the most words into the smallest ideas better than any man I ever met."

Caught with His Pants Down

Abraham Lincoln was attending the circuit court in Bloomington, Illinois. The prosecuting attorney was Ward H. Lamon, a man of great physical strength, who took great pleasure in contact sports. He was so fond of wrestling that his power and experience rendered him a formidable and generally successful opponent.

One pleasant day in the fall, Lamon was wrestling near the courthouse with someone who had challenged him to a trial, and in the scuffle made a large rent in the rear of his unmentionables. Before he had time to change his clothes he was called into court to take up a case.

The evidence was finished, and Lamon got up to address the jury. He had on a somewhat short coat, which made his misfortune rather apparent. One of the lawyers, for a joke, started a subscription paper, which was passed from one member of the bar to another as they sat at a long table fronting the bench, to buy a pair of pantaloons for Lamon, "a poor but worthy young man." Several put their names down with some ludicrous subscription, and finally the paper was placed by someone in front of Lincoln, on top of a plea that he was engaged in writing at the time. He quietly glanced over the paper, and immediately took up his pen and wrote after his name: "I can contribute nothing to the end in view."

Smartass

A great big Irish lawyer once said to John Curran: "If you go on, I'll put you in my pocket." "Egad! if you do," Curran came back, "you'll have more law in your pocket than ever you had in your head."

BAD APPLES

Hanging Judge

Justice Francis Page (1661-1741) lived in an age when even petty offences automatically drew capital punishment, and it was easy to earn the epithet of "hanging judge." When he was old and decrepit, Justice Page was coming out of the court one day and ran into a friend, who asked him about his health. "My dear sir," said the old man, who had not lost his sense of humor, "you see I keep just hanging on—hanging on."

Hanging the Judge

One day at dinner, John Curran sat opposite to John Toler (later Lord Norbury), who was also called "the hanging judge." "Curran," asked Toler, "is that hung-beef before you?" "Do you try it, my lord, and then it's sure to be."

No More Mr. Nice Guy

From hanging judges to hangmen: Mist's Weekly Journal, *which counted Daniel Defoe, the author of* Robinson Crusoe, *among its contributors, reported on April 26th, 1718:*

On Sunday the Lord Mayor was taken so ill at dinner, that he was carried away by his servants, but is so well recovered that he sat in Court this week at the Sessions House in the Old Bailey, where the former hangman was tried for the murder of an old woman that sold nuts and apples in Bunhill Fields. Who making a resistance when he robb'd her, he beat one of the eyes out of her head, broke one of her arms, of which she died; he was found guilty, and is such a harden'd villain that he appeared not at all concerned, and went afterwards upon the leads, and took the present hangman by the hand, telling him he hang'd a great many, and now he must hang him. The old woman that he robb'd had but five shillings upon her.

Seventeen months later, the same paper reported that yet another hangman was in trouble:

On Saturday night last Robert Marvel, the late hangman (who beheaded the Earls of Derwentwater and Kenmure on Tower Hill, and who was arrested in going to Tyburn with three malefactors, who by that means were brought back and not executed, and for which he was turned out of his office), was committed to Newgate, and being unruly, was put into the condemn'd hold.

Marvel was sentenced to transportation. He requested to be whipped as an alternative, but he was both whipped and transported. William Kent, the London antiquarian in the middle of this century, cites other hangmen in trouble, including this item from The Times, *from January 4th, 1884:*

Bartholomew Binns, the public hangman, and Alfred Archer, his assistant, were brought up yesterday morning at the Dewsbury Court House and fined 20 shillings each and costs for defrauding the London & North-Western Railway Company by traveling on their line without tickets with intent to escape payment.

The Unsuccessful Applicant

Sir Walter Scott recalled once seeing an advertisement for a hangman in a Scottish newspaper. It concluded: "None but persons of respectable character need apply." Clearly the English were less discriminating. In 1883, when the job of public hangman was open, one gentleman wrote in his application: "I am by profession a scaffolder. Would you honor me with the appointment, I will do my best to please all parties."

Otherwise He Was Great

Lord Kenyon's hasty and ungovernable temper, and his partialities and antipathies, made him widely disliked by the Bar, while his absurd misapplication of a few stock Latin quotations made him notoriously ridiculous. He had, however, the singular good fortune to elicit two *bon-mots* from George III, who on one occasion said to him: "My lord, by all I can hear, it would be well if you would stick to your good law, and leave off your bad Latin."

And on another occasion, the king remarked: "My lord Chief Justice, I hear that you have lost your temper, and from my great regard for you I am very glad to hear it, for I hope you will find a better one."

Presumed Guilty Until Proven Guilty

Scottish judge Lord Braxfield (1722-1799) was presiding at a criminal trial, and the counsel for the defense was about to begin his argument when his lordship was heard to mutter, loud enough to be heard by several people in the court: "You may spare your pains; we're determined to hang the scoundrel at any rate!"

Judicial Murder

In early eighteenth-century Malta, a judge named Cambo was roused one morning by a fracas just under his window. Looking out, he saw one man stab another. The wounded man, who had been fleeing for his life, staggered and fell. At this moment the assassin's cap flew off, exposing fully his face for a moment to the judge above. Then, quickly picking up his cap, he ran on, throwing away the sheath of his knife, and turning into another street, he disappeared.

While still doubtful how he should act, the judge now saw a baker, carrying his loaves for distribution, approach the scene of the murder. Before he reached the place where the corpse lay, he saw the sheath of the stiletto, picked it up, and put it into his pocket. Walking on, he came upon the corpse. Terrified at the sight, and losing all self-control, he ran and hid himself, fearing he might be charged with the crime. But at the moment a police patrol entered the street and saw him disappearing just as they came upon the body of the murdered man. They naturally concluded that the fugitive was the criminal and made close search for him. When they presently caught him, they found him confused and incoherent. He was searched, and the sheath of the stiletto was discovered in his pocket. When tried, it was found that the sheath exactly fitted the knife lying by the side of the corpse. The baker was taken into custody and carried off to prison.

All this went on under the eyes of the judge, yet he did not interpose to protect the innocent man. The police came and reported both murder and arrest; still he said nothing. He was at the time the presiding judge in the criminal court, and the wretched baker was eventually tried before him. Cambo had conceived the curious idea that he was forbidden somehow to act from his own private knowledge in the matter brought before him—that he must deal with the case according to the evidence of the witnesses. So he sat on the bench to hear the circumstantial proofs against a man whom he knew beyond the shadow of a doubt to be innocent. When he saw that the evidence was insufficient, amounting to no more than *semi prova*, half-proof, according to Maltese law, he used every endeavor to make the accused confess his crime. Failing in this, he ordered the baker to be "put to the question," with the result that under torture the man confessed to the murder he had not committed.

Cambo was now perfectly satisfied; the accused, who had been innocent in fact, was now guilty according to law, and having thus satisfied himself that his procedure was right, he carried his strange logic to the end and sentenced the baker to death. Sometime after the baker had been executed, the real murderer was convicted and condemned for another crime, and he confessed that he was also guilty of the murder for which the baker had wrongly suffered. He appealed to Judge Cambo himself to verify the statement, for he knew that the judge had seen him. The Grand Master of the Knights of Malta, who then ruled the island, called upon Judge Cambo to defend himself against this grave imputation. The judge freely admitted his action, maintaining that he had merely done his duty in sending an innocent man to his death rather than do violence to his own legal scruples. The Grand Master thought differently, and he stripped the judge of his office and ordered him at the same time to provide handsomely for the family of his victim.

Bribes

Lord Chancellor Francis Bacon, before he was impeached in 1621 and removed from the highest judicial office in England, in appointing Serjeant Hutton a judge of the Common Pleas, solemnly cautioned him that "your hands, and the hands of your hands, I mean those about you, be clean and uncorrupt from gifts, from meddling in titles, and from serving of turns, be they great ones or small ones."

Lord Bacon had a marked preference for "great ones" and he used to refer to bribes as New Year's gifts. In admitting to the charges of corruption, which were in part politically inspired, Bacon, one of the great intellects of the English renaissance, excused himself that "though he made justice pay more than he ought to have done, he never for money showed favor to injustice."

Indeed, it was difficult in those days to distinguish between gifts, bribes, and so-called court fees, which greased the wheels of justice. One of the trumped-up charges against Sir Thomas More, when Henry VIII used the Privy Council to get rid of his chancellor, was that he had received a gift-cup from Mistress Vaughan, the wife of a successful suitor in a case. More admitted that he had received the cup as a New Year's gift. "But my lords," he continued in his self-defense, "hear the other part of my tale. After having drunk to her of wine, with which my butler had filled the cup, and when she had pledged me, I restored it to her, and would listen to no refusal."

In another case, a Mrs. Crocker presented Sir Thomas with a pair of gloves containing forty pieces of gold, to help settle her suit against Lord Arundel. More, the man for all seasons, courteously accepted the gloves, but insisted on returning the gold.

It is curious how several of these early anecdotes of bribery involve women. Chief Justice Markham, who was dismissed from office in 1470, was petitioned by a lady, whose husband had lost a suit. He thought the judgment fair, but she was unhappy with the results and, according to Fuller's *Worthies*, "invited the judge to dinner, and (though thrifty enough herself) treated him with sumptuous entertainment. Dinner being done, and the cause being called, the judge gave it against her. And when, in passion, she vowed never to invite the judge again, 'Nay, wife,' said the husband, 'vow never to invite a just judge any more.'"

After the Fall

The most famous example of widespread corruption in modern times was fifty years ago, when Martin Manton, chief judge of the Court of Appeals for the Second Circuit, was removed from the bench. New York attorney Milton Gould, in his retelling of the case, which he played a minor role in prosecuting, calls it "the most momentous judicial disgrace in the Anglo-American judicial system since Francis Bacon was impeached in 1621"; a full account is to be found in Joseph Borkin's *The Corrupt Judge*. The disbarred Martin Manton served time without parole at Lewisburg, was released and died in 1946. Five years later, his former colleague, Judge Learned Hand, enormously respected for his probity, was testifying to a Senate subcommittee about ways of raising ethical standards in public life. He tried delicately to refer to the painful fall of his fellow judge:

Judge Hand: There lingers in the back of my memory some things that happened very close at home, but they shall not be mentioned.
Senator Fulbright: If there is anything wrong, it has been better concealed. At least, I am not aware of anything wrong.
Judge Hand: All right, then, I will not bring it to your attention. I could a tale unfold.
Senator Douglas: There is a former judge from New York who is serving in the penitentiary.
Judge Hand: He has gone now I would not say to a greater penitentiary.

Shysters

The term shyster derives, according to some, from the name of a certain New York attorney by the name of Scheuster (pronounced "shoister"). Back in the 1840s this lawyer so irritated Justice Osborne of the Essex Market Police Court that he would rebuke other attorneys for "their Scheuster practices." The most legendary shysters in legal history were William Howe and Abraham Hummel, who terrorized New York during the Gilded Age. Richard H. Rovere, in his highly entertaining series of profiles in the New Yorker, *chronicled their extraordinary exploits:*

Howe & Hummel found loopholes large enough for convicted murderers to walk through standing up. Once in 1888, Howe produced a state of terror in the city by invoking a technicality, which, if it had been allowed by the higher courts, would have set free not only the murderer he was defending but every other first-degree murderer then awaiting execution and every defendant then awaiting trial for first-degree murder. On another occasion, Hummel almost depopulated the city prison on Blackwell's Island by discovering a technical error in the procedure by which two hundred and forty petty criminals had been committed. After collecting a small fee from each man, they obtained the release of the entire group. Only sixty-some-odd prisoners were left on the island. During the investigation of Judge Albert Cardozo, the most villainous of the Tweed Ring judges who were forced from the bench in 1872, it was revealed that he had received bribes to spring more than two hundred Howe & Hummel clients from prison.

The firm specialized in breach-of-promise blackmail, and it employed informers to collect backstage gossip about prominent gentlemen:

Howe & Hummel affidavits alleging "seduction under promise of marriage" troubled the morning-after thoughts of playboys and stage-struck businessmen for a quarter of a century . . . It cost anywhere from five to ten thousand dollars to redeem a Howe & Hummel affidavit; the heart balm was split fifty-fifty between the injured lady and her attorneys. Howe & Hummel process servers often turned up disguised as Western Union messengers, scrubwomen and milkmen. A favorite way of delivering a notice of judgment was to have the server pose as a man who had lost his way or was in desperate need of a drink of water. After being admitted to the victim's premises, he would hang around a while, so that the victim would be sure to remember him later on, and surreptitiously plant the notice in a desk drawer or between the pages of some handy book. When the time was up and the adjudged complained that he had never been notified of the action against him, Howe & Hummel would confront him, in court, with the lost or thirsty stranger. The victim would betray the fact that he recognized the man. If he still insisted that no papers had been served on him, Howe & Hummel would suggest that the court authorize a search of his home or office. The papers would be found in the drawer or the book.

Influence

Arthur Train, as public prosecutor for the City of New York, was frequently up against Howe & Hummel:

Part of the firm's repute was due to a belief in their pull with the police and their closeness to the bench. It is said that Hummel had an unconnected set of telephone apparatus hanging on the wall of his office through which he used to hold imaginary conversations with judges and city officials for the benefit of clients who were in search of "in-floo-ence." A client would timidly inquire if Mr. Hummel by any chance knew the judge before whom the case in which he was interested would be tried.

"Sure I know him. I lunch with him practically every day," Hummel would say, reaching for the transmitter. "Hello—hello? Is this Judge Nemo? O, hello, Jack! Yes, it's me—Abe. Say, I want to talk over a little matter with you before we go into court. How about lunch?—One o'clock? I'll be there. S'long, old man. See you later."

The client by virtue of such an aurical demonstration of intimacy would naturally be convinced that his success or liberty was "in the bag" and that Howe & Hummel were cheap at any retainer they might choose to name.

Fleas

George Wilson, a nineteenth-century New York lawyer, was called before the euphemistically named Court for the Correction of Errors, which monitored in those days the professional standards and practices of members of the bar. Wilson had failed to account promptly for a large amount he had received from a client, which he argued had been offset by the value of his professional services. Some leading lawyers who had heard him declared that his declamation and force were marvelous and that one of his figures of speech was so graphic, vivid, and powerful that it brought some of the court to their feet.

Wilson's language was, however, erratic. In a case before a New York jury he commenced in a charming strain and was prettily coming down to describe life and its enjoyments and then its ills—and though he began by touching on these tenderly, poetically and affectingly, he concluded with:

Great fleas have little fleas
Upon their backs to bite 'em,
And these again have lesser fleas,
And so *ad infinitum.*

Blatant Prejudice

Few cases in the twentieth century have been more controversial than the trial
and execution of Nicola Sacco and Bartolomeo Vanzetti, convicted for a murder
and robbery they had allegedly committed in South Braintree, Massachusetts,
April 15, 1920. Convicted in an atmosphere of Red-baiting on July 14, 1921,
they were executed amid a flood of protest in 1927. The presiding judge, Superior
Court Justice Webster Thayer, behaved with such open hostility and prejudice
against the accused that Frank P. Sibley, the dean of the Boston journalistic
corps, felt compelled to detail in an affidavit the ways the judge had sought to
influence the press: ''It is nothing you can read of in the record. In my thirty-five
years I never saw anything like it . . . His whole manner, attitude, seemed to be
that the jurors were there to convict the men.'' Louis Stark was assigned to the
case by his editor at the New York Times *in 1922. He immediately asked for an*
interview with Judge Thayer:

After greeting me cordially the Judge said: "I hope the *New York Times*
is not going take the side of these anarchists." He pronounced the first
syllable of the word 'anarchist' as if it were spelled 'on.'

While I was rather taken aback that he should think the *Times* would
be interested in 'crusading' for two convicted radicals, I soon realized his
remark was merely an introduction to a denounciation of all radicals. My
reply to his question was that the *Times* was not concerned with taking
either side of the case but that it was interested in having prepared a fair
and impartial summary of the evidence on which the convictions were
returned.

Judge Thayer then launched into a detailed discussion of the case,
making no attempt to conceal his aversion for economic or political dissenters and particularly foreigners. His lips trembled with emotion and
his yellow and deeply wrinkled face darkened as he spoke of the need for
the defense of American institutions. It was obvious that to him a
philosophical anarchist was the same as a murderer. He went on in this
way for an hour, jumping from the trial testimony to criticism of aliens,
anarchists and radicals. They all seemed to be lumped together in his
mind.

The Judge stipulated that I was not to quote him. But the measure of his extraordinary prejudice against Sacco and Vanzetti was obvious . . .

New evidence was uncovered year after year to prove that the two men were innocent, to prove that they had not had a fair trial, that Judge Thayer had denounced them as 'bastards' and anarchists in conversation outside the courtroom. The Judge was begged to allow another member of the Supreme Court to pass on appeals since he was charged with prejudice. He ruled that he was not prejudiced. Affidavits to prove that important witnesses whose testimony helped convict the men had lied were submitted to Judge Thayer. He turned them down. The head of the State Police, who had told the jury that one of the fatal bullets was 'consistent' with being fired from Sacco's pistol, said that the question which elicited this answer had been framed by him and the prosecutor but that if he had been asked directly if the so-called mortal bullet had passed through Sacco's pistol, "I should have answered them, as I do now without hesitation, in the negative."

. . . Judge Thayer completely lacked judicial temperament in this case. His prejudice overflowed to reporters, acquaintances, and friends whom he sought out during lunch, whom he invited to his chambers. In a Boston club, on the golf links, wherever he went, something impelled him to denounce the prisoners before him. He sought to sway an observer for the Boston Federation of Churches to disbelieve Sacco's employer, who had given him a fine character.

Robert Benchley, then dramatic editor of *Life*, whose family knew the Judge well, said that in the summer of 1921 his friend Loring Coes told him "that Web [Thayer] has been saying that these bastards down in Boston were trying to intimidate him. He would show them that they could not and that he would like to get a few of those Reds and hang them too."

The Judge was unable to keep his violent language out of the record of the trial. In his charge he went out of the way to compare the duty of the jurors with that of our soldiers in France. His lack of restraint and judicial temper even led him to exclaim to a friend after he had turned down a plea for a new trial:

"Did you see what I did to those anarchist bastards?"

Vengeance Is Mine

In late 1957 there occurred a vacancy on the U.S. Court of Appeals, and Justice Felix Frankfurter found out through his friends Learned Hand

and John Harlan that a *bête noire* of his, district court Judge Irving Kaufman, was a prime candidate for the post. The pair's personal hostility dated back to Frankfurter's disagreement with Kaufman's handling of the Rosenberg espionage trial in 1952. A firm opponent of capital punishment, Frankfurter particularly resented Kaufman's manner in sentencing the two convicted atomic spies to death. "I despise a judge who feels God told him to impose a death sentence." Frankfurter wrote to Judge Learned Hand, and he added his intention to block Kaufman's advancement to the Supreme Court by extreme measures if necessary: "I am mean enough to try to stay here long enough so that Kaufman will be too old to succeed me."

And What a Way to Go

Percy Hagel practiced law after his own fashion in Winnipeg, Canada. In 1914 he helped a client on a murder charge to escape from jail, by smuggling in a rope and pistol for him. The man was recaptured and convicted, and Hagel was disbarred and sent to join his client in prison.

After his release, the ex-lawyer became an itinerant preacher, ranting against the evils of the flesh and of alcohol, subjects he continued to study firsthand. He used his gift of the silver tongue to persuade the Manitoba Law Society to reinstate him in his profession. Back in court one day, Percy asked the accused where he had been on a certain day in 1915.

"You should know," the man shot back, "you were in the next cell block!"

Percy Hagel's picaresque adventures became part of legend in Manitoba, and his end, which came in 1944, seemed appropriate. Peter Macdonald writes that he was found locked in the embrace of a scarlet woman, who later told a reporter: "When he trembled, I thought he was coming. But I guess he was going."

The Respectable Judge

Melvin Belli, the San Francisco attorney known as King of the Torts for the well-publicized injury awards he had obtained for many of his clients, was involved in a case back in 1949 which took him to Paris. Not knowing his way around the French court system, he retained a local *avocat* to join the case. When Belli landed in Paris, the lawyer was there to greet him, and as they drove away, he said that the outcome was practically assured:

"We can't lose; I've given the judge a hundred thousand francs."

Belli was somewhat taken aback; this was certainly not what he had been used to in California. Still, he was worried that the other side might have done the same thing:

"And what did he receive from the other lawyer?"

"But Monsieur Belli," the French advocate was shocked, "we are dealing with a respectable judge, a man of honor. He would not think of taking from *both* sides."

· 3 ·
CAREERS

LEARNING

Education of a Lawyer

In an English pamphlet, The Character of an Honest Lawyer, *published in 1676, an anonymous author states his view of the ideal training for the legal profession:*

As his profession is honourable, so his education has been liberal and ingenious, far different from that of some jilting pettifoggers, and purse-milking law-drivers, whose breeding, like a cuckoo's, is in the nest of another trade, where they learn wrangling and knavery in their own causes, to spoil those of other men, and, with sweetened ingredients of mechanic fraud, compound themselves (though simple enough) fit instruments for villainy. But his greener years were seasoned with literature and can give better proofs of his university learning, than his reckoning up the colleges, and boasting his name in the buttery book. He understands logic (the method of right reasoning) and rhetoric (the art of persuasion), is well seen in history (the free school of prudence), and no stranger to the ethics and politics of the ancients. He is skilled in other languages besides Declaration Latin and Norman gibberish: he read Plato and Tully before he saw either Littleton or the Statute Book, and grounded in the principles of Nature and customs of nations, came (*lotis manibus*) to the study of our common municipal law, which he found to be *multorum annorum opus,* a task that requires all the nerves of industry, and therefore employed his time at the Inns of Court better than hunting after new fashions, starting fresh mistresses, haunting the playhouses, or acquiring the other little town accomplishments which render their admirers fine men in the opinion of fools, but egregious fops in the judgement of the wise.

Oh, Take Me to the Bar

In a little book called The Barrister *(1930), Sir Harold Morris explains the mysteries of a traditional legal education at the Inns of Court:*

Everyone knows that, before a barrister is called to the Bar, he has to eat dinners. There are some who believe that eating dinners is all that is necessary, but there is more to be done and it takes time, work and money to get called to the Bar. The Honourable Societies of Lincoln's Inn, the Inner Temple, the Middle Temple and Gray's Inn regulate the admission of students, the mode of keeping terms, the education and examination of students, the calling of students to the Bar and the taking out of certificates to practise under the Bar.

A student keeps his terms by dining in the Hall of his Inn of Court. There are four students' terms during the year, each of about a month in length, and they fall usually in January, April, June and November. They are in fact the old legal "terms" when the Courts used to sit at Westminster and the Guildhall, though in those days they had "after term" sittings as well. The Judicature Acts created the present "sittings" of the Courts. It is curious that the old legal "term" should survive as dining periods and for no other purpose.

A member of a university can keep a term by dining in the Hall on any three days in each term, but others have to dine on six days in each term. To make the attendance at Hall available for the purpose of keeping term, the student must be present at the grace before dinner, during the whole of the dinner, and until the concluding grace shall be said. The proceedings start with the usual formality of a Hall dinner. Silence is called and the barristers and students stand while the Benchers in order of seniority walk in and take their places at the high table.

Students dine in Messes of four and the wine is allotted to each Mess, which has the choice of a bottle of port, a bottle of sherry, or two bottles of claret. A bottle of claret equals a half-bottle of port or sherry, and the changes can be rung on these according to the desires of the Mess. There is an ancient courtesy when the wine is opened. The members of the Mess drink the health of one another, and then the whole Mess drinks to the health of the Mess dining on each side of them.

One Good Turn Deserves Another

From a sketch of the life of Edward Thurlow, Lord Chancellor of England, published in 1790, comes the following story:

Having been absent from chapel, or committed some other offence which came under the cognizance of the Dean of the college, the Dean, who, though a man of wit, was not remarkable for his learning, set Thurlow, as a punishment, a paper in the Spectator into Greek. This he performed extremely well, and in very little time, but instead of carrying it up to the Dean, as he ought to have done, he carried it to the Tutor, who was a good scholar, and very respectable character. The Dean was exceedingly wrath at this and complained to the Fellows of the insult, and insisted that Mr. Thurlow should be convened before the Masters and Fellows, and receive a severe reprimand. They were convened accordingly, and the Master of the college accused him of the insult above stated, to which Thurlow coolly replied that what he had done proceeded not from disrespect to the Dean but merely from motives of pity, an unwillingness to puzzle him. The irritated Dean ordered him immediately out of the room, and then insisted that the Masters and Fellows ought immediately to expel or rusticate him. This request was nearly complied with, when two of the Fellows, wiser than the rest, observed that expelling or rusticating a young man for such an offence would perhaps do much injury to the college, and expose it to ridicule, and that as he would soon quit college of his own accord to attend the Temple, it would be better to let the matter rest than irritate him by such severe measures, which advice was at length adopted. One of the gentlemen who recommended lenient measures was the present Master for whom Lord Thurlow procured the chancellorship of the diocese of Lincoln.

Never Idle

John Philpot Curran, the great Irish advocate at the turn of the nineteenth century, got the usual, desultory education at Trinity College, as his biographer Charles Phillips remarked:

That Mr. Curran passed through this university without much distinction can hardly be considered as very derogatory to his character. He passed through it as Swift, and Burke, and Goldsmith did before him—"The glory of the College, and its shame." But though uncheered by any encouragement, and undistinguished by any favor, by the anonymous superintendants of the day, he was not altogether unvisited by their severity. He was called before their board on the slightest suspicion of irregularity, and generally proved himself more than an overmatch for them. At one time the charge was that he kept *idle women* in his rooms! "I never did, please your reverences," said the embryo

advocate, with the expression of a modern saint upon his countenance—
"I never did keep any woman *idle* in my room, and I am ready to prove
it." Their reverences, I believe, did not require the corroboration.

Water Torture

*After his years at Trinity, John Curran went to study law at the Temple. He
described his pursuits in London in a letter to a friend:*

I have made some additions to my wardrobe, and purchased a fiddle,
which I had till then denied myself. Do not think, however, from my
mentioning these indulgences, that I have diminished my hours of reading. All I have done by the change, is, employing the time that must
otherwise be vacant, in amusement, instead of solitude. I still continue to
read ten hours every day—seven at law, and three at history and the
general principles of politics; and that I may have time enough, I rise at
half past four. I have contrived a machine after the manner of an hour-
glass, which perhaps you may be curious to know, which wakens me
regularly at that hour. Exactly over my head I have suspended two vessels
of tin, one above the other. When I go to bed, which is always at ten, I
pour a bottle of water into the upper vessel, in the bottom of which is a
hole of such a size as to let the water pass through so as to make the
inferior reservoir overflow in six hours and a half. I have had no small
trouble proportioning these vessels, and I was still more puzzled for a
while how to confine my head so as to receive the drop, but I have at
length succeeded.

Extra Vacation

When Salmon P. Chase was at Dartmouth in the 1820s, a classmate was expelled by the faculty of the college on a charge that Chase
knew to be unfounded. He first went to the president of Dartmouth and
tried in vain to argue with him. Finally, the future chief justice told him
that he would have to leave, too, since he would not stay in an institution
where his friends were treated with such injustice. The two youths
packed up their earthly goods and drove off in a carriage. Almost before
they had got out of the village, the faculty sent word after them that the
sentence of expulsion had been rescinded and that they might come
back. But Chase and his friend said that they must take time to consider
whether they would return; so they took a week off for a pleasant vacation, after which they returned to their studies.

Advice

When Daniel Webster was visiting back home from college, his father sent him to find John Hanson, a neighbor who had moved away and whose sons had been schoolmates with Daniel. The young man made his inquiries, and, as he liked to tell the story:

One Saturday afternoon I thought I would trudge up there through the woods, and spend Sunday with my old friends. After a long, tedious walk, I began to think I should never find the place, but I finally did: and when I got there, I was pretty well tired out with climbing, jumping over logs, and so on. The family were not less delighted than surprised to see me; but they were as poor as Job's cat. Their house contained but one apartment with a rude partition to make two rooms. I saw how matters were, but it was too late to go back, and they seemed really glad to see me. They confessed to me that they had not even a cow or any potatoes. The only thing they had to eat was a bundle of green grass and a little hog's lard, and they actually subsisted on this grass fried in the hog's fat. But it was not so bad after all. They fried up a great platter of it, and I made my supper and breakfast off it.

About a year and half afterwards, just before graduating, I thought that before leaving Hanover I would go and pay another visit to the Hansons. I found that they had improved somewhat, for they now had a cow and plenty of plain, homely fare. I spent the night, and was about to leave the next morning, when Hanson said to me:

"Well, Daniel, you are about to graduate. You've got through college, and have got college larnin'—and now, what are you going to do with it?" I told him I had not decided on a profession.

"Well", he said, "you are a good boy; your father was a kind man to me, and was always kind to the poor. I should like to do a kind turn for him and his. You've got through college, and people that go through college either become ministers, or doctors, or lawyers. As for bein' a minister, I would never think of doin' that: they never get paid anything. Doctorin' is a miserable profession: they live upon other people's ailin's, are up nights and have no peace. And as for bein' a lawyer, I would never propose that to anybody. Now," said he, "Daniel, I'll tell you what! You are a boy of parts, you understand this book-larnin', and you are bright. I knew a man who had college larnin' down in Rye, where I lived when I was a boy. That man was a conjurer—he could tell, by consultin' his books, and study, if a man had lost his cow, where she was. That was a great thing; and if people lost anything, they would think nothin' of payin' three or four dollars to a man like that, so as to find their property. There is not a conjurer within a hundred miles of this place, and you're a bright boy, and have got this college larnin'. The best thing you can do, Daniel, is to study that, and become a conjurer!"

So You Want To Be a Lawyer
Sir Walter Scott wrote in his journal in December, 1825:

There is a maxim almost universal in Scotland, which I should like much to see controlled. Every youth, of every temper and almost every description of character, is sent either to study for the bar, or to a writer's office as an apprentice. The Scottish seem to conceive Themis the most powerful of goddesses. Is a lad stupid, the law sharpen him;—is he too mercurial, the law will make him sedate;—has he an estate, he may get a sheriffdom;—is he poor, the richest lawyers have emerged from poverty;—is he a Tory, he may become a deputy-advocate;—is he a Whig, he may with far better hope expect to become, in reputation at least, that rising counsel Mr. —, when in fact he only rises at tavern dinners. Upon some such wild views lawyers and writers multiply till there is no life for them, and men give up the chase, hopeless and exhausted, and go into the army at five-and-twenty, instead of eighteen, with a turn for expense perhaps—almost certainly for profligacy, and with a heart embittered against the loving parents or friends who compelled them to lose six or seven years in dusting the rails of the stair with their black gowns, or scribbling nonsense for twopence a page all day, and laying out twice their earnings at night in whisky-punch.

The Mason and the Architect
Senator Sam Ervin's father was also a country lawyer, who practiced for sixty-five years. Unlike his son, he was largely self-taught. Sam recalled:

Like most Southerners of his generation, he was denied a college education by the hard times that prevailed in most areas of the South for many years after the Civil War. He more than surmounted his deprivation by being a voracious reader all of his life. He loved to quote these words from Sir Walter Scott's *Guy Mannering*: "A lawyer without history or literature is a mechanic, a mere working mason. If he possesses some knowledge of these, he may venture to call himself an architect."

My father studied law without an instructor. After he was admitted to the North Carolina bar in 1879, he read every statute in Battle's *Revisal of*

the Public Statutes of North Carolina and every decision in the eighty existing volumes of the *North Carolina Supreme Court Reports*. If he disagreed
with the court reporter's analysis of a decision, he wrote his own analysis
on the margin of the page of his book.

He always maintained that a lawyer owes to his clients, the courts, the
law, and himself the duty to know the facts and the law of his cases, and
that cases are won by the diligence of the lawyer in preparing them for
trial and not in the courtroom. When I became his law partner, he gave
me this instruction on the first duty of a lawyer: "Salt down the facts; the
law will keep."

Lesson

Lord Brampton, the distinguished British judge who practiced at the Bar as (Sir)
Henry Hawkins, never forgot an incident he witnessed as a small schoolboy in
1830, and which formed an indelible impression on his mind for the next seventy
years:

I saw, emerging from a by-street that led from Bedford Jail, and coming
along through the square and near the window where I was standing, a
common farm cart, drawn by a horse which was led by a labouring man.
As I was above the crowd on the first floor I could see there was a layer of
straw in the cart at the bottom, and above it, tumbled into a rough heap,
as though carelessly thrown in, a quantity of the same; and I could see
also from all the surrounding circumstances, especially the pallid faces of
the crowd, that there was something sad about it all. The horse moved
slowly along, at almost a snail's pace, while behind walked a poor, sad
couple with their heads bowed down, and each with a hand on the tail-
board of the cart. They were evidently overwhelmed with grief.

The cart contained the rude shell into which had been laid the body of
this poor man and woman's only son, a youth of seventeen, hanged that
morning at Bedford Jail for setting fire to a stack of corn! He was now
being conveyed to the village of Willshampstead, six miles from Bedford,
there to be laid in the little churchyard where in his childhood he had
played. He was the son of very respectable labouring people of
Willshampstead; had been misled into committing what was more a
boyish freak than a crime, and was hanged. That was all the authorities
could do for him, and they did it.

Years afterwards, when I became a judge, this picture, photographed
on my mind as it was, gave me many a lesson which I believe was turned
to good account on the judicial bench. It was mainly useful in impressing

on my mind the great consideration of the surrounding circumstances of every crime, the *degree* of guilt in the criminal, and the difference in the degrees of the same kind of offence.

School for Judges

Unlike lawyers, judges are not trained specifically for their job. Yet judges are appointed or often elected in America not because of their legal skills but because of politics. In the 1960s a number of colleges, institutes and summer schools sprang up to upgrade the professional skills of judges. Donald Dale Jackson visited a course at the National College of the State Judiciary in Reno, Nevada:

Following the discussion, according to their printed schedule, the judges were to engage in "corridor conferences." The faculty envisioned excited huddles of judges extending and deepening their classroom dialogues at impromptu meetings. The sportier members of Discussion Group K, however, eschewed the corridors. Instead, Judges Tennessee, Colorado, and Michigan [not their real names, obviously] went to a nearby beer-and-pizza emporium called The Library, where they drank several pitchers of beer and conferred through the afternoon.

They discussed juries. "I believe in 'em," said Tennessee. "I think you can go out and stop five people on the street, any five people, and they know what justice is. They can do justice as well as we can. We don't have to hold back anything with 'em, or send 'em out so they don't hear some technicality. They know what's right."

"But we have to protect the little guy," Michigan said. "It's like Cassius Clay fighting some hundred-twenty-pound guy. We have to make sure that it's a fair fight. And we know more than the jurors do."

Judge Tennessee, the defiant democrat, shook his head. "I don't," he drawled. "I'm no damn better than the people on that jury. Oh, maybe I know a little law that they don't, but they know some things I don't, too."

The three had taken different routes to the bench. Tennessee won his job in a Democratic primary ("I had to kiss a few of those politicians' asses"), Michigan was selected on a non-partisan ballot ("The Republican organization supported me"), and Colorado, also a Republican, was chosen by his local city council.

Despite the range of their political and geographic backgrounds, they had more similarities than differences. All believed, for example, that judicial sternness was important in the face of increasing crime, that "respect for law and order" was declining, that all lawyers secretly yearned to be judges, and that a judge was a fine thing to be.

"The prestige, the robe, all that means a lot," said Judge Michigan, "and don't believe them if they tell you differently."

"I got tired of watching them other sonsabitches playin' God," Tennessee explained. "*I* wanted to play God awhile."

. . . I asked if they aspired to be federal judges. "Hell, yes," said Michigan, "that's the best deal around. But it's a long shot for somebody like me. You have to know the big boys or be a big contributor. With the kind of system we have, it's lucky we get as good federal judges as we have."

"What's wrong with the system?" Tennessee wanted to know. "It's politics. That's how it works. That's what it's all about. If I was going for it, I'd become friendly with everyone who could possibly help me, and so what? I ain't proud."

The talk drifted into descriptions of their somewhat tepid adventures the night before. Colorado and Michigan had visited a topless bar and discovered three brother judges there. "They were buying drinks for the girls," Colorado said. Michigan shook his head. "I can't even go into a place like that at home," he sighed. They had watched discreetly from the bar, played the slot machines briefly, and left before eleven.

"Only one of those girls was good-looking, if you noticed," Colorado said. "One of the others looked like her mother and the other looked like her grandmother."

Tennessee smiled broadly and raised his glass. "Why, you-all are just plain *devils*, you know that?"

Later that evening, on my way to accompany a group of judges to a teenage drug-rehabilitation center, I passed the motel where Judge Tennessee was staying. He was in front of the building, leaning against a wall. I stopped and asked if he wanted a ride.

"Where you heading'?" he asked.

I told him.

"Naw, I reckon I'll pass on that," he said. "You're answering the call of duty. I'm feeling the call of desire." He waved cheerfully as I drove off.

Inductive Thinking

Louis Brandeis graduated from the Louisville public schools at age fifteen with a gold medal for excellence. When the family business was dissolved by his father, Adolph, in 1872 to conserve capital, the Brandeis family was sent on what turned out to be a three-year trip to Europe. Seeking higher education but lacking the necessary preparation, Louis failed the entrance exam to the *Gymnasium* in Vienna; after a year of travel and self-education he convinced the proctor at the *Annen Realschule* in Dresden to admit him. Studying there from 1873 to 1875, Brandeis later claimed that it was in that period that he learned to think inductively—to derive new ideas from close attention to the facts presented.

Despite his lack of formal college training, bad health and failing eyesight so severe that doctors advised him to give up the law entirely, Louis Brandeis achieved the highest grade-point average in the history of the Harvard Law School. In so doing, he outperformed classmates who had the advantage of being both older than he (though he was first in his class, the trustees had to pass a special rule to allow him to graduate because he was not yet twenty-one) and from much higher social stations.

Not a Horatio Alger Story

Justice Benjamin Cardozo credited his success in gaining admission to Columbia University at the age of fifteen to the tutoring of Horatio Alger, a friend of his parents, who had studied divinity at Harvard. He had already begun writing those optimistic success stories about newsboys becoming bank presidents, and young Benjamin devoured these inspirational thrillers. He got his master's degree at nineteen and passed his bar exam with high honors at twenty-one.

"My preparation for college was the work of Horatio Alger," the Justice confided to a friend in later life, "but he did not do as successful a job for me as he did for his newsboy heroes."

Pearls Before Swines

The legendary Harvard law professor Edward "Bull" Warren was so enthusiastic about his subject that he always went on after the bell at the end of class. His students were continually late to their next class, so they decided to start shuffling their feet to let the prof know when to stop. The first time they tried it, "Bull" roared: "Quiet! I still have a few more pearls to cast!"

Why Some Lawyers Turn Out So Nasty

Sam Ervin recalled that on opening day each year, Bull Warren would say to his students,

"Look at the students on your right and left. One of the three of you won't be back next year because of poor grades."

Each teacher in the Harvard Law School had charts that revealed the names of his students and their respective seats in his classrooms. During my days at Harvard, most of the law students were veterans of the First World War who had endured the perils of battle. When Bull Warren questioned his students, he took up the chart and proceeded to question the students in the exact sequence in which their names appeared in one of its rows. Consequently, each student could anticipate when he was about to be subjected to interrogation. Sometimes students who had faced German machine guns without faltering descended to the floor and crawled under the seats to the door and made their exits from the classroom rather than endure the sarcasm that they anticipated Warren would visit on them if they gave an erroneous answer to a question.

One day a student made a poor response to one of his questions, and Warren commented, "Some students will never become lawyers. They ought to choose another vocation. I suggest that you study music or write poetry."

On another occasion he told a student he was going to interrogate him on law and that he hoped the student would make a noise like a lawyer in answering. He then proceeded to state three times in rapid succession the facts in cases, reveal the rulings the courts handed down in such cases, and ask the student whether he deemed the rulings to be legally sound. The student gave this succinct reply to each question, "I can conceive of the court making its ruling on the facts." Warren exploded, "You've conceived three times and haven't given birth to a single thought."

Common Law
Robertson Trowbridge, a civilized gentleman and lawyer who privately published in 1937 Forty-Eight Years: Anecdotes and other Oddments, *fantasized about his law professor in late nineteenth-century America:*

"A man cannot commit a rape upon his own wife." I glanced up quickly from my note-book, instead of following the example of most of my class-mates who were scribbling vigorously in theirs, and stole a look at the lecturer.

We rather enjoyed our first year lectures in Common Law, an easy, discursive commentary on a much abridged Blackstone, which made few demands on our thinking powers. The lecturer was a remarkably handsome old man, powerfully built, clear eyed and of a sanguine complexion framed in beautiful snow-white hair. He had a fashion of flashing on a benevolent smile, like an electric light, at the beginning and end of each section of his discourse.

When I looked up from my note-book after he had pontificated this horrifying pronouncement of the Common Law I must have expected to see the usual smile. If so I was not disappointed: it was there, augmented to sixty-four candle-power, a veritable *feu de joie* of triumph, cruelty, lechery. Not all this was apparent to me at the time. I was an extremely callow youth, just under age, 'unaware' to a degree that would now be unusual in a lad of sixteen. It was only later, when I had picked up a little elementary psychology that our venerable, white-bearded Law Professor was clearly revealed to me as an old satyr who systematically violated the person of his wife.

I have recently looked him up in the *Dictionary of American Biography*. He is there, with a long and laudatory account of his career and a beautiful vignette portrait. I was a little disappointed in not finding that he had been married three or four times—even six, like Henry VIII. His monogamy is very briefly noted. His wife's parentage is given, but there is no mention of children. I should have expected the poor lady to have died in bringing into the world her twenty-first infant.

The Ties That Bind

When the future U.S. Chief Justice Harlan Stone was Dean at the Columbia Law School (1910-23), he was probably the busiest man on campus, teaching several classes, with a downtown law practice and attending to all the administrative details that a dean is heir to. An unknown student from Yakima, Washington came to see him about his financial problems. He needed advice on how to complete his studies. Stone could easily have referred him to an assistant or another office on campus. Instead, he saw the young man immediately, and for two hours he dropped everything while he discussed the options of working part-time during his law studies, or of dropping out from school to make money, as Stone himself had done, teaching in Vermont, until he had saved enough money to return.

The young man decided to follow the Dean's example, and found a teaching job in Plainfield, New Jersey. Just before leaving campus, he dropped by the employment office, and found that there was a job advertisement to help someone write a law book. He applied, and the $600 he earned enabled him to finish his studies at Columbia. A few years later that student was teaching at Yale, the highest paid law professor in the country. And in 1939 William O. Douglas, as the young man was called, joined Justice Stone, his former dean, on the bench of the Supreme Court.

Storyteller

In his book of reminiscences, Senator Ervin paid tribute to a fellow storyteller, the Dean of the Harvard Law School 1916-1936:

Dean Roscoe Pound had a most remarkable memory. He could lecture for an hour without notes explaining the niceties of the law and citing by volume cases from all Anglo-American jurisdiction in support of what he said. He gave this exhortation to his students: "You must know the law like a sailor knows his ship, drunk or sober."

Sometimes Dean Pound would relax and tell this story. As a young lawyer, he practiced with an established law firm in Omaha, Nebraska, which represented all the railroads serving the area. He was sent to a rural community to try a petty case for a railroad before an old justice of the peace, who happened to be a good friend of the senior member of the firm. As plaintiff, the railroad sought to recover demurrage from a merchant on a shipment of freight.

The justice of the peace ruled in favor of the plaintiff. Dean Pound said that it was unusual for a railroad to win a lawsuit in those days and that he bragged of his victory before the justice of the peace on his return to the offices of the firm in Omaha.

His opportunity for boasting proved short-lived. After a few days, the old justice visited the senior member of the firm and told him: "You sent a young whipper-snapper to try a case before me a few days ago. He tried to make me believe that the railroad was the plaintiff. He couldn't fool me. I knew the railroad could not be a plaintiff, and so I gave judgement for the plaintiff as usual."

Deanliness

Writes Milton D. Green in It's Legal to Laugh:

Deans are a special breed. That is because they are required to represent conflicting interests: while looking after the welfare of the students they must also support the faculty, satisfy the alumni, and create a good public image so that legislatures and donors will be generous to the school. It has been said that a dean must be a contortionist—he must at all times keep his ear to the ground, his eye to the future, his nose to the grindstone, straddle the fence, and swim with the tide. Thurman Arnold, himself an ex-dean, sent the following telegram to his brother, who had just been appointed Dean of the University of Wyoming School of Law:

"CONGRATULATIONS STOP DEANLINESS IS NEXT TO GODLINESS STOP BUT UNEASY LIES THE HEAD THAT LAYS THE GOLDEN EGG."

Robert L. Stearn served with distinction as Dean of the University of Colorado School of Law and later as President of the University. While in that office he received a letter from a high school principal requesting names for a commencement speaker. The letter said, "We want nothing lower than a dean." Bob Stearn is supposed to have quipped back, "There *is* nothing lower than a dean."

Black Sheep

Milton Green throws further light on the sad status of law deans by quoting in extenso a letter composed and propagated by one of them, the famous author of The Judicial Humorist:

Dean William L. Prosser,
Law School,
University of California,
Berkeley, California

Dear Dean:
    I am writing to ask your advice on a problem, because I have a cousin who is a law school dean.
    I am a sailor in the U.S. Navy at Treasure Island. I have had a rather unfortunate family history. My father has epilepsy and my mother is insane, so that neither of them can work and they are both in state institutions in the east. They are totally dependent upon my two sisters, who are in burlesque, because my only brother is serving a life term in prison for rape and murder.
    I am in love with a streetwalker who operates off the end of the Bay Bridge. She knows nothing of my background, but says that she loves me. We intend to get married as soon as she can get out of her bigamy case, which is in court now. When I get out of the Navy, we intend to move to Detroit and open a small gambling house.
    The question I want to ask you is this: in view of the fact that I intend to make this girl my wife and bring her into the family, should I or should I not tell her about my cousin who is a law school dean?

Yours truly,
Henry (Illegible)

Written in Blackstone

For two hundred years all lawyers throughout the English-speaking world were educated on Sir William Blackstone's Commentaries on the Laws of England, *which he began publishing in 1765 as Vinerian Professor at Oxford. It became almost immediately, as Daniel J. Boorstin wrote in* Mysterious Science of the Law, *his early book on Blackstone,*

. . . the most influential and systematic statement of the principles of the common law. For generations of English lawyers, it has been both the foremost coherent statement of the subject of their study, and the citadel of their legal tradition. To lawyers on this side of the Atlantic, it has been even more important. In the first century of American independence, the *Commentaries* were not merely an approach to the study of law; for most lawyers they constituted all there was of the law. The influence of Blackstone's ideas on the framers of the Federal Constitution is well known. And many an early American lawyer might have said, with Chancellor Kent, that "he owed his reputation to the fact that, when studying law . . . he had but one book, Blackstone's *Commentaries*, but that one book he mastered."

The Commentaries *went through eight editions in his lifetime (Blackstone died in 1780) and countless more afterward. His work won extravagant praise from some, such as Lord Avonmore:*

He it was who first gave to the law the air of science. He found it a skeleton, and clothed it with life, color and complexion; he embraced the cold statue, and by his touch it grew into youth, health and beauty.

This was elaborated upon by the great reformer Jeremy Bentham:

He has taught jurisprudence to speak the language of the scholar and the gentleman; put a polish upon that rugged science; cleansed her from the soot and cobwebs of the office, and if he has not enriched her with that precision which is drawn only from the sterling treasury of the sciences, he decked her out, however, to advantage from the toilet of classic erudition; enlivened her with metaphors and allusions, and sent her abroad in some measure to entertain, the most miscellaneous and even the most fastidious societies.

But Blackstone attracted some prominent critics. John Austin said:

. . . the arrangement is a slavish and blundering copy of Sir Matthew Hale's; in the whole work there is not a single particle of original discriminating thought; its flattery of English institutions is a paltry but effectual artifice which has made it popular.

And Thomas Jefferson, writing to Judge Tyler in 1812, showed an acute understanding of the danger posed by such commentaries replacing the direct study of the law itself:

Though the most eloquent and best digested of our catalogue, it has been perverted more than all other to the degeneracy of legal science. A student finds there a smattering of everything, and his indolence easily persuades him that if he understands that book he is master of the whole body of the law.

Trust Nobody

Joel Prentiss Bishop (1811-1884), the author of many major legal works, advised students of the law not to trust authority: "A lawyer to be anything must enlarge his view by reading, and, above all, by thinking. And let me caution you not to believe everything you read in a law book. Take the caution with you in reading my books. I know that they are more accurate than our books average, but nobody is to be trusted. True, I trust myself, but God has given me nobody else to trust. And he has done the like with you. You must trust yourself . . ."

On Exams

Lord Birkenhead, Lord Chancellor of England, had this to say about bar exams:

"No one can pass an examination except people who have been working for two or three years in order to do so. It would be the most staggering performance ever known if the Archbishop of Canterbury could pass an examination in theology. As for a Lord Chancellor who could pass the final examination for the Bar, I do not believe that such a man ever existed."

That's Different

In 1830 Salmon P. Chase was examined for admission to the bar. At the close of the examination, the future chief justice was told that he had better read for another year. He replied that he could not do that, as he was all ready to start a practice in Cincinnati.

"Oh, at Cincinnati!" the judge replied, as if any law or no law was enough for such a backwoods settlement—"well then, Mr. Clerk, swear in Mr. Chase."

Only in California

A story told by a former secretary of the California Board of Bar Examiners recalls an applicant who had failed the exam three times. He was granted a special permission to try once more, but he died before his papers were graded. The widow applied to have his license granted posthumously. It turned out that she and her husband were both spiritualists, and she said that he had communicated to her that it would greatly enhance his standing in the spirit world to have his professional license.

Jeopardy!

Milton Green tells the story of a student being asked during an exam on criminal law, "What is double jeopardy?" He really had no idea but thought he would give it a try. So he wrote: "The question is 'What is double jeopardy?'" This technique of repeating the question is not uncommon among students who do not know the answer and are sparring for time to think. So far, of course, he was absolutely right. He next wrote: "In order to determine what double jeopardy is, one must first know what single jeopardy is." Again he has put off the evil moment. Finally he came out with it: "Single jeopardy is the sound made by one jeopard, so double jeopardy is the sound made by two jeopards."

In a class about property law, the students had been studying the cases which held that apples, while on the tree, were real property, but upon falling on the ground they became personal property. The instructor then asked, "Is manure real or personal property?" A student promptly responded, "Personal. Nothing is more personal than manure."

STARTING OUT

Capital Argument

When Melville W. Fuller was growing up in mid-nineteenth-century Maine, he belonged to a debating club in Oldtown. One evening there was a debate on capital punishment. The deacon of the local church was in favor of hanging; young Fuller was opposed.

"Whoso sheddeth man's blood," the deacon argued, quoting the law of Moses, "by man his blood shall be shed." Thinking this to be a bombshell to his opponents he dwelt upon it until his time had expired, when Fuller sprang to his feet, and said:

"Supposing we take the law which the gentleman has quoted and see what the logical deduction would come to. For example, one man kills another; another man kills him, and so on, until we come to the last man on earth. Who's going to kill him? He dare not commit suicide, for the same law forbids. Now, Deacon, what are you going to do with that last man?"

The boy's logic called out rounds of applause, and vanquished the deacon, and the victor went on to become chief justice of the United States.

Contract

In accepting each year a law clerk or secretary from Harvard's graduating class, Justice Oliver Holmes made only one condition: the clerk had to agree not to marry during that one year of employment. As he grew older, the justice added that he reserved the right to die or resign.

Pupils

Sir Harold Morris, an English barrister early in this century, once asked his older colleague, Sir Charles Gill, if he ever took on pupils. "Yes," Gill said, in his slow way, with characteristic pauses, "but I have one rule—which I tell 'em—before I agree to take 'em—they must never"—and here the pause was longer—"ask questions."

Devils

Morris himself became a pupil with Edward Beaumont:

"Mens sana in corpore sano" [A sound mind in a sound body] was a motto with Edward Beaumont, and to carry it into effect he kept some sets of Indian clubs in his chambers, for exercise, for himself and his pupils. On most mornings if he was not in Court we had to swing Indian clubs in his room for about ten minutes, and then he dealt out a set of papers to each of us and we went up to the pupil room to draft a conveyance or write an opinion. In the evening the pupils were sent for and their efforts examined and corrected.

He had a pupil-room on the top floor of the house where he had his chambers, and we pupils sat there and worried at his papers: one of his chief "devils" shared the room with us. Every junior barrister in a big practice has to have one or two other barristers called "devils" to assist him in drafting his pleadings, getting up his cases and doing them in Court when he is called away to some other case. Except for drafting work "devils" are usually unpaid. In Court cases it is considered that the honor and glory of doing the case, the experience and the chance of picking up a client, are sufficient payment. I am not sure how the word "devil" originated, but I am inclined to think it comes from the old "Devil's Advocate" (*Advocatus Diaboli*) who was originally employed to find out the worst that could be alleged against a person or a cause. The "devil" finds out the worst that can be said against the other side's case.

My fellow pupil when I was with Edward Beaumont was a sergeant in the Inns of Court Rifle Volunteers, generally known as the "Devil's Own". It got the nickname because most of the members had been "devils" or hoped to be "devils" at some time in their careers at the Bar. We all joined the "Inns of Court" and hilarious times we used to have at camp. I remember Viscount Hailsham, Mr. Justice Roche, Mr. Justice McKinnon, Sir William Leese, and Sir Owen Seaman, the editor of *Punch*, to name only a few of the distinguished men who were in the ranks of the Inns of Court. Arthur Roberts, the comedian, had a very popular song, the chorus of which went:

> Someone ought to speak to Milly Simpson,
> Someone ought to tell her, if they could,
> That it isn't ladylike
> To ride feet up on a bike,
> A word or two might do the lady good.

How to Get an Unpaid Job

The American lawyer Arthur Train got his law degree from Harvard in 1899, spent some bored months working at a Boston law firm, then moved to New York, where more boredom followed.

Then I had a piece of undeserved luck—if the luck of an opportunist is ever undeserved—Governor [Theodore] Roosevelt removed Asa Bird Gardiner, the erratic district attorney of New York County, and appointed in his place Eugene A. Philbin.

I was in bed, suffering from a bad case of flu, when I read the piece of news which was eventually to determine the whole future course of my life. I had never heard of Mr. Philbin, only vaguely of Mr. Gardiner. I knew nothing of the district attorney save that it was his office to prosecute crime. But I broke out in a cold sweat. Here was the chance I was looking for. My father had been a public prosecutor. Why should not

I? Was this perhaps the something I had been looking for beyond the legal ranges?

I leaped out of bed, dressed and hurried downtown, where I secured a letter of introduction to the new encumbent from Mr. Lewis L. Delafield, then one of the leaders of the junior New York Bar, a prominent figure in reform politics. Armed with this I paid my first visit to the grimy old building on Lafayette Street where I was destined to spend so many active years.

Mr. Philbin, a grave, handsome man, received me courteously. He had, he regretted to say, already filled all the vacancies upon his official staff. His salary appropriation was entirely exhausted. Perhaps the flu intensified the disappointment upon my face, for he added in a kindly way:

"I'm really sorry! I'd have been glad to appoint any one so highly recommended by Mr. Delafield."

"Then I'll work for you for nothing!" I exclaimed eagerly. Mr Philbin, taken thus by surprise, hesitated.

"Listen, Mr. District Attorney," I said. "You don't really know anything about me, but this is the kind of work I want to do and I think I can do it. Give me a chance and I promise you faithful service. If I don't make good, fire me. It won't have cost you anything."

He must have been impressed with my eagerness.

"All right!" he replied. "It isn't exactly regular, but I'll do it. When do you want to go to work?"

"Now."

Mr. Philbin rang a bell and a process server entered.

"If there is an office vacant anywhere give it to Mr. Train," he said.

How to Attract Attention

On August 20, 1931, the late Robert Kenny of California was appointed a municipal court judge. Not quite thirty years old, he had not practiced law for the required five years, but he persuaded the governor to post-date his commission to September 13, by which time he was able to qualify. (It was Kenny who once defined a judge as ''just a fellow who knew the governor.'') Biographer Janet Stevenson tells how the young man used his unpromising office for advancement.

A few months later, Kenny was assigned by the presiding judge of the department to the small claims court, a position which was not considered desirable . . . but which turned out to be a gold-rich Siberia for an ex-newspaperman. No attorneys were permitted there. Controversy was served up raw. The sums of money involved were insignificant, so the press usually neglected to cover the proceedings. But Kenny found and exploited a vein of "human interest stories": cases involving pets—dogs, cats, snakes, birds, even alligators. His colleagues of the Fourth Estate knew a good thing when it was offered them, and soon Kenny's image was being presented several times a week to the animal-loving public.

Kenny also heard cases involving the shrinking or stretching of ladies' dresses by cleaners. He made it a rule that no claims for damages of this type would be honored in his court unless the plaintiff was willing to model the garment in court or in chambers, so that his Honor could determine the degree to which its fit had been distorted. Photographers found that sort of bait irresistible.

Acquiring a Taste for the Law

The following strange story is found in Manning and Bray's *History of Surrey*. Mr. Serjeant Davy was buried in Newington Church in 1780. He was originally a chemist at Exeter, and when a sheriff's officer came to serve on him a process from the Court of Common Pleas, he civilly asked him to share a drink. While the man was drinking, Davy contrived to heat a poker, and then told the bailiff that if he did not eat the writ, which was of sheepskin and as good as mutton, he should swallow the poker. The man preferred the parchment, but the Court of Common Pleas, not then accustomed to Mr. Davy's jokes, sent for him to Westminster Hall and for contempt of their process committed him to the Fleet Prison. From this circumstance, and some unfortunate man whom he met there, he acquired a taste for the law. On his discharge he applied himself to its study in earnest, and was called to the Bar, made serjeant, and was for a long time in good practice.

Sea Change

Lord Erskine delighted in relating to his friends the following history of his first lucky hit:

I had scarcely a shilling in my pocket when I got my first retainer. It was sent to me by a Captain Baillie of the Navy, who held an office at the Board of Greenwich Hospital, and I was to show cause in the Michaelmas term against a rule that had been obtained in the preceding term, calling on him to show cause why a criminal information for a libel, reflecting on Lord Sandwich's conduct as governor of that charity, should not be filed against him. I had met, during the long vacation, this Captain Baillie at a friend's table, and after dinner I expressed myself with some warmth, probably with some eloquence, on the corruption of Lord Sandwich as First Lord of the Admiralty, and then adverted to the scandalous practices imputed to him with regard to Greenwich Hospital. Baillie nudged the person who sat next to him and asked who I was. Being told that I had just been called to the Bar, and had been formerly in the Navy, Baillie exclaimed with an oath, 'Then I'll have him for my counsel!'

I trudged down to Westminster Hall when I got the brief, and being the junior of five, who should be heard before me, never dreamt that the court would hear me at all. The argument came on. Dunning, Bearcroft, Wallace, Bower, Hargrave, were all heard at considerable length, and I was to follow. Hargrave was long-winded, and tired the court. It was a bad omen; but, as my good fortune would have it, he was afflicted with the strangury, and was obliged to retire once or twice in the course of his argument. This protracted the cause so long that when he had finished Lord Mansfield said that the remaining counsel should be heard the next morning. This was exactly what I wished. I had the whole night to arrange in my chambers what I had to say the next morning, and I took the Court with their faculties awake and freshened, succeeded quite to my own satisfaction, (sometimes the surest proof that you have satisfied others) and as I marched along the Hall after the rising of the judges, the attorneys flocked around me with their retainers. I have since flourished, but I have always blessed God for the providential strangury of poor Hargrave.

Erskine turned his brief service in the Navy to good account. He was engaged to draw up the successful defense of Admiral Keppel, who was court-martialed in 1778 for not engaging a French fleet. Although Erskine wrote the defense, it was spoken by the Admiral. For this service he received a bank note for 1,000 pounds, which he ran off to flourish in the eyes of his friend Reynolds, exclaiming, ' 'Voilà the non-suit of cow-beef!"

Taking Action

After Daniel Webster opened an office in Boscawen, New Hampshire, his first writs were served by Sheriff Kelley upon Messrs. Purdy and Currier, traders in Boscawen. While the young attorney and the sheriff were at dinner, the former proprietors, with a reckless accomplice, expelled the keeper left in possession by the officer of the law, and by force recovered possession of the shop. Returning to the scene of action, the sheriff began a parley with the intruders and tried to convince them of the magnitude of their offense. But Daniel Webster resolved to vindicate the majesty of the law in a more practical way, and accordingly he ran for an axe to batter down the door. Before his return the door was unbarred, and the sheriff, having recovered possession of the property, levied—without judge or jury—a fine of thirty dollars upon the owners for forcibly excluding him.

The First Brief

Sir Henry Hawkins remembered a lesson he learned his first time out when a colleague had referred a hopeless case to him:

A father never looked on his firstborn with more pleasure than a barrister on his first brief. I was instructed to defend a man at Hertford Sessions for stealing a wheelbarrow, and unfortunately the wheelbarrow was found on him; more unfortunate still—for I might have made a good speech on the subject of the *animus furandi*—the man not only told the policeman he stole it, but pleaded "Guilty" before the magistrates. I was therefore in the miserable condition of one doomed to failure, take what line I pleased. There was nothing to be said by way of defence, but I learnt a lesson never to be forgotten.

Being a little too conscientious, I told my client, the attorney, that in the circumstances I must return the brief, inasmuch as there was no defence for the unhappy prisoner.

The attorney seemed to admire my principle, and instead of taking offence, smiled in a good-natured manner, and said it was no doubt a difficult task he had imposed on me, and he would exchange the brief for another. He kept his word, and by-and-by returned with a much easier case—a prosecution where the man pleaded "Guilty." It was a grand triumph, and I was much pleased.

Those were early days to begin picking and choosing briefs, for no man can do that unless he is much more wanted by clients than in want of them; but I learned the secret in after life of a great deal of its success.

I was, however, a little chagrined when I saw the mistake I had made. Rodwell was leader of the sessions, and ought to have been far above a guinea brief; judge then of my surprise when I saw that same brief a few minutes after accepted by that great man—the brief I had refused because there was nothing to be said on the prisoner's behalf. My curiosity was excited to see what Rodwell would do with it, and what defence he would set up. It was soon gratified. He simply admitted the prisoner's guilt, and hoped the chairman, who was Lord Salisbury, would deal leniently with him.

I could have done that quite as well myself, and pocketed the guinea. From that moment I resolved never to turn a case away because it was hopeless.

Poor But Proud

When John Curran, the celebrated Irish wit and barrister, lived upon Hog-hill, he used to say that his wife and children were the chief furniture of his apartments, and as to his rent, it stood pretty much the same chance of liquidation as the national debt.

Judge Robinson, a coarse-minded man, had the bad taste to sneer at Curran's poverty, by telling him that he suspected his "law library was rather contracted." Curran replied:

"It is very true, my lord, that I am poor, and the circumstance has certainly somewhat curtailed my library: my books are not numerous, but they are select, and I hope have been perused with proper dispositions. I have prepared myself for this high profession rather by the study of a few good works than by the composition of a great many bad ones. [Judge Robinson was the author of many slavish and scurrilous, anonymously authored political pamphlets, and by his demerits was raised to the eminence which he thus disgraced.] My books may be few, but the title-pages give me the authors' names, and my shelf is not disgraced by any such rank absurdities that their very authors are ashamed to own them. I am not ashamed of my poverty; but I should be ashamed of my wealth, could I have stooped to acquire it by servility and corruption. If I rise not to rank, I shall at least be honest; and, should I ever cease to be so, many an example shows me that an ill-gained elevation, by making me the more conspicuous, would only make me the more universally and the more notoriously contemptible."

"Sir," said the judge, "You are forgetting the respect which you owe the dignity of the judicial character."

"Dignity!" exclaimed Curran, "my lord, upon that point I shall cite you a case from a book, of some authority, with which, perhaps, you are not acquainted." He then briefly related the story of Strap in *Roderick Random*, who having stripped off his coat to fight, entrusted it to a bystander. When the battle was over, and he was well beaten, he turned to resume it, but the man had carried it off. Mr. Curran thus applied the tale: "So my lord, when the person entrusted with the dignity of the judgment-seat lays it aside for a moment to enter into a disgraceful personal contest, it is in vain when he has been worsted in the encounter that he seeks to resume it—it is in vain that he tries to shelter himself behind an authority which he has abandoned."

"If you say another word, I'll commit you," replied the angry judge, to which Curran retorted:

"If your lordship shall do so, we shall both of us have the consolation of reflecting that I am not the worst thing that your lordship has committed."

Nerves

U.S. Chief Justice Salmon P. Chase made his first argument before a United States court in 1834, in Columbus, Ohio. There was so much riding on the case for him and he became so nervous that when he rose to make his argument, the young lawyer could not utter a single word. He had to sit down and, after composing himself, he tried again and made his plea. After he was through, one of the judges came up to him and sincerely congratulated Chase. The novice, suprised and suspecting irony, asked why. "On your failure," the judge answered, adding: "A person of ordinary temperament and abilities would have gone through his part without any such symptoms of nervousness. But when I see a young man break down once or twice in that way, I conceive the highest hopes for him."

Starting Over

After the collapse of the Confederacy, Judah P. Benjamin (1811-1884) became a famous barrister in England. The man who began as a penniless lawyer's clerk in New Orleans made three fortunes and lost two of them. He lost *Bellechasse*, his Louisiana sugar plantation, because he had endorsed a friend's dishonored note for sixty thousand dollars. He was already 55 when he arrived in London; within five years he was making ten thousand dollars a year, eighty thousand by 1880. He built houses in Paris and in London, where he died in 1884. *The Times* wrote in its obituary:

"When he first settled in London he practiced in all the courts, and made many masterly addresses to juries; but in the very difficult art of examining and cross-examining witnesses and managing a case at *nisi prius*, he did not shine. This requires a special experience with the peculiar class of jurymen to be influenced . . . The Privy Council was perhaps his favorite tribunal; his wide acquaintance with foreign systems of law qualified him in an eminent degree to deal with the cases from the colonies and dependencies of Great Britain which came before the Judicial Committee in Downing Street.

"His great faculty was that of argumentative statement. He would so put his case, without in the least departing from candor, that it seemed impossible to give judgment except in one way. It must be confessed that this is a dangerous power, and sometimes imposed on himself. His 'opinions' were, in consequence, sometimes unduly sanguine, or at least, seemed so in cases which he had not the opportunity of arguing himself. When he did argue he often justified by his advocacy that which had seemed the hardest."

Pierce Butler, his biographer, wrote that "Mr. Benjamin was never in a hurry; never important with this big thing or that big thing, never pretentious, always the same, calm, equable, diligent, affable man, getting through an enormous mass of work, day by day, without ostentation and without friction."

Late Bloomer

Lord Camden's (1713-1794) father presided in the Court of King's Bench. He himself, then known as Charles Pratt, was called to the Bar in his twenty-fourth year, and he continued to await the arrival of clients—"their knocks at his door while the cock crew"—for fourteen long years; but to wait in vain. In his thirty-eighth year he was, like Lord Eldon, on the point of retiring from Westminster Hall and had resolved to shelter himself from the frowns of Fortune within the walls of his college, there to live upon a fellowship till a vacant living in the country should fall to his share.

This resolution he communicated to his friend Lord Henley, afterwards Lord Northington, who vainly endeavored to rally him out of a despondency for which, it must be confessed, there seemed good ground. He consented, however, at his friend's solicitation, to go once more the western circuit, and through his kind offices received a brief as his junior in an important cause. The leader's illness threw upon Mr. Pratt the conduct of the cause, and his great eloquence, and his far more important qualifications of legal knowledge and practical expertness in the management of business, at once opened for him the way to a brilliant fortune. He obtained the verdict and received several retainers before he even left the Hall. He was made a King's Counsel in 1755, and in 1757 was appointed attorney-general by his old friend William Pitt, who was prime minister. He now had an opportunity of acting upon the great principles of justice for which he had contended so long. When John Wilkes was seized and committed to the Tower for publishing the *North Briton*, No. 45, His Lordship granted him a *habeas corpus*; and when the prisoner was brought before the Common Pleas he discharged him from his confinement, amid the shouts of the people, which were heard with dismay at St. James's. After the liberation of Wilkes, he condemned, successfully, "general warrants," and "search-warrants for papers," which rendered him the idol of the nation. Busts and prints of him were hawked through remote villages; a Reynolds portrait of him was hung in the Guildhall; he had the Freedom of London presented to him in a gold box; he grimly laid down the law from signposts; English journals and travelers carried his fame over Europe. He was raised to the peerage and next year made Lord Chancellor.

No Kidding

Early in his career, Clarence Darrow was up against an old veteran of a prosecuting attorney who kept belittling him before the jury by always referring to Darrow as "my beardless adversary." In his summation, the young man decided to answer him: "My opponent seems to condemn me for not having a beard. Let me tell you a story. The king of Spain once entrusted a young man with an important message he wanted delivered to a royal brother in a neighboring kingdom. Even before hearing him out, the monarch flew into a rage and yelled:

'Does His Most Catholic Majesty of Spain lack men, that he sends me a beardless boy?' To which the young envoy answered with great poise:

'Sire, had my king but known that you imputed wisdom to a beard, he would have sent you a goat.'"

Darrow won his case.

POLITICS

Beyond Deniability

During the 1856 presidential campaign, one Mr. Hughes of Hagerstown, an intimate friend of Chief Justice Roger Taney, wrote to the judge in the heat of the political campaign, saying that it was affirmed all through the country that Judge Taney had declared himself in favor of Mr. Douglas for the presidency. Consequently the Irish Catholic voters were going pell-mell for Mr. Douglas. And Mr. Hughes, who believed the contrary to be the predilections of the chief justice, wrote to him for permission to deny that he had expressed himself in support of the Little Giant, as he was called. Judge Taney replied:

> Sir:
> I am Chief Justice of the United States. As such, since the year 1836, I have never cast a vote. I never permit any retainer or under-officeholder of mine to converse with me upon candidates and their prospects. I never give advice or render service voluntarily or involuntarily, upon any side. And so particular am I sir, that my name shall never appear, with my consent, appended to any politics, that I refuse to permit you to deny that I am for or against anybody at this juncture. If any man has affirmed anything on the credit of my name, I hold to my neutrality so tenaciously that I refuse to let my name be used for any denial, even of an unauthorized falsehood.

Not a Good Time to Go to the Aid of the Party

At one time the marshal of Chief Justice Taney's court, who was a stout partisan, wanted to go to the polls in his official capacity, to keep order, for the Democrats were hard pressed and required physical aid. The chief justice said to him:

"Mr. Marshal ———,"—he always gave every man his official term, and insisted upon being entitled to his own name officially, in like manner—"Mr. Marshal, you can go to the polls, sir, like every citizen, but if you go as marshal of my court, you go at your peril."

Hobson's Choice

Giving the reason for appointing Lloyd Kenyon (1732-1802) the Chief Justice in preference to Justice Buller, Lord Eldon said: "I hesitated long between the corruption of Buller and the intemperance of Kenyon, and decided against Buller. Not, however, that there was not a great deal of corruption in Kenyon's intemperance."

Courtesy

In the early 1840s, Horace Binney and John Sargent were arguing the Girard Will case before the U.S. Supreme Court, when a vacancy occurred on the Court. President Tyler offered Henry Baldwin's seat to

John Sargent, who declined the honor. But believing that it would be offered to his co-counsel, Horace Binney, he requested that the fact that he had been offered it first be kept secret during their lifetime. Then the position was indeed offered to Binney, who also declined it with the same request, in case the post was then offered to Sargent.

Murphy's Law

In 1916 Justice Charles Evans Hughes was persuaded to resign from the bench and run against Woodrow Wilson as the Republican nominee for president. On election night, convinced that he had won, Hughes went to bed. Just after midnight, a reporter called at his house, with news that the California vote, essential to his victory, looked doubtful.

"The president cannot be disturbed," said the candidate's son, young Charles Hughes, Jr. But the newsman persisted, so the young man repeated: "You will have to come back in the morning; the president cannot be disturbed."

"Well, when he wakes up just tell him that he isn't president."

(Wilson won the election by only 23 electoral votes.)

A Maneuver Backfires

Charles Evans Hughes became a distinguished Secretary of State after the First World War. Later, in private practice, he represented cases before his former colleagues on the Supreme Court. In 1930 he went back to join them under circumstances described by journalists Drew Pearson and Robert S. Allen:

Shortly after Chief Justice Taft died, Joseph P. Cotton, Undersecretary of State, was called to the White House by Herbert Hoover for advice as to whom he should appoint as Taft's successor. Hoover, who leaned heavily upon Cotton in all important matters, told him that he wanted to elevate his old friend Justice Stone to that office, but considered himself under obligation to Charles Evans Hughes, who had campaigned most effectively in his behalf, and who, he felt, carried great prestige throughout the nation.

Cotton agreed emphatically that Stone was the man for the chief justiceship, and mentioned the idea of elevating Judge Learned Hand, of the United States Circuit Court in New York, as a successor to Stone as associate justice.

"What I would like to do," said Hoover, "is to offer Hughes the appointment but make sure that he will turn it down."

"That's very simple," suggested Cotton. "Hughes's son, Charles Evans,

Junior, is Solicitor General and argues the government's cases before the Supreme Court. If his father became Chief Justice he would have to resign, and I'm sure Hughes wouldn't have him do that. Hughes is almost seventy years old. He has lived his life. He has received almost every honor there is to receive. He doesn't need the job, while being Solicitor General means a great deal to his son who is just at the start of his public career. So you can offer Hughes the appointment and be sure that he will turn it down."

Hoover thought this was sound reasoning and got Mr. Hughes on the long-distance telephone immediately.

"Mr. Hughes," he said, "I would like to offer you the chief justiceship of the Supreme Court."

Without a moment's hesitation, Hughes replied:

"Mr. President, this is a very great honor, indeed. I accept."

Hoover and Cotton looked at each other in astonishment. Then the latter exploded:

"Well, I'll be damned! Can you beat that? The old codger never even thought of his son!"

Spite

When James G. Blaine was running for the White House in 1884, a friend of his approached Roscoe Conkling, a famous lawyer and senator from New York, to make some campaign speeches on Blaine's behalf. "I can't," Conkling declined ungraciously, "I've retired from criminal practice."

But Blaine got even by telling a story about Conkling's vanity: "One day, when Conkling and I were still friends," said Blaine, "the proud attorney asked Sam Cox whom he thought were the two greatest characters America ever produced?"

"I should say," said Sam Cox solemnly, "I should say the two most distinguished men in America have been General Washington and yourself."

"Very true," said Roscoe Conkling, "but I don't see why you should drag the name of Washington into it."

God Listened

Justice Edward White was appointed to the Supreme Court in 1894 in part because he was a good Catholic. He was staying for a weekend party at the home of Senator Bayard of Delaware, which was also attended by

President Grover Cleveland. White, who was then a senator from Louisiana, asked his host whether he knew of a Catholic church in the neighborhood where he could attend Sunday morning Mass. The president overheard him and he later confided to Professor Bliss Perry of Harvard that he had made up his mind that "there was a man who was going to do what he thought right; and when a vacancy came, I put him on the Supreme Court."

Fighting Congress

Journalists Drew Pearson and Robert Allen captured the backstage maneuvering behind Justice Benjamin Cardozo's appointment:

Cardozo was first mentioned for the Supreme Court in 1922. The Dean of the Columbia Law School and other prominent lawyers urged Harding to appoint him, but the notorious [Attorney General] Harry Daugherty was permitting no liberal jurist, no matter how able, to get by him to a place on the Supreme bench. When Justice Holmes retired ten years later the renewed demand for Cardozo's appointment came from men of every viewpoint, including such liberals as Senators Norris and Borah and such conservatives as ex-Senator James Watson and the late George Wickersham.

Hoover, however, was not at all enthusiastic.

To Justice Stone, to whom he broached the subject one morning after a medicine-ball workout, Hoover explained his reluctance on the ground that two New Yorkers already were on the Court—Hughes and Stone. Without hesitation, Stone offered to resign.

Hoover voiced the same objection to Borah when the Senator from Idaho pressed Cardozo's appointment at a White House reception. "Mr. Cardozo," Borah shot back, "belongs as much to Idaho, or California, as he does to New York. It is not a question where the man comes from, but what he is, Mr. President."

Hoover then raised another point. He expressed the fear that Cardozo's selection might add fuel to anti-Semitism in the country.

"Mr. President," Borah replied, "there is only one way to deal with anti-Semitism. That is not to yield to it."

Several days later, Hoover telephoned to Borah to say that he was considering the names of two federal judges, one in New Mexico and the other in California. He asked Borah his opinion on the two men.

"If you appoint either of them," Borah replied, "I will defeat his confirmation."

"What is the ground of your objection?"

"Obscurity," was the terse answer.

Fearing another Parker or Hughes fight, Hoover finally swallowed his personal antipathy and appointed Cardozo.

Meanwhile, Justice Cardozo was just as anxious not to be appointed as Hoover was anxious not to appoint him. Walking through the streets of Albany with Herbert Cohen, confidential clerk of the Court of Appeals, at the time the appointment was definitely reported, they went over all the reasons why Cardozo should not and could not become a justice of the Supreme Court. By the time they returned to Cardozo's office they had planned a letter they would send President Hoover when they received his proffer of the justiceship.

Suddenly the telephone rang. Cardozo picked up the receiver, and Cohen heard his chief say:

"Why . . . yes, Mr. President. Yes, Mr. President."

With a dazed look, the new justice of the Supreme Court hung up the telephone.

"Why didn't we realize," he said, "that he could use the long-distance telephone?"

Influencing FDR

Although Justice Felix Frankfurter had a great deal of influence, especially in recommending to President Roosevelt appointments to the bench and to the Supreme Court, he failed in several efforts to promote the widely admired Judge Learned Hand. In 1942, to fill a vacancy left by James Byrnes, FDR ignored Frankfurter's strenuous urgings and appointed federal appeals court Judge Wiley Rutledge. As Roosevelt told William O. Douglas at a poker party several days before announcing the new appointment to the Court, "This time Felix overplayed his hand . . . Do you know how many people asked me today to name Learned Hand? . . . Twenty, and every one a messenger from Felix Frankfurter." Then with an expression of hardening, FDR added, "And by golly, I won't do it."

You Must Be Joking, Mr. President!

In 1936 President Roosevelt put Samuel Mandelbaum, a poor Jewish immigrant from Poland who became a champion of the huddled masses on the Lower East Side, on the bench of the Southern District of New York. Milton Gould, the famous trial lawyer, tells the story of this appointment:

A newspaper reporter in Albany told Sam in the spring of 1936 that his Washington office had a leak that FDR was going to give Sam one of the three new judgeships. Would Mandelbaum comment on this?

"Ridiculous!" said Mandelbaum. "I have never been in the federal court!"

A few days later he was invited to lunch at the White House. Before lunch, he found himself sitting across the desk from the President.

"Sam, how would you like to be a federal judge?" asked FDR.

"Who, me?" said Mandelbaum. "That is ridiculous. I've never even been in the federal court."

Roosevelt threw his head back and roared the famous leonine laugh.

"Don't move, Sam," he said, "and don't say a word." The President reached forward and pressed all the buttons on his desk. In came the White House entourage: Missy LeHand, Steve Early, Marvin McIntyre, Eleanor, half a dozen Secret Service men.

Roosevelt: "Now, Sam, I'm going to repeat what I said to you and I want you to repeat what you said. Sam, how would you like to be a federal judge?"

Mandelbaum: "Who, me? It's ridiculous!"

The imperial court burst into laughter.

"Well, Sam," said the President, "ridiculous or not, you are hereby appointed to be a judge of the United States District Court for the Southern District of New York."

Ambition

An ambitious young lawyer in New York State once approached Judge Samuel Seabury for his recommendation for a legislative post. Since the judge did not know much about the young man, he said only half in jest:

"If you will give your word that you won't steal when you get to Albany, I'll see what I can do for you."

"I go to Albany," said the lawyer with great dignity, "absolutely un-pledged, or I don't go at all."

Civil Rights

In 1967 Thurgood Marshall became the first and so far the only black man appointed to the Supreme Court of the United States. Bob Woodward and Scott Armstrong, in their book The Brethren, *sketch how he got there:*

Marshall had headed the Inc. Fund for twenty-two years, from its founding in 1939 until 1961, when John F. Kennedy appointed him to the second Circuit Court of Appeals. The great-grandson of a slave, son of the steward at a fashionable all-white Chesapeake Bay yacht club, Marshall pioneered the civil rights battle against segregation in housing, public accommodations and schools. He won 29 of the 32 cases he argued before the Supreme Court for the Inc. Fund.

In 1965, Lyndon Johnson appointed Marshall Solicitor General. When Marshall hesitated, Johnson's closing argument was, "I want folks to walk down the hall at the Justice Department and look in the door and see a nigger sitting there." Two years later Johnson appointed Marshall to the Supreme Court. Marshall had not sought and had not wanted the appointment. He preferred the more active give-and-take of public-interest law . . . On the Court, he had little interest in perfecting the finer points of the law. He often told his clerks, only half jokingly, "I'll do whatever Bill [Brennan] does," sometimes even jotting "follow Bill" on his notes. He trusted Brennan's resolution of the detailed, technical questions of legal scholarship. The clerks had taken to calling Marshall "Mr. Justice Brennan-Marshall." Often he would follow [Justice Byron] White on antitrust cases. But on discrimination cases, Marshall followed no one.

When in 1969 President Richard Nixon appointed the more conservative Warren Burger to replace Chief Justice Earl Warren, Thurgood Marshall's sense of feeling out of place on the Court made him engage in some unusual antics:

For Burger there were no more intimidating experiences than his first few encounters with Marshall in the marble corridors of the Court.

"What's shakin', Chiefy baby?" Marshall would sing out. Puzzled, Burger mumbled a greeting of his own. It did not take Burger long to realize the pleasure Marshall got from making him uncomfortable. Marshall had many similar stories of putting people on. A favorite of his involved unsuspecting tourists who mistakenly entered the Justices' private elevator. Finding a lone black man standing there, they said, "First floor please." "Yowsa, yowsa," Marshall responded as he pretended to operate the automated elevator and held the door for the tourists as they left. Marshall regularly recounted the story, noting the tourists' puzzlement and then confusion as they watched him walk off, and later realized who he was.

The Lawyer Who Couldn't
Sam Ervin, Jr., told the story about his friend Marvin Ritch, who was running for the Democratic nomination for United States senator. Shak-

ing hands in search of votes one day he was asked by a voter what his profession was.

"I'm a lawyer," Ritch replied.

"I can't vote for you then," said the proverbial man in the street. "I swore a long time ago I'd never vote for a lawyer for public office."

But the lawyer was prepared even for this eventuality. He patted the man on the shoulder, assuring him:

"If that's all you've got against me, my friend, you can vote for me with a clear conscience. I'm not enough of a lawyer to hurt."

MAKING A DIFFERENCE

Their Finest Hour

U.S. Solicitor General James Beck, in a 1915 speech to the Bar of Canada, gave as perhaps the most potent reason for the unpopularity of the lawyer, the fact that

. . . he is the great conservative force in a nation, and is constantly called upon to defend the individual against the tyranny of the majority. He must frequently defy and defeat public opinion by protecting the individual from its unreasonable demands. Erskine sacrificed his social popularity and political prestige by accepting a retainer to defend the then despised Tom Paine, while Brougham in the teeth of royal displeasure and social persecution espoused the cause of the unfortunate Queen Caroline. One of the finest chapters in the history of the American Bar is the fact that after the Boston Massacre and amid all the tumult which culminated in the Revolution, two leaders of the popular party, John Adams and Josiah Quincy, offered to defend the British soldiers, who were charged with murder, and it is to the greater credit of a Boston jury that it so far rose above popular passion that the soldiers were acquitted.

You will remember the splendid exhibition of professional loyalty when Louis XVI was arraigned before the National Convention during the Reign of Terror, and it was clearly understood that any advocate who defended him would forfeit his own life with that of his client. The great advocate [Christian William] Malesherbes, in volunteering his services, nobly said: "I was twice called to the council of the King when all the world coveted the honor and I owe him the same service now when it has become dangerous."

He gave to his royal client the sacrifice of his own life and perished with him on the guillotine.

Duty

John Adams describes how and why he came to defend one of the eight British soldiers:

The next morning, I think it was, sitting in my office, near the steps of the town-house stairs, Mr. Forest came in, who was then called the Irish Infant. With tears streaming down from his eyes, he said:

"I am come with a very solemn message from a very unfortunate man, Captain Preston, in prison. He wishes for counsel, and can get none. I have waited on Mr. Quincy, who says he will engage, if you will give him your assistance; without it, he positively will not. Even Mr. Auchmuty declines, unless you will engage."

I had no hesitation in answering that counsel ought to be the very last thing that an accused person should want in a free country; that the Bar ought, in my opinion, to be independent and impartial at all times and in every circumstance, and that persons whose lives were at stake ought to have counsel they preferred. But he must be sensible, this would be as important a cause as was ever tried in any country of the world; and that every lawyer must hold himself not only to his country, but to the highest and most infallible of all tribunals for the part he should act. He must, therefore, expect from me no art or address, no sophistry or prevarication, in such a cause, nor anything more than fact, evidence and law would justify.

"Captain Preston," he said, "requested and desired no more, and that he has such an opinion from all he had heard from all parties of you that he would cheerfully trust his life with you upon those principles. And," added Forest, "as God Almighty is my judge, I believe him an innocent man."

"That must be ascertained by his trial," I replied, "and if he thinks he cannot have a fair trial of that issue without my assistance, without hesitation he shall have it."

At this time I had more business at the Bar than any man in the Province. My health was feeble. I was throwing away as bright prospects as any man ever had before him, and I had devoted myself to endless labor and anxiety, if not to infamy and to death, and that for nothing, except indeed was and ought to be in all, a sense of duty. In the evening I expressed to Mrs. Adams all my apprehension. That excellent lady, who has always encouraged me, burst into a flood of tears, but said she was very sensible of all the danger to her and to our children, as well as to me, but she thought I had done as I ought; she was very willing to share in all that was to come, and to place her trust in Providence.

When John Adams was asked why he defended the eight British soldiers for murder in the Boston Massacre, he replied: "If I can but be the instrument of preserving one life, his blessing and tears of transport shall be sufficient consolation for me for the contempt of all mankind."

The Rights of Man

In 1792 the British government decided to prosecute Thomas Paine for sedition in his pamphlet *The Rights of Man*, in which he advocated a republican form of government. At the time of his trial, Paine was defending the revolution in France, so he was tried *in absentia*. Thomas Erskine was offered the brief to defend Paine, and despite all his friends in and out of government urging him not to endanger his own career, he undertook to defend Paine in a jury trial. He explained his action to the Lord Chief Justice—Lord Kenyon—and his court at Guildhall:

"I will for ever and at all hazards assert the dignity, independence and integrity of the English Bar, without which impartial justice, the most valuable part of the English constitution, can have no existence.

"From the moment that any advocate can be permitted to say he will or will not stand between the Crown and the subject arraigned in the Court where he daily sits to practise—from that moment the liberties of England are at an end.

"If the advocate refuses to defend from what he may think of the charge, or of the defence, he assumes the character of a judge; nay, he assumes it before the hour of judgment, and in proportion to his rank or reputation puts the heavy influence of perhaps a mistaken opinion into the scale against the accused in whose favor the benevolent principle of English law makes all presumptions, and which commands the very judge to be his counsel."

Erskine spoke for four hours. At one point he paused and said: "I will now lay aside the role of advocate and address you as a man."

"You will do nothing of the sort," Lord Kenyon interrupted him. "The only right and licence you have to appear in this Court is as an advocate."

The jury, which was hostile to Paine's cause, found him guilty, and the Court sentenced Thomas Paine to be outlawed. Yet Erskine found himself vindicated in the court of public opinion. As he left Guild Hall unrobed, an enormous crowd greeted him, swept him up and carried the courageous advocate on their shoulders toward St. Paul's cathedral.

Wall Street Lawyer

John W. Davis, the great conservative lawyer, who was the Republican presidential nominee in 1924, served on the boards of a great many corporations during his days as a Wall Street lawyer. Although often accused of being too interested in making money, he claimed that his goal was not the filthy lucre itself but the "glorious privilege of being independent." Once, as he was leaving the Supreme Court, he said to the clerk in a stage whisper: "Tomorrow I have a date with J.P. Morgan, the day after that with Rockefeller. God, how I hate to take their money."

Integrity

A great jurist can exercise profound moral force in a society, as we have seen during great constitutional crises and Senate confirmation hearings for appointments to the federal judiciary. Within the profession the impact may be more quiet but it is continuous and cumulative. William H. Harbaugh in his book Lawyer's Lawyer: The Life of John W. Davis, *profiles such a man:*

By precept and example, Davis also imbued the associates and younger partners with an urgent sense of the majesty of the law and the courts. He was especially fond of a paper by Lord Moulton on law and manners, a key passage of which reads: ". . . to my mind the real greatness of a nation, its true civilization, is measured by the extent of this land of Obedience to the Unenforceable." So strongly did Davis subscribe to that view that he tended to invest the advocate's supporting role in rendition of that almost mystical concept, "justice," with a kind of priestly sanction. In the 1940s, for example, as Davis and a young associate left the courtroom, the associate expressed wonder that Davis had bothered to make a polished argument and smooth and subtle presentation of an extremely complex point before an ex-Tammany judge of limited legal background. To his great surprise, Davis stopped and said: "Young man, never let me hear you say that again. I couldn't be a lawyer and argue cases as I do unless I believed that the man on the bench, no matter what his origins, was doing his level best to do the right thing."

Davis's attitudes and values had an elevating impact on everyone he touched; the firm's reputation for integrity, always high, became so fixed during his tenure that even the courts were prone to defend it. Once, about 1940, an opposing counsel charged one of Davis's partners with making a fraudulent contention in argument. Immediately, the judge interrupted him. "Wait a minute, counsel," he said. "The firm you're talking about is Davis Polk Wardwell Gardiner & Reed. You can't charge them with fraud!"

Good Will

Fanny Holtzmann, the diminutive woman from Brooklyn who was trusted alike by the royalty of Europe and of Hollywood, was the first entertainment lawyer in the contemporary sense. She got her way by quiet finesse, as Margaret Case Harriman describes one of her famous coups *in her* New Yorker *profile:*

In 1933, when *As Thousands Cheer* opened on Broadway with a sketch that sensationally kidded the British royal family, Fanny Holtzmann, who happened to be in London, heard that the British government proposed making a formal protest to Washington. Although no one had consulted her legally, she managed to communicate with the earl of Cromer, the Lord Chamberlain, and to point out to him that a formal protest would be a mistake. "It will simply give the revue tons of publicity," she said, "and one dislikes obliging the producer to that extent." Lord Cromer thanked Fanny, but the protest was made anyway, through the British ambassador at Washington. Every newspaper printed it, with counter-protests from Sam Harris, producer of the show, and *As Thousands Cheer* got off to a good start under a momentum of nationwide notoriety. Two seasons later, when Harris was rehearsing *Jubilee!*, a revue concerned, unmistakably, with King George V and his Queen, Fanny was in London again. In one of her daily telephone calls to New York, she learned that Walter Winchell's Monday column had carried the following item: "England's king and queen will be violently ribbed in *Jubilee!*" A few days later Winchell printed another crack. "*Jubilee!*" he said, "which ribs Britain's king and queen, shows them holidaying incognito, doing the things they've always wanted to do for the last twenty-five years . . . and how they do carry on!" Fanny called up Winchell in New York to verify what he had printed, and then broke the news to Lord Cromer. "Surely, dear Lord Cromer," she said, mildly, "the British government doesn't want to come another frightful cropper like that last one. Why not let me see if I can't wangle something?" Visibly shaken, Cromer authorized her to do what she could, unofficially, and

Fanny called up Sam Harris in New York. "Listen dear," she said, "what are you trying to do, buck the British government? Maybe you don't want to put on a show in London ever again. Listen," she said, while Mr. Harris listened, "suppose you want to sell your lousy show to Hollywood, so what? So the British are laying for you, and they'll see that the picture is banned all over the British Empire." Mr. Harris saw the truth of Fanny's argument, and besides he had no real desire to keep on affronting England. He changed the locale of *Jubilee!* to a mythical kingdom and trusted his audience to suspect that it meant England just the same. The British were pacified, and after the New York opening, the London *Daily Telegraph* had this comment to make: "Fears that the play would attempt to caricature the British royal family were dissipated, although it is rumored that extensive cuts were made at the last moment at the suggestion of Washington officials." Fanny's name was never mentioned publicly in connection with the incident, and she got no fee from the Lord Chamberlain. But the goodwill was worth thousands.

Cowardice

Following a rash of wife-beating cases (called wife-bashing in Australia), a New South Wales divorce court judge, Mr. Justice Bonney, made the public observation that "boys and men should have it instilled into them that to strike a woman is the lowest imaginable form of cowardice." In one case during World War II, a wife was suing for divorce after repeated assaults and cruel beatings by her soldier husband every time he came home or was A.W.O.L. from the army.

"Did he serve overseas?" asked Justice Bonney.

"No, only in Sydney," he was told.

"So he never got the opportunity to hit anyone except a woman," the judge remarked sardonically.

Shame

In another Australian story, a man was asking Judge Parker for exemption to serve in the war, as a conscientious objector. He said he would rather go to jail than take the oath.

"Would you shoot a Japanese soldier if he attacked your wife?" the court asked him.

"No," replied the man, "but I would try to rouse in him a sense of shame."

Gallows Humor

Sir Thomas More was Chancellor of England and a good Catholic who refused to go along with Henry VIII's plans to divorce his wife and found his own church. As a result, in 1535, Henry locked him up in the Tower and ordered to have his head cut off. According to William Winstanley, the seventeenth-century barber who wrote in England's Worthies:

The day was appointed for his execution being come, about nine of the clock he was brought out of the Tower, ascending the scaffold, he seemed so weak that he was ready to fall; whereupon he merrily said to the Lieutenant, "I pray you Mr. Lieutenant see me safe up, and for my coming down let me shift for myself." Then desired he all the people to pray for him, and to bear witness with him, that he should then suffer death, in, and for the Faith of the Holy Catholic Church, a faithful servant both of God and the King. Which done, he kneeled down, and after his prayers ended, he turned to the executioner, and with a cheerful countenance, said, "Pluck up thy spirits, man, and be not afraid to do thine office. My neck is very short, take heed therefore thou strike not awry for saving thine honesty." Then laying his head upon the block he had the executioner stay until he had removed his beard, saying that it had never committed any treason. So with much cheerfulness he received the fatal blow of the axe, which at once severed his head from his body. This jest at his death the Catholics so much distasted, that at so serious a time he should be so airy and light, that he had almost been scratched out of their Canonisation for a saint."

Thomas More was finally canonized in 1935.

Impeachment

During the impeachment trial of President Andrew Johnson on the U.S. Senate floor, Senator George Sewall Boutwell of Massachusetts wanted to consign the unfortunate president to a black hole in the heavens for punishment: "that place, that terra incognita in the sky where there are no stars, no light, no life—and there let him be confined through all eternity."

Then Senator William M. Evarts of New York rose and said: "Yes, it is meet, if the innocent president is to be punished, that he be taken to that unknown hole in the sky, where there is no law, where there is no justice, and where no statutes can be broken. And even now," continued Evarts in one of his forensic flights of eloquence, "I see the president, the innocent president, passing up the dome of the Capitol—his left foot kicks the Goddess of Liberty, and while all the people shout—*sic itur ad astra*—away he flies to the stars!"

Speech from the Heart

It was William S. Groesback's closing speech for the defense that probably acquitted Andrew Johnson by a single vote. At one point he looked tearfully at the assembled Senate and with all the solemn tones of Mark Antony at the funeral of Caesar said: "The president is not a learned man, like many of you, senators; his light is the feeble light of the Constitution."

When asked about the speech later in life, William Groesbeck said: "It was only a short speech—say two-thirds of a column, and it was really an extemporaneous speech. Boutwell and Evarts had been talking for days to the tired Senate. I had a long speech prepared, but saw the folly of using it. I was full of ideas and sympathy, for I liked Andrew Johnson. But I threw away all notes, gave up all thought of oratory or my own reputation, and lost myself in that personal plea for a friend who tried to be as just as Aristides."

For Whom the Cock Crows

The old Russian rabbi Reb Zolmuna of Rachmanifka used to settle even severe disputes in an offhand way, and usually to the satisfaction of all parties concerned, thereby restoring peace and order to the community.

The greatest fame Reb Zolmuna gained was through a tangled affair between two outstanding Jews of Rachmanifka. This is what happened:

Reb Todros Foigel, a rich, pious and respectable man, bought for himself a rooster, for the sole purpose of being awakened by its crowing at midnight, so that he might then recite the *Chatsot* prayers and lamentations, which tradition sets for that exact hour.

Reb Todros had a neighbor, Reb Zarach Tobeles by name, who was of the same conditions as himself—rich, pious and respectable. A chance remark revealed to Reb Todros that his neighbor, instead of going to the trouble of purchasing a rooster of his own to awaken him at midnight for the *Chatsot* prayer, made use of the crowing of Reb Todros' rooster.

"What merit can there be in Reb Zarach's prayer," thought Reb Todros to himself, "when his opportunity of reciting it is, so to say, a stolen one? Can a merit be acquired through a sin? For it says in Berakot 47b, that one may not fulfill a religious duty through the means of a transgression."

So when he next met Reb Zarach he said to him:

"I will allow you to contribute toward my rooster's keep, in order that you may lawfully share in his summoning you for the recital of *Chatsot.*"

Great was Reb Todros' astonishment when Reb Zarach replied:

"Why should I? Does not the Talmud say in Baba Kamma 20b, that one may even be compelled to permit his neighbor to receive a benefit, so long as the owner of the property has no additional expense thereby? It costs you no more to feed a rooster just because I also am awakened by its crowing."

These differing viewpoints were taken up by Reb Todros's and Reb Zarach's families, and then by the scholars at the Bet-HaMidrash, and finally divided Rachmanifka into two camps. The principals, Reb Todros and Reb Zarach, applied to the rabbi for a Din Torah, or legal arbitration.

Reb Zolmuna heard both sides, and said:

"I am ready for a decision, but as this is a difficult problem, I must demand a high price for 'Psak-Gelt' (fees); you must, as the law requires, pay equally—it will be a whole ruble from each of you."

Each litigant placed his ruble before the rabbi, and he continued:

"You, Reb Todros, claim that your rooster must crow only for you; you, Reb Zarach, claim that it crows for whomsoever may hear it. My decision is that it crows for neither of you, but for me, in order that I may receive two rubles in fees."

The litigants sat speechless for a moment, and when they saw where the decision left them, each began to laugh. The rabbi joined in with them, and seeing that they were satisfied gave each one back a ruble and dismissed them. When the people heard the rabbi's decision they also laughed, and peace and harmony were restored in Rachmanifka.

· 4 ·
THE JOY OF SUING

LITIGATION

Admonition

Doctor Johnson once compared plaintiff and defendant to two men ducking their heads in a bucket and daring each other to remain longest under water.

Their Long Suit

The Berkeley suit lasted more than one hundred and ninety years. It started shortly after the death of Thomas, the fourth earl of Berkeley, in the fifth year of the reign of King Henry V (1416), and terminated in the seventh of James I (1609). It arose out of the marriage of Elizabeth, only daughter and heiress of Lord Berkeley with Richard Beauchamp, earl of Warwick. Their descendants sought continuously to gain possession of the castle and lordship of Berkeley, which not only occasioned the famous lawsuit, but was often attended with the most violent quarrels on both sides, at least during the first fifty years or so of the dispute. In 1469, Thomas Talbot, Viscount Lisle, great-grandson of Elizabeth, residing at Wotton-under-Edge, was killed at Nibley Green in a furious skirmish between some five hundred of his own retainers and about as many of those of William, then Lord Berkeley, whom he had challenged to the field. Apart from young Thomas, scarcely of legal age, about one hundred and fifty of their followers were killed and three hundred injured. Lord Lisle's claim passed on to his sisters, whose husbands kept the suit alive, as did their descendants, until Henry, the eleventh earl of Berkeley, obtained a decree in favor of his claims and got full possession of the lands and manors in dispute.

There is no record of how much all this cost in legal fees, or whether in the end it was worth it.

Libel

In 1817 Aaron H. Palmer was a counselor and attorney in New York, and he ran one day into a portrait painter named Francis Mezzara. The painter proposed to draw a portrait of Palmer, claiming that there was a very striking peculiarity in his forehead, and the head was a study, expressing this in French—*une tête d'étude*. The lawyer sat somewhat reluctantly for his portrait and the result was exhibited at the Academy of Arts.

Palmer's friends did not like the picture and pronounced it a caricature. Mezzara, hearing of these comments, rudely refused to accept his fee for the portrait. Later the painter changed his mind, but by then Palmer refused to pay him. So Mezzara brought an action for the price of the painting, but it failed. Some time afterwards, the two litigants met, and Mezzara invited Palmer and the two friends he was with back to his room to inspect the picture. During this private exhibition, the painter became abusive again, took chalk and sketched ass's ears on the head of the portrait and promised to paint them on and then expose it on Broadway.

Palmer and his friends left, and later Palmer had the picture seized by the sheriff. Thereupon a notice appeared in the *Republican Chronicle*:

"CURIOUS SHERIFF'S SALE.—We have been requested to mention, that there will be sold this forenoon, at public vendue, at No. 133 Water Street, a picture *intended* for the likeness of a gentleman in this city, who ordered it to be painted. But as the gentleman disclaimed it, it remained the property of the painter and is now seized by execution. In order to enhance its value, the painter, who is an eminent artist from Rome, has decorated it with a pair of *long ears*, such as are usually worn by a certain stupid animal. The goods can be inspected previous to the sale."

Mezzara, it was discovered, had caused the notice to be inserted in the newspaper, and he was promptly indicted for libel. Martin Wilkins was one of the counsel on behalf of the prosecution, and in the course of summing up, he said, "Gentlemen of the jury, what is to be done with the man? Should you acquit him, he still continues to hold up the respectable citizen, this distinguished counselor, to public contempt and ridicule. Should you find him guilty, I am not certain but that, to revenge himself, he will draw your pictures with his ass's ears!—And," the counsel added, casting his eyes toward the court with that peculiar gravity which he could put on, "I fear their honors on the bench will share the same fate."

The mayor, Jacob Radcliff, told the jury tersely that any publication, picture or sign, made with a mischievous or malicious design, which holds up any person to public contempt or ridicule is denominated a libel. The jury found Mezzara guilty, and he was sentenced to pay a fine of one hundred dollars.

Beauty and the Beast

Another litigation in England involving a portrait painter took place in 1810. Thomas Hope, a novelist and a man about town, had married a beautiful woman and engaged an artist named Du Bost to immortalize her beauty. The husband was so disappointed with the result that he refused to pay the painter, who then went ahead and painted next to the lady's head a caricature of the husband, and called the picture *La Belle et la Bête* (Beauty and the Beast). He then had it exhibited at a gallery in Pall Mall and charged people to see it. A great many came, including a Mr. Beresford, the brother of Mrs. Hope, who attacked the picture with a knife and destroyed it.

Du Bost brought an action against him, not only for the value of the picture but for the profits he would have derived from the exhibition. Mr. Beresford saw it differently, insisting that the exhibition was a public nuisance, which everyone had the right to abate by destroying the picture. The case was tried by Lord Ellenborough, who said that the material question was what value to set upon the article destroyed. If it was a libel upon the persons introduced into it, the law would not consider it valuable as a picture; upon application to the lord chancellor an injunction would have been granted against its exhibition, and the plaintiff would be both civilly and criminally liable for having exhibited it. And he instructed the jury not to consider the picture a work of art in assessing the damages, but to award the plaintiff merely the value of the canvas and paint. Verdict was for the plaintiff; damages five pounds.

Vanity

The various trials of Polly Bodine for murder and arson were the talk of New York in the 1840s. She was in her mid-thirties, a handsome woman who prided herself on her good looks. After her indictment for the double murder of her brother's wife and child, P.T. Barnum exhibited in his museum a wax figure that he claimed was an accurate likeness of

Polly, although it looked like a hideous old woman. After she had somehow caught sight of this statue, it became a great source of mortification to Polly's vanity, and the wax work continued to occupy her mind much more than the mortal peril she found herself in. Before her last trial, she had importuned her counsel to bring an action of libel against Barnum, but they told her that it was idle to think of such a proceeding while she was soon to be tried for her own life.

Still, she was not easily pacified. Finally the last day of her last trial came. The counsel closed. The court very solemnly charged the jury and they retired. The agitated prisoner with pallid countenance took her seat by the side of her counsel. The clerk of the court asked the jury, if they had agreed on their verdict: "We have." The prisoner was commanded to rise and look on the jury and the jury were directed to look on the prisoner.

"How say you, gentlemen of the jury, do you find the prisoner guilty or not guilty?"

"Not guilty."

The prisoner sank down, tears streaming down her face. But very soon she recovered herself, and leaning her head over to one of her counsel she asked with great eagerness, "Can't I now sue Barnum for libel?"

The Theatrical Season

Actors' Equity in Australia once took a theatrical management to court for an alleged breach of contract, which revolved around the issue whether the company was on tour or not.

"How long is a theatrical season?" was one question put to the defendant by Hal Alexander, who appeared for the actors' union.

"Any length of time," replied the defendant. "It might mean any-thing—two years or two months."

"It's a loose term, is it?" asked Mr. Alexander. "Would you call two days a season?"

"No," put in Mr. H.L. O'Neill, solicitor, who appeared for the defendant, "that's a frost."

Everybody Wins

In her book, The Suing of America, *Marlene Adler Marks describes the benefits of litigation, in the most publicized of the ''palimony'' suits:*

Michelle Triola Marvin, whose name has come to symbolize legal rights for unmarried lovers, spent years trying to become an entertainer before her lawsuit thrust her into the public spotlight. With long dark hair, wide eyes, she advanced an image that was part Annette Funicello and part Elizabeth Taylor, yet her singing career proved eminently forgettable and she was consigned to bit parts, mostly in "B" movies.

Michelle might not have sued her former lover, Academy Award-winning Lee Marvin (*Cat Ballou*) to gain stardom for herself. (She legally adopted his name when she started singing professionally.) But people should be held responsible for the attorneys they select. Michelle took her woes to Marvin Mitchelson, a Los Angeles attorney known for his publicity cases involving the wives of big-name stars (among them Tony Curtis, Rod Steiger, and Alan Jay Lerner) . . . She claimed that Lee had promised her half of everything he earned during the nearly six years they lived together. She insisted she gave up her singing career at his request, and was his wife in all but name.

It so happened that live-in love was a big issue for feminists during the late 1970s. Michelle soon found herself the woman of the hour, the champion of legal and social rights for unmarried lovers everywhere. Her epic "palimony" lawsuit played for eleven media-packed weeks during the spring of 1979 in the Los Angeles Superior Court. By trial's end, Michelle was nationally famous, a star of *People* magazine, the *Enquirer*, and the *California Family Law Reporter*. As they say in the movie business, she had true "crossover" potential, meaning she had appeal to audiences of many stripes.

Incidental to her newfound fame, Michelle also ended the trial with a judgment for $104,000 against the actor, which kind-hearted Judge Arthur K. Marshall had awarded her so she might "rehabilitate" herself. That $104,000, however, remained a paper judgment for at least two years, while Lee appealed to a higher court. Michelle's financial plight came to light in the summer of 1980, when she was arrested for shoplifting in Beverly Hills.

As for Mitchelson, he may be remembered as the first member of his profession to be shown taking a bubble bath in his office on the television show "60 Minutes." He obviously had no concept of invasion of privacy. His five-year investment in the Marvin case more than paid off in new clients rushing to his antique- and art-laden offices. Within a year, he was handling the affairs of Bianca Jagger and the wife of an Arab sheik whose estate was reportedly worth more than $1 billion. Nevertheless, Mitchelson asked the state of California to pay him half a million dollars in legal fees for representing Michelle, claiming his lawsuit was a public service. His request was denied.

Advice to Litigants

Robert Kenny, the late distinguished California judge, began his career in small claims court, where he introduced several innovations. Foremost, he established a different tone and demanded it from even the most bellicose litigants. Janet Stevenson describes in her book about Judge Kenny how in January 1932, only a few months after his appointment, he had a notice posted in the clerk's office, which read:

TO LITIGANTS IN THE SMALL CLAIMS COURT

With the holidays over, I face the prospect of hearing about 20,000 small claims cases during the 1932 year. I hope that the litigants in this court will help me get through the year by observing the following suggestions:

1st, to forget all they have read about courtrooms being arenas, and lawsuits being battles in which everything is fair and no holds are barred;

2nd, to regard the small claims court as a place where two persons who may honestly disagree can submit their difference to a disinterested third person, remembering that in most lawsuits neither side is wholly right or wholly wrong;

3rd, to present only honest claims and defenses without quibbling;

4th, to remember that this court can only give judgement up to $50, and that while $50 is a lot more money than it used to be, it is not yet a matter of life and death;

5th, to present cases truthfully, but briefly, and to furnish the court light, not heat;

6th, to treat your opponent not as an enemy or a liar, but as another human being with whom you have a sincere disagreement over a question of law or fact;

7th, to stifle hatred and ill will, but if you must give vent to it, to aim it at the judge instead of your opponent. The judge is paid for that sort of thing, and if there must be ill will, it is better that it be focused on him than diffused throughout the community;

8th, to indicate your willingness to accept these principles by offering to shake your opponent's hand when you are called before the judge to present your case.

I am not trying to be a Pollyanna judge, and I don't expect Clerk John Dugan or Bailiff Max Richman to be Happiness Boys, but I am appalled at the prospect of hearing 20,000 petty, bickering lawsuits and neighborhood quarrels this year, with each side using every sort of unfair means to take advantage of the other. It is not unreasonable to ask litigants to adopt the attitude of sportsmanship toward each other. If they do, cases can be expedited and crowded calendars cleared. Expressions of personal animosity take up much of the time of this court that should be devoted to arriving at the truth. ——Robert W. Kenny, Judge.

The results of this approach were not all that Kenny had hoped. While a few of the litigants were willing to shake hands on request, so many refused that it became embarrassing, and Kenny did not press the matter. Worse was what happened after judgment had been rendered. So many of the losers lurked outside the courtroom waiting to take a poke at the winners that the bailiff nicknamed the hall near the elevator bank "the Appellate Court."

Kenny decided that this situation was incompatible with judicial dignity and devised a stratagem to cure it: he had his bailiff detain the loser for a few minutes after decision had been rendered to give the winner time to escape unscathed. Another tactic was to announce that "the Court will take the matter under advisement and send you a postcard." In such cases the judge claimed that both parties left the courtroom "happily confident of eventual victory; when the bad news came to the loser, he was at home or in his office and had only his family or fellow workers to tie into."

Before long Kenny's wisecracks had begun to make news, and people came to his court expecting to enjoy themselves. Courtroom laughter became such a problem that eventually he had to add another to his list of suggestions to litigants:

> 9th, Don't be provoked to anger when the audience laughs during your trial. Stick around and enjoy a few grins at the expense of the next victim.

How to Avoid Lawyers

Abraham Lincoln advised lawyers to discourage litigation. "As a peacemaker, the lawyer has a superior opportunity of becoming a good man. There will always be enough business. Never stir up litigation. A worse man can scarcely be found than one who does this. Who can be more nearly a fiend than he who habitually overhauls the register of deeds in search of defects in titles, whereon to stir up strife and put money in his pocket? A moral tone ought to be infused into the profession which should drive such men out of it."

Lincoln practiced what he preached. A farmer who got into a boundary dispute with a neighbor once went to Lincoln to secure his services. But Lincoln told him:

"Now, if you go on with this, it will cost both of your farms, and will entail an enmity that will last for generations and perhaps lead to murder. The other man has just been here to engage me. Now, I want you two to sit down in my office while I am gone to dinner and talk it over, and try to settle it. And, to secure you from any interruption, I will lock the door." As the farmer told it, Lincoln did not return for the rest of the afternoon, and "we two men, finding ourselves shut up together, began to laugh. This put us in good humor, and by the time Mr. Lincoln returned, the matter was settled."

A Lesson Learned

One of the most controversial events of the past hundred years has been the so-called *Affaire Dreyfus*. Captain Alfred Dreyfus, falsely accused of treason by anti-Semitic elements in the French army, was tried and convicted at the end of the nineteenth century. He was sent to rot on the penal colony of Devil's Island. Finally, after many trials and ceaseless efforts by several people, including Émile Zola (who wrote his famous letter *J'accuse*) demanding justice, Dreyfus was rehabilitated. Living in the twilight of his years high up in a Paris apartment building, Dreyfus was visited one day by his nephew, Louis Weill. Not for the first time, the elevator was out of order and Weill puffed his way up several flights of stairs. After embracing and greeting his uncle, he suggested:

"You know, if they don't fix that elevator, you should think about taking the owners of the building to court."

Dreyfus looked at him with a twinkle in his sad eyes, and shook his head:

"Well, Louis, you know me and trials . . ."

CLIENTS

The Carriage Trade

One night Sarah, the duchess of Marlborough, called without an appointment at the Temple chambers of her lawyer, who was called Murray. She waited till past midnight in the hope of seeing him. But Murray was at an unusually late supper party, and did not return until the formidable Sarah—cofounder of the great dynasty that has given us Sir Winston Churchill—had departed in a towering rage. When the lawyer returned, his clerk described Her Grace's appearance and manner, adding:

"I could not make out, sir, who she was, for she would not tell me her name; but she swore so dreadfully that I am sure she must be a lady of quality."

Selling a Practice

Until recently there has been a great debate whether lawyers should be allowed to advertise their services, and in many countries the practice is either forbidden or frowned upon. In a book published more than a century ago we find the following notice:

"To be sold, on the 8th of July, 151 suits in law, the property of an eminent attorney, about to retire from business. Nota bene: the clients are rich and obstinate."

Criminal Ambition

Lord Cockburn describes in his journal, published in 1874, the kind of client who would disgust even his lawyer:

I had a client, David Haggart, who was hanged in Edinburgh for murdering his jailer in Dumfries. He was young, good-looking, gay, and amiable to the eye; but there was never a riper scoundrel—a most perfect miscreant in all the darker walks of crime. Nevertheless his youth (about twenty-five) and apparent gentleness, joined to an open confession of his sins, procured him considerable commiseration, particularly among the pious and the female. He employed the last days of his existence in dictating memoirs of his life, with a view to publication. The book was published; and my copy contains a drawing of himself in the condemned cell, by his own hand, with a set of verses of his own composition, which he desired to be given to me as a token of his gratitude for my exertions at his trial. Well, the confessions and the whole book were a tissue of absolute lies—not of mistakes, or exaggerations, or of fancies, but of sheer and intended lies. And they all had one object—to make him appear a greater villain than he was. Having taken to the profession of crime he wished to be at the head of it. He therefore made himself commit crimes of all sorts, which, as was ascertained by inquiry, were never committed at all. A strange pride; yet not without precedent, and in nobler walks of criminal ambition.

Honest Old Abe

Judge Samuel Treat passed on to posterity the occasion that got Lincoln his epithet. He was trying a simple case of collection on a note. The defendant went on the stand and showed a receipt of payment in full, given him by the plaintiff. Abraham Lincoln asked his client:

"Did you know he held this receipt?"

"Yes, but I thought he had forgotten it."

Lincoln left the courthouse abruptly and went back to his hotel. A few minutes later the judge sent a messenger to ask him to return and finish the case. Lincoln sent back word:

"You go tell that judge that I am washing my hands."

Ethics

It was not uncommon for Louis Brandeis to win a case for a client and then lecture him on the need to change his ways, according to Bruce Allen Murphy's recent book on him. Further, he organized and led numerous citizen reform organizations seeking to better the conditions of mankind. For Brandeis, this was just another function of a concerned lawyer, and he encouraged others to follow the same road. However, he carefully separated these public activities from his private business. Whenever engaged in *pro bono publico* work, Brandeis, who was one of the first attorneys to perform such services, would financially compensate his law firm for the time he had spent on the project. On these occasions, to preserve the necessary separation of functions, he simply considered himself to be a client of the law firm.

How to Deal with Clients

Reginald Hine, in his entertaining Confessions of an Un-common Attorney, *discussed the problems of clients:*

Some clients are more than unreasonable; they are downright angry: 'chafed and irritable creatures with red faces,' as [Ralph Waldo] Emerson well described them. With such, one has a difficult *tête-à-bête*, but one learns in time not to lose one's temper. If I am provoked beyond bearing, I make an excuse to leave my room, take a turn round St. Mary's Church, practise deep breathing, and, as I come back, repeat the words of that long-suffering and sweet-natured lawyer Sir Walter Scott: "If God bears with the very worst of us we may surely endure one another." Then if the client is still impossible I show him the door and charge up a double attendance fee.

One of the queerest of those half-certifiable clients was a woman whose habit it was, the moon being at the full, to get out of bed at midnight, take off her night-gown, descend the stairs, open the door, proceed along the pavement for two hundred yards until she came to a red pillar box; and then, falling reverently upon her knees, she would pray fervently to that strange postal deity. This was all very well so long as the devout lady remained unobserved. But one night the local police constable caught her in the act of praying naked and unashamed and, after thumbing his note-book, decided that, under section 28 of the Town Police Clauses Act, 1847, his duty was to take her into custody; after which I was called in and consulted. It was a case that required careful handling, with the co-operation of a psycho-analyst, and a priest; and let me say in passing how wise solicitors would be in such circumstances to make more use of the friendly offices of the Church.

Beyond the Call of Duty

E. S. P. Haynes, author of The Lawyer's Notebook, *demonstrates what English solicitors used to do for their clients, in the early years of this century:*

A client of mine, an elderly spinster, died in a cheap hotel in Paris and as her only surviving relation was too old to undertake the journey, I was despatched with the parish clergyman and his wife and daughter, who, although in a state of decent melancholy, were at the same time interested in seeing Paris. On arrival we found the body in exactly the same position as when death occurred, and the authorities had put seals on her personal possessions, although the deceased lady's watch was never found.

For various reasons we decided to bury the lady in a Paris cemetery; and then the trouble began. The State undertakes burial in France, and ordains nine different classes of funerals on a scale suitable to the rank and fortune of the deceased. After reading a vast quantity of regulations, I came to the conclusion that the fifth class, with a hearse and two mourning coaches, was the proper class to choose. I then had to fill up an interminable series of documents about the deceased's family history and my own.

I flatter myself that there were only two serious hitches in the proceedings. The first was in regard to the funeral ceremony itself. Unfortunately, the clergyman's wife had a predilection for incense, and knowing that incense had been used in Ely Cathedral up to 1750, I did not see why she should not have it if she wanted it. This, however, excited violent indignation in the verger, who was present at the Embassy Church, and he nearly created what in ecclesiastical circles is known as a brawl. It took some time to soothe him before the funeral service could be carried out.

In the second place, I seriously offended the driver of the coach which conveyed us to the cemetery and back. The hotel-keeper had told me that we could take the coach wherever we liked so long as we did not come near the hotel, where the death had been carefully concealed. Consequently I considered myself at liberty to show my friends some of the sights of Paris, with which I was more familiar than they. The clergyman's daughter had seemed a little distressed by the fact that she had never seen a dead body, and particularly that of the lady who had been buried. So I benevolently directed the coach to go to the Morgue, which in those days was quite a popular show. At this stage I did not notice any discontent on the part of the coachman, who may have supposed that we were a kind of burying party looking out for deceased Englishmen and women. As we were all getting hungry I gave him the name of a restaurant in the Latin Quarter, and on arrival asked him if he would wait half an hour. But by this time the outraged dignity of a professional funeral-coachman, suitably arrayed in deep mourning and a streamer, asserted itself, with a wealth of gesticulation which attracted a large crowd on the pavement and in the road. He asserted that as a professional coachman in the service of the French Republic, he considered it necessary to maintain the dignity of that Republic by refusing to allow himself and the State coach to be used for the purpose of sightseeing. He finally ended an impressive oration with the searching but rhetorical question whether, after the meal, we proposed that he should drive us to the Moulin Rouge?

I ultimately succeeded in soothing this gentleman and dispersing the crowd, who seemed rather too sympathetic to let us enjoy our meal in peace. On returning to the hotel it became necessary to effect a settlement with the hotel-proprietor, who required an indemnity of no less than a hundred pounds in respect of a lady who died suddenly and quietly of heart failure, and whose life would probably have been saved if the servants, who had presumably taken her watch, had not left her alone for at least thirty-six hours while she was alive. I will not repeat the proprietor's arguments in detail, but may mention that he began by stating that his nerves had so entirely broken down owing to the death that he had not been able to sleep in the hotel while the dead body was there. He was unable to share the British phlegm which had enabled four English persons to sleep in the rooms with which he had accommodated us. However, I may cut a long story short by saying that he ultimately accepted twelve pounds in full satisfaction of his claim after being told that if he disputed the amount the question should be referred to a *juge de paix*. For a foreigner could always obtain justice in Paris, though very rarely in Berlin, before 1914.

After the Fact

One of Cicero's most admired speeches, *Oratio pro Milone*, had been held up as a model of forensic argument and rhetoric to countless generations of law students. It is a lesser known fact that Cicero wrote the speech after he lost the case for Milo, who stood accused of murdering the demagogue Clodius. And he lost it because he did not adequately prepare himself, but relied—as unprepared advocates often do—on the inspiration of the moment. The result was that Milo was exiled to Marseilles. When Cicero finally got around to writing down his defense speech long after the fact, he had the bad taste to send it to Milo, who sent back his sarcastic gratitude: "For had you spoken as you wrote," his client observed, "I would not be enjoying these exquisite mullets of Marseilles now."

The Recidivist

Roger Baldwin, director of the American Civil Liberties Union in the 1930s, began his career as a probation officer in St. Louis. Among his numerous clients was an engaging young crook for whom Baldwin once did a small favor that was perfectly consistent with his role as a social worker. The young man was extravagantly grateful—perhaps a bit more so because Baldwin made no effort to reform him—and he rapidly developed a pronounced case of hero-worship.

About ten years after their last meeting, the young man suddenly turned up at his former probation officer's apartment in New York. He was still young, still engaging, still a worshiper. After much mutual back-slapping the two men sat down for a talk. Somewhat to his surprise, Baldwin found that the young man's business in New York seemed to be legitimate, with no apparent relation to his more than shady past. He was to be in New York, he said, for some weeks—could he be of service? Was there anything he could do for his friend and hero?

"Say, Rodge," he offered, "isn't there something you want done? Isn't there anybody you want bumped off?"

"It is very good of you, Jack, but I really can't think of anyone I would like to have bumped off."

"Isn't there! I—I could make it a sure thing, Rodge. There wouldn't be any come-back on either of us. I'd like to do something for you, Rodge . . . honest!"

Darrow Loses Case, Wins Repartee

Clarence Darrow, when a very young man and starting out to practice law, was retained by a merchant to defend him in a suit brought by an employee. Unfortunately for Darrow, his client completely lost his head under cross-examination, furnishing evidence so favorable to the prosecution as to result in a four-thousand dollar verdict. The merchant was highly indignant and, blaming his attorney for losing the case, allowed but a very short time to elapse before he acquainted him of his feelings about the matter.

"If I had a son born an idiot," he blustered, "I'd make him a lawyer."

"Your father seems to have been of another opinion," Darrow came back smoothly.

Where the Buck Stops
Activist San Francisco lawyer Charles Garry has a little sign on his desk that says: THE ONLY CLIENTS OF MINE WHO GO TO SAN QUENTIN ARE THE ONES WHO LIE TO ME.

One Way to Terminate a Relationship
In May 1988, Reynard Jones, frustrated with long delays in his civil suit concerning some injury insurance claims, went to his lawyer's Century City office in west Los Angeles and took a secretary hostage. After an eight-hour standoff, the SWAT team used explosives to blow the door off and arrested Jones, who was later charged on five criminal counts ranging from kidnaping to extortion and assault. Viewing the wreckage caused by the explosion—scorched walls, carpets, the mangled artwork and disembowelled lawbooks—attorney Herbert L. Michel told *The Los Angeles Times* that "he would probably withdraw as Jones's lawyer."

FEES

The Lawyer's Prayer
Senator Sam Ervin used to tell the story of the young lawyer who turned up at a revival meeting and was asked to deliver a prayer. Unprepared, he gave a prayer straight from his lawyer's heart: "Stir up much strife amongst the people, Lord, lest thy servant perish."

Costly Entertainment
John Horne Tooke, the eighteenth-century English political writer, had remarked that the "law ought to be not a luxury for the rich but a remedy

to be easily, cheaply and speedily obtainable for the poor." When somebody observed to him how excellent are the English laws, because they are impartial and the courts are open to all persons without distinction, Horne Tooke replied: "And so is the London Tavern, to such as can afford to pay for their entertainment."

Strong Hints

According to one nineteenth-century antiquarian,

the payment of English barristers has varied much more than the remunerations of English physicians. Whereas medical practitioners in every age have received a certain definite sum for each consultation, and have been forbidden by etiquette to charge more or less than the fixed rate, lawyers have been allowed much freedom in estimating the worth of their labor. This difference between the usages of the two professions is mainly due to the fact that the amount of time and mental effort demanded by patients at each visit or consultation is very nearly the same in all cases, whereas the requirements of clients are much more various. To get up the facts of a law case may be the work of minutes, or hours, or days, or even weeks; to observe the symptoms of a patient, and to write a prescription, can be always accomplished within the limits of a short morning call. In all times, however, the legal profession has adopted certain scales of payment that fixed the minimum of remuneration but left the advocate free to get more, as circumstances might encourage him to raise his demands. Of the many good stories, told of artifices by which barristers have delicately intimated their desire for higher payment, none is better than an anecdote recorded of Serjeant Hill. A troublesome case being laid before this most erudite of George III's serjeants, he returned it with a brief note that he "saw more difficulty in the case than he could well solve under all the circumstances." As the fee marked upon the case was only a guinea, the attorney readily inferred that its smallness was one of the circumstances which occasioned the counsel's difficulty. The case was returned with a fee of two guineas. Still dissatisfied, Serjeant Hill wrote that he "saw no reason to change his opinion."

Small Change

A client once brought a brief and his fee to John Fitzgibbon, who later became Attorney General and Lord Chancellor for Ireland. The man wanted personally to apologize for the smallness of the fee, receipt of which Fitzgibbon acknowledged with a rather discontented look.

"I assure you, Counsellor," said the client mournfully, "I am ashamed of its smallness, but in fact, it is all I have in the world."

"Oh, then", said the lawyer, "you can do no more; as it is all you have in the world—why—hum—I must take it!"

Perversity

Abraham Lincoln's fellow lawyers used to say that he was in professional matters, "perversely honest." If a man desired to retain him whose cause was bad, he declined and told the applicant not to go to law. A lady once came to him to have him prosecute a claim to some land and gave him the papers in the case for examination, together with a retainer in the form of a check for two hundred dollars. Next day she came to see what her prospects were. Mr. Lincoln told her that he had examined the documents very carefully, that 'she had not a peg to hang her claim on,' and that he could not conscientiously advise her to bring an action. Having heard this opinion, the lady thanked him, took her papers, and was about to depart.

"Wait a minute," said Lincoln, "here is the check you gave me."

"Mr. Lincoln," said she, "I think you have earned that."

"No, no," he answered, insisting on her receiving it, "that would not be right. I can't take pay for doing my duty."

House Call

In his old age, Judah P. Benjamin (1811-1884), feeling the absolute necessity of restricting his exertions, refused to go into any court other than the House of Lords and the Privy Council, except for a fee of $500, and if a client demanded a home consultation, the fee was $1,500.

Benjamin used to explain his four-stage scale of collecting fees, as follows: "First, I charge a retainer; then I charge a reminder; next I charge a refresher, and then I charge a finisher."

Contingency

The heirs of A. T. Stewart, one of the wealthiest Americans in the last century, wanted to bring a suit against Judge Hilton for his way of handling the estate. They went to William M. Evarts, one of the most distinguished lawyers of his day who later served in the Senate and as secretary of state, and asked him to manage their case.

"Well, I will take a contingent fee."

"And what is a contingent fee?" asked one of the heirs.

"My dear, sir," Evarts replied mellifluously, "I will tell you what a contingent fee to a lawyer means. If I don't win your suit, I get nothing. If I do win it, you get nothing."

Frankness

Chief Justice Morrison Waite delighted to tell the story about the young Roscoe Conkling coming to see his mentor, William M. Evarts, one day in quite a nervous state.

"You seem to be very much excited, Mr. Conkling," said Evarts, as Roscoe walked up and down the room.

"Yes, I am provoked—I am provoked," said Conkling. "I never had a client dissatisfied about my fee before."

"Well, what's the matter?" asked Evarts.

"Why, I defended Gibbons for arson, you know. He was convicted, but I did hard work for him. I took him to the Superior Court and he was convicted, then on to the Supreme Court, and the Supreme Court confirmed the judgment and gave him ten years in the penitentiary. I charged him $3,000, and now Gibbons is grumbling about it, says it's too much. Now, Mr. Evarts," he asked the older lawyer, "I ask you if I really charged too much?"

"Well," said Evarts, very slowly and deliberately, "of course you did a good deal of work, and $3,000 is not a very big fee, but to be frank with you, Mr. Conkling, my deliberate opinion is . . . that . . . he might have been convicted for less money."

How to Make Money at the Supreme Court

How the value of stocks can be affected by court decisions is well illustrated by Charles Henry Butler in the so-called New York City 80 cent Gas Case, which a lower court had declared unconstitutional. The appeal was argued in the Supreme Court in November, 1908 (Willcox v. Consolidated Gas Co. 212 U.S. 19.):

For seven Mondays after the New York case had been argued, a New York lawyer friend of mine sat within the Bar, listening attentively to the decisions. Early in January 1909 Justice Moody read an opinion adverse to the [similar] Knoxville case (Knoxville v. Water Co. 212 U.S. 1.). My friend immediately disappeared, but returned shortly to hear Justice Peckham announce the decision refusing to set aside the New York ordinance.

When the Court opened Consolidated Gas was selling at about 160, and my friend, as he told me afterward, had left sufficient margin with his brokers either to buy 1000 shares of Consolidated Gas, or to "go short" of the market for the same number of shares with a stop order to sell or cover at ten points' profit.

Before the New York Stock Exchange closed that day, Consolidated Gas had dropped to 130 and my friend, who had given his order to sell the stock short had covered it by buying it in, and had made $10,000 on the day's transaction. This, he said, made it very worth while for him to come from New York to Washington every one of the seven Mondays on which the Court had sat and delivered opinions between the time of the argument and the decision of the case.

Where to Begin

A heavily marked brief was once delivered to Mr. Justice Hawkins's chambers, where it sat for six weeks unopened. The hearing of the case was approaching, so the clerk wrote on Justice Hawkins's behalf to the solicitor, suggesting that a check for the fee was both desirable and in accordance with the usual practice of the profession. The solicitor replied by return mail suggesting that if Mr. Hawkins had taken the trouble to open the brief he would have found the check inside.

Mere Money

British attorney Reginald Hine tells the story of one of his clients who was a man of taste.

He had not spent twenty years with William Morris's firm for nothing. He paid up like a Christian. I took his hand and his cheque. We parted the best of friends.

The tale does not end upon that mercenary note. There was a charming sequel. Four years later, in came the same little man with the same big heavenly smile.

"You will have quite forgotten me," he modestly began.

"Not in the least," I broke in, "you are Sheldrick. We don't forget the interesting clients."

"There's no business to bring you this time," he explained, "but I have a month's leave from the firm, and should like to spend it making you a piece of tapestry. If you haven't forgotten, I haven't either. I want you to have from me something more lasting than mere money."

Common Knowledge

Lloyd George was still a young lawyer in Wales when one day he offered a ride to a little girl whose family he knew. In trying to make conversation with her, he found her practically inarticulate, answering all his questions with barely a yes or a no. A few days later, the future prime minister of Great Britain ran into the little girl's mother. As they chatted he mentioned her daughter's strange silence, and the mother said that her little girl had also talked about her ride in the carriage, adding, "I couldn't talk with Mr. George because everybody knows that he charges a fee when one talks with him, and I had no money."

Once Bitten

Bennett Cerf, the founder of Random House, knew of a fellow publisher who received an enormous legal bill after what he had considered an informal consultation with Max Steuer, the famed New York attorney. The next day they met in the elevator.

"Mr. Steuer," said the publisher, "it's good to see you again." And then he quickly added:

"Mind you, Mr. Steuer, I am not asking your opinion about this. I'm merely stating a fact."

No Combat Pay

During the acrimonious confirmation hearings in the U.S. Senate concerning President Reagan's nomination of Judge Robert Bork to the Supreme Court, Senator Orrin Hatch asked the combative candidate:

"As a professor of law, are you not paid to be provocative?"

"Yes," replied Judge Bork gravely, "though I should say that on that basis I was grossly underpaid."

· 5 ·
TRIALS AND ERRORS

TALK TO THE ANIMALS

Animal Trials

There has been a rash of municipal ordinances recently directed against pit-bull dogs, which have killed or maimed both children and grown-ups. Even though the ultimate penalty is often paid by the dog, it is generally the owner who is held responsible for having let the animal loose, and who must therefore face charges in court. This has not always been the case. In the French code of laws it was the animal, not the owner, that had to answer for its misdeeds.

Thomas Frost, in an 1897 essay on the *Trials of Animals*, culled from the records of the criminal tribunals of France ninety-two such judicial processes between 1120 and 1741, when the last of these grotesque trials took place in Poitou. The practice seems to have been based on the Mosaic law that "if an ox gore a man or a woman that they die, then the ox shall be surely stoned, and his flesh shall not be eaten: but the owner of the ox shall be quit." (Exodus, 21:28). Oxen and pigs were the animals that most frequently were the subjects of these strange proceedings, the indictment against the former being for goring persons, while the latter suffered for killing and sometimes devouring very young children. The scriptural commands were codified into law, with the finest legal minds adding refinements and technicalities. For instance, when a bull had caused the death of a man, the animal was seized and incarcerated. A lawyer was appointed to plead for the delinquent and another as counsel for the prosecution. Witnesses were bound over, the case was heard in court, the bull was declared guilty of willful murder, and the sentence was pronounced by the judge—death by hanging or burning. There is no record whether the bull paid counsel for his defense.

M. Carlie preserves in his history of the Duchy of Valois the proceedings of an early instance of another case, from 1314. It seems a bull escaped from a farmyard in the village of Moisy and gored a man to death. Charles, comte de Valois, heard of the accident at his château in Crépy, and he ordered the bull seized and committed for trial. The officers of the count gathered all requisite information, received the affidavits of witnesses, established the guilt of the bull, condemned it to be hanged, and executed it on the gibbet of Moisy-le-Temple.

But matters did not stop there. An appeal against the sentence of the count's officers was lodged before the Candlemas parliament of 1314—drawn up in the name of the procureur de l'hôpital at Moisy, declaring the officers to have been incompetent judges, having no jurisdiction within the confines of Moisy, and as having attempted to establish a precedent. The parliament received and investigated the appeal and decided that the condemnation of the bull was perfectly just but found that the comte de Valois had no judicial rights within the territory of Moisy and that his officers had acted illegally in taking part in the affair.

Cock and Bull Stories

The Reverend Sabine Baring-Gould gives several examples of medieval French animal trials in his Curiosities of Olden Times:

A.D. 1266. A pig burned at Fontenay-aux-Roses, near Paris, for having devoured a child.

1386. A judge at Falaise condemned a sow to be mutilated in its leg and head, and then to be hanged, for having lacerated and killed a child. It was executed in the square, dressed in man's clothes. The execution cost six sous, six deniers, and a new pair of gloves for the executioner, that he might come out of the job with clean hands.

1389. A horse was tried at Dijon, on information given by the magistrates of Montbar, and condemned to death, for having killed a man.

1499. A bull was condemned to death at Cauroy, near Beauvais, for having in a fury killed a little boy fourteen or fifteen years old.

From a Swiss chronicle from Basle comes the story of a cock being brought to trial. There have always been widespread country superstitions that cocks lay eggs from which they hatch basilisks or horrible winged serpents. The poor birds also were thought to be in league with the devil, a belief that survives in voodoo. A cock was the offering made by witches at their sabbaths, and as these eggs were reputed to contain snakes—reptiles being particularly grateful to devils—it was taken as a proof of the cock having been engaged in the practice of sorcery.

This particular Swiss cock was accused of having laid such an egg and was brought before the magistrates in August 1474, tried, convicted and condemned to death. The court delivered the culprit to the executioner, who burned it publicly, along with its egg, in a place called Kohlenberger, amidst a great crowd of citizens and peasants assembled to witness the execution.

In the annals of Ireland is found an earlier story of a cock having been convicted of a similar offense in 1383. As it was burning at the stake, the heat of the flames supposedly burst the egg, "and there issued forth a serpent-like creature," which, however, perished in the fire without a trace.

Some Pigs Are More Equal Than Others

In 1457 a sow and her six young pigs were tried at Lavegny, on the charge of having killed and partially eaten a child. The sow was convicted and condemned to death; but the six piglets were acquitted on the ground of their tender age, the bad example of their mother, and the absence of direct evidence of their having partaken of the unnatural feast.

In 1494, sentence of death was pronounced on a pig by the Mayor of Laon for having mutilated and destroyed an infant in its cradle. The act of condemnation ends with these words:

"We, in detestation and horror of this crime, and in order to make an example and satisfy justice, have declared, judged, sentenced, pronounced, and appointed that the said hog, being detained a prisoner, and confined in the said abbey, shall be by the executioner, strangled and hanged on a gibbet, near and adjoining the gallows in the jurisdiction of the said monks, being near their copyhold of Avin. In witness of which we have sealed this present with our seal."

The document was sealed with red wax and endorsed: "Sentence on a hog, executed by justice, brought into the copyhold of Clermont, and strangled on a gibbet at Avin."

Three years later, a sow was condemned to be beaten to death for having mutilated the face of a child in the village of Charonne. The act of condemnation in this case directed further that the flesh of the sow should be given to the dogs of the village and that the owner of the sow and his wife should make a pilgrimage to the Church of Our Lady at Pontoise and bring on their return certificate that this injunction had been duly followed.

Who Needs Pesticides?

In bygone times, domesticated animals could be prosecuted singly and their owners held responsible. It was different with locusts, ants and other vermin. Fighting these required a combination of the finest legal minds and the power of the Church. The Rev. Baring-Gould recounts (in his 1866 book, Curious Myths of the Middle Ages*) such a case based on notes made by Bartholomée de Chasseneux (sometimes spelled Chassanée), a celebrated French lawyer of the late sixteenth century:*

After having spoken, in the opening, of the custom among the inhabitants of Beaune of asking the authorities of Autun to excommunicate certain insects larger than flies, vulgarly termed *hureburs*, a favour which was invariably accorded them, Chasseneux enters on the question whether such a proceeding be right. The subject is divided into five parts, in each of which he exhibits vast erudition.

The lawyer then consoles the inhabitants of Beaunois with the reflection that the scourge which vexes them devastates also other countries. In India the *hureburs* are three feet long, their legs are armed with teeth, which the natives employ as saws. The remedy found most effectual is to make a female, in the most *dégagé* costume conceivable, perambulate the canton with bare feet. This method, however, is open to grave objections on the score of decency and public morality.

The advocate then discusses the legality of citing insects before a court of justice. He decides that such a summons is perfectly justifiable. He proceeds to inquire whether they should be expected to attend in person, and, in default of their so doing, whether the prosecution can lawfully be carried on. Chasseneux satisfies himself and us that this is in strict accordance with law.

The sort of tribunal before which the criminals should be cited forms the next subject of inquiry. He decides in favor of the Ecclesiastical Courts. The advocate proceeds to convince his readers, by twelve conclusive arguments, that excommunication of animals is justifiable; having done so, he brings forward a series of examples and precedents. He asserts that a priest once excommunicated an orchard, whither children resorted to eat apples, when—naughty chicks!—they ought to have been at church. The result was all that could have been desired, for the trees produced no fruit till, at the request of the Dowager Duchess of Burgundy, the inhibition was removed.

He mentions, as well, an excommunication fulminated by a bishop against sparrows, which, flying in and out of the church of St. Vincent, left their traces on the seats and desks, and in other ways disturbed the faithful. Saint Bernard, be it remembered, whilst preaching in the parish church of Foligny, was troubled by the incessant humming of the flies. The saint broke off his sermon to exclaim, "O flies! I denounce you!" The pavement was instantaneously littered with their dead bodies.

Saint Patrick, as every one knows, drove the serpents out of Ireland by his ban.

This is the form of excommunication as given by Chasseneux: "O snails, caterpillars, and other obscene creatures which destroy the food of our neighbors, depart hence! Leave these cantons which you are devastating, and take refuge in those localities where you can injure no one. *In Nomine Patris*, etc."

The Exterminator

Chasseneux's first famous case involved rats. Being a good lawyer, he could represent either party to a dispute with equal facility; this time he was appointed by the authorities of the diocese of Autun to represent rats and to plead their cause in their trial for eating the harvest over a large portion of Burgundy.

The rats did not appear on the first citation, and in his opening gambit Chasseneux showed that they had not received formal notice. Before proceeding with the case, their advocate argued that the summons was of too local a character, and that, as all the rats in the diocese of Autun were interested in the case, they should be summoned throughout the diocese. This plea being admitted, he obtained a decision that all the priests of the afflicted parishes should announce an adjournment and summon the defendants to appear on a fixed date. When the day arrived and the rats still failed to appear, Chasseneux explained that, as all his clients were summoned, including old and young, sick and healthy, great preparations had to be made and certain necessary arrangements effected, and he had to ask, therefore, for an extension of time. This also being granted, another day was appointed, but again not a single rat put in an appearance.

Chasseneux now made an objection to the legality of the summons. A summons from that court, he said, implied full protection to the parties called, both on their way to it and on their return to their homes; and his clients, the rats, though most anxious to appear in obedience to the court, did not dare to leave their homes to come to Autun, on account of the number of evil-disposed cats kept by the plaintiffs. If the latter would enter into bonds, under heavy pecuniary penalties, that their cats should not molest his clients, the summons would be immediately obeyed. The court acknowledged the validity of this plea, but the plaintiffs declined to be bound for the good behavior of their cats. The further hearing of the case was therefore adjourned *sine die*, and thus Chasseneux won his case. The enterprising lawyer later wrote up the full particulars of these proceedings in Latin, and published them in 1588.

The Late Great Jones County Calf Case

From an account published in 1887:

A time-honored lawsuit has just come to a conclusion at Waterloo, Iowa. It is known as the "great Jones County calf case." This litigation arose out of the theft of four calves, eleven years ago, belonging to a man named Foreman, of Jones County. The stolen calves were bought by a neighboring farmer, by name Johnson, for a friend in Green County. Johnson was prosecuted by the "Anti-Horse-Thief Association" for the theft of the calves. He was tried twice and acquitted, and in 1877 brought an action against his prosecutors for damages. Ever since that date the case has been from time to time before the law courts. It has been tried five times, and each time, except one, Johnson has been victorious, receiving verdicts in his favor of from 3000 to 7000 dollars. These verdicts were on each occasion set aside, but Johnson was still persistent, and has at last been awarded him 7000 dollars damages, and the great calf case will be heard of no more in the courts. It will be sadly missed by the legal profession in Iowa. The costs, attorneys' fees and expenses entailed upon all parties to the litigation amount, it is stated, to over 20,000 dollars, and several prosperous farmers have been reduced to bankruptcy. The estimated value of the calves was 50 dollars.

What About Pit Bulls?

A city magistrate in old Los Angeles once was listening to a suit about a horse biting a stranger's hand. The judge ruled against the plaintiff, referring to a city ordinance which stated that a horse was entitled to one bite.

TALK OF THE TOWN

Suffer Little Children

One of the great cases argued before the Supreme Court in the nineteenth century was in 1844, known as the Girard Will Case, which pitted Walter Jones and Daniel Webster against Horace Binney and John Sargent. In a newspaper account, the scene is described:

It is said that there were never so many persons in the court room. Hundreds were turned away. Senators, members of the House, foreign ministers, cabinet officers, social leaders of both sexes were there to hear the Olympian Webster argue with the first of Philadelphia's lawyers. Mr. Binney, in the course of his argument, quoted from one of Mr. Webster's arguments in a preceding case, and Webster laughingly replied: "That was a bad case, and I had to make my argument to suit my case."

Under the rule, Webster, having the closing argument, was obliged to furnish his points and authorities to Mr. Binney before the latter commenced his argument. This he did, just as Binney was about to begin. In so doing, Webster apologized for his tardiness, and when he had concluded, Binney sarcastically said, with a slight wave of his hand, that he "fully excused his brother for his delay of citation, for he [Binney] would have no occasion to touch a single point or anything cited by him."

Binney argued for two days, and as he proceeded with his masterly exposition of a very difficult subject, to which he had given many months of research, Webster was literally stunned by the power of an argument to which he could make no adequate reply. As a contemporary said of the argument: "It was like a huge screw slowly turning around on its threads."

Webster's response was a masterpiece of rhetoric, and it produced thrills and tears throughout the audience. A congressman recorded in his diary:

"One day a Member came into the House and exclaimed that 'preaching was played out. There was no use for ministers now. Daniel Webster is down in the Supreme Court room eclipsing them all by defense of the Christian religion.' As I entered the court room, here are his words: 'And these words which I command thee this day shall be in thy heart.' Then again: 'Suffer little children to come unto me,' accenting the word 'children.' He repeated it, accenting the word 'little.' Then rolling his eyes heavenward and extending his arms, he repeated it thus: 'Suffer little children to come unto *Me*, unto *Me*, suffer little children to come.' So he went on for three days, and it was the only three days' meeting that I ever attended where one man did all the preaching and there was neither praying nor singing."

Webster failed to win the case.

Crocodile Tears

At the trial of political writer John Horne Tooke, Lord Eldon, speaking of his own reputation, said: "It is the little inheritance I have to leave my children, and, by God's help, I will leave it unimpaired." Here he shed tears, and to the astonishment of those present, Mitford, the attorney general, began to weep.

"Just look at Mitford," said a bystander to Horne Tooke, "what on earth is he crying for?" Tooke replied: "He is crying to think what small inheritance Eldon's children are likely to get."

The Value of Art

One of the celebrated trials in the annals of libel and art was when the American artist James McNeill Whistler sued the British critic John Ruskin for his attacks and demanded one thousand pounds in damages for the harm his reputation suffered. The case, which came before Lord Huddleston on November 15, 1878, had its origin in a piece Ruskin had brought out in a publication called *Fors Clavigera*, in which he reviewed a group exhibit at London's prestigious Grosvenor Gallery, organized by Sir Coutts Lindsay.

"For Mr. Whistler's own sake," Ruskin wrote among other unkind things, "no less than for the protection of the purchaser, Sir Coutts Lindsay ought not to have admitted works into the gallery in which the ill-educated conceit of the artist so nearly approached the aspect of wilful imposture. I have seen and heard much of Cockney impudence before now; but never expected to hear a coxcomb ask two hundred guineas for flinging a pot of paint in the public's face."

Now toward the end of his life, Ruskin was the most famous and opinionated art critic in England. He could never conceive of himself being in the wrong, though posterity has not borne out many of his judgments. For example, he hated Rembrandt: "It is evident," he pronounced, "that Rembrandt's system of colours is all wrong from beginning to end. Vulgarity, dullness, impiety will indeed always express themselves through art, in brown and gray, as in Rembrandt."

Whistler, known as an iconoclast and wit, absolutely detested critics.

"Art," he once exclaimed at no one in particular, "that for ages has been its own history in marble and written its own comments on canvas, shall it suddenly stand still and stammer and wait for wisdom from the passer-by?—for guidance from the hand that holds neither brush nor chisel? Out upon the shallow conceit."

Ruskin, who was too ill to attend the libel trial, sent a long essay arguing for the social usefulness of the critic, comparing it to impartial canons of justice: "The Bench of Honourable Criticism is as truly a seat of judgment as that of the Law itself, and its verdicts, though usually kinder, must sometimes be no less stern."

The attorney general represented Ruskin, and in his questioning of Whistler, who was testifying on his own behalf, the following famous exchange took place about one of the artist's paintings, which he had titled *A Nocturne*:

"Now, Mr. Whistler. Can you tell me how long it took you to knock off that nocturne?"

"I beg your pardon—"

"Oh! I am afraid I am using a term that applies rather perhaps to my own work. I should have said: "How long did you take to paint that picture?"

"Oh, no! permit me, I am too greatly flattered that you apply to work of mine any term that you are in the habit of using with reference to your own work. Let us say then how long did I take to —'knock off,' I think that is it—to knock off that nocturne; well, as well as I remember, about a day.

"Only a day?"

"Well, I won't be quite positive; I may have still put a few more touches to it the next day if the painting were not dry. I had better say then, that I was two days at work on it."

"Oh, two days! The labour of two days, then, is that for which you ask two hundred guineas!"

"No, I ask it for the knowledge of a lifetime."

The jury brought in a verdict of one farthing for Whistler. Technically he had won. Each party was ordered to pay his own costs. Ruskin felt deeply wounded by the result. He resigned his post as Slade Professor of Art at Oxford and went into virtual retirement.

Poseur

Few events rocked British society more than the three trials of Oscar Wilde in 1895, which led to his disgrace, imprisonment, and early death.

In the first case, Wilde was the plaintiff against the Marquess of Queensberry, who was outraged by the intimate relationship between his son, Lord Alfred Douglas, and the Irish writer, which both of them flaunted. Just after Wilde's greatest success in the London theater with *The Importance of Being Earnest*, the Marquess (who wrote the rules for modern boxing) left an insulting and misspelt card at Wilde's club, the Albemarle. It read: "To Oscar Wilde, posing as a somdomite."

Unmindful of the warning that in libel cases truth is a defense, Wilde denied to his counsel, the urbane Sir Edward Clarke, that he had ever engaged in homosexual activities. Representing the defendant was the formidable Edward Carson, one of the most relentless cross-examiners of the time, who knew Wilde from their school days. In fact, when Wilde heard who he was up against, he remarked: "No doubt he'll be attacking me with all the animosity of an old school friend."

Carson exploited Oscar Wilde's infatuation with his self-image as an esthete and wit. Confronting him with an extravagant and compromising letter written to Lord Alfred Douglas, the barrister asked sneeringly: "Is that an ordinary letter?"

"Everything I write is extraordinary. I do not pose as being ordinary, great heavens!" Wilde replied, mainly for the benefit of the gallery.

Carson and the Marquess won easily, making it unavoidable for the Crown to prosecute Wilde for homosexuality, which was until recently a criminal offense. Wilde was advised to flee England, but he refused and was arrested with a young man named Alfred Taylor. Though legally still innocent, Wilde was helpless while his creditors took over his house and auctioned off all his possessions, while his name was reviled by the hysterical press and street mobs. Deserted by his wife and most of society, Wilde was touched by the fact that Sir Edward Clarke, now more or less in possession of the facts, continued to defend him at no charge.

But Wilde was still trying to turn his trial into an artistic and philosophical discussion. When the prosecutor asked him to explain the line in a poem to Lord Alfred—"I am the Love that dare not speak its name"—the poet made this famous defense:

"The Love that dare not speak its name" in this century is such a great affection of an elder for a younger man as there was between David and Jonathan, such as Plato made the very basis of his philosophy, and such as you find in the sonnets of Michelangelo and Shakespeare. It is that deep, spiritual affection that is as pure as it is perfect. It dictates and pervades great works of art like those of

Shakespeare and Michelangelo, and those two letters of mine, such as they are. It is in this century misunderstood, so much misunderstood that it may be described as "the Love that dare not speak its name," and on account of it I am placed where I am now. It is beautiful, it is fine, it is the noblest form of affection. There is nothing unnatural about it. It is intellectual, and it repeatedly exists between an elder and a younger man, when the elder man has intellect, and the younger man has all the joy, hope and glamour of life before him. That it should be so the world does not understand. The world mocks at it and sometimes puts one in the pillory for it.

The prosecution was unimpressed by such outbursts. Relentlessly it produced sordid evidence that Wilde had spent time with a succession of very young men, some of them probably prostitutes:

Q. Do you remember a young man named Scarfe?
A. Yes. Taylor brought him to see me. Scarfe represented himself as a young man who had made money in Australia.
Q. Why was he brought to you?
A. Because many people at that time had great pleasure and interest in seeing me.
Q. Did he call you Oscar?
A. Yes.
Q. At once?
A. I had to ask him to. I have a passion for being called by my Christian name.

Wilde realized that Victorian society was almost as scandalized by someone deserting his class as its morals. During his first trial, after Edward Carson's fierce cross-examination forced him to admit intimacy not just with Lord Alfred but with "low life," Wilde ran into an actor friend, Charles Goodheart, near Piccadilly Circus, where placards and newsboys were proclaiming his latest confessions. Goodhart launched into an embarrassed discussion of the weather, but Wilde immediately set him at ease: "You've heard about my case? All is well. The working classes are with me . . . to a boy."

Give Me That Old-Time Religion

One of the most famous American trials in the twentieth century was the so-called "Monkey Trial" of John T. Scopes, a biology teacher in Dayton, Tennessee who was arrested in 1925 for teaching the theory of evolution. The case was dramatized into a successful Broadway play, Inherit the Wind, *and made into a great film, in which Spencer Tracy, playing Clarence Darrow, is pitted against William Jennings Bryan, played by Paul Muni. Clarence Darrow describes the setting:*

The bailiff was calling the court to order, "Tennessee versus Scopes." The judge was sinking into his seat beneath a monster sign, saying, "READ YOUR BIBLE DAILY." He had a palmleaf fan in one hand, and in the other the Bible and the statutes. As he laid these down on his desk I wondered why he thought he would need the statutes. To the end of the trial I did not know. Judge Raulston wriggled down into his high-backed chair and two tall policemen hopped forward close to his shoulder with Southern courtesy and big palm fans, which they fluttered above and around his serious, shining brow. The policemen seemed to appreciate the arduous mental labor going on beneath the skull of the man under their wings.

. . . The courtroom was packed, and still the people crowded together in the hallways, on the staircases; and the yard, too, was filling up. Spectators had come from near and far. "Hot dog" booths and fruit peddlers and ice-cream vendors and sandwich sellers had sprung into existence like mushrooms on every corner and everywhere between, mingling with the rest, ready to feed the throng. Evangelist tents were propped up at vantage points around the town square, where every night one not knowing what was going on would have thought hordes of howling dervishes were holding forth. In reality, they were crying out against the wickedness of Darwin and the rest of us, and advocating as substitutes cool meadows and melodious harps in KINGDOM COME. There was no reason why they should not be prohibitionists, for they were so elated and intoxicated by their religious jags that they needed no other stimulants. Then, too, they had become so immunized to common liquor through their brand of "White Mule" that it required something else to give them any "kick," and religion was doing the trick for some of the most hard-soaked, or sun-baked sinners.

When the courtroom was packed just short of bursting apart, it seemed, the judge ordered the doors closed over the sweltering audience, and with great solemnity and all the dignity possible announced that Brother Twitchell would invoke the Divine blessing. This was new to me. I had practiced law for more than forty years, and had never before heard God called in to referee a court trial. I had likewise been to prize fights and horse races, and these were not opened to prayer. After adjournment we went to the judge and told him that in a case of this nature, especially, we did not consider it fair or suitable to play up their side by opening court proceedings with prayer; it was not a form of church service; it was a trial in a court; and at best it was an unfair weapon to introduce, particularly as the case had a religious aspect.

The lawyers for the prosecution seemed shocked that such an objection and request should be presented. Prayer surely could do no harm. But, of course, it is easy for a lawyer to seem shocked.

At the next session Darrow objected once again to the opening prayer but was overruled by the judge. He next took on, with greater success, the ubiquitous slogan that greeted him at every turn:

The jury was given front seats, and right before them was a great sign flaunting letters two feet high, where every one could see the magic words: "READ YOUR BIBLE DAILY." As for the improved accommodations for the audience—well, there were now acres of audience, branching off into the surrounding streets, waiting for the curtain to rise.

I began the proceedings by calling attention to the flaming instructions to the populace and the jury to *"READ YOUR BIBLE DAILY"* and made a motion, for the sake of getting it into the record, pointing out the very evident purpose of influencing the jury, and asked to have the banner removed. Every one paused in awe at the audacity, but it was not a rainy day so that I was taking no chance with lightning. The judge and all the rest of the prosecution expressed great astonishment at any such motion; Mr Bryan's voice rose above all the others. However, we stood our ground until the attorneys for the prosecution rather thought that we might be right about its being "a bit thick" and consented to the removal of the blessed banner.

BOREDOM AND COMIC RELIEF

A Long Story

The famed American lawyer Louis Nizer had a simple but rarely heeded advice for making speeches: "If you haven't struck oil in 15 minutes, stop boring."

In the early days the U.S. Supreme Court permitted lawyers appearing before it to consume an unlimited amount of time in arguing their cases, rather than the 30 minutes allowed now. This was due partly to the scarcity of cases. During its first three semi-annual terms, no cases came before the Court. In the decade between 1793 and 1803 the justices decided upon sixty-four cases; in the period between 1809 and 1815, the Court sat about thirty days a year, and between 1822 and 1846 the annual load was still only 40 cases. (By the last decade of the nineteenth century there were around fifteen hundred cases on the docket and it took three years to reach a case for argument.)

The justices were not unconscious (as James Beck, one of the solicitors general of the United States remarked in a speech to the Philadelphia Bar), of the inordinate length of the arguments on questions which, while important as pioneer decisions, were not inherently difficult. Justice Story thus wrote at the very beginning of his judicial career in 1812: "The mode of arguing cases in the Supreme Court is exceedingly prolix and tedious." Again, in 1831, when the Charles River Bridge Case was before the Court, he wrote: "We have been sadly obstructed of late in our business by very long and tedious arguments, as distressing to hear as to be nailed down to an old-fashioned homily."

It was not until March 1849, that the long-suffering Court adopted a rule that limited the length of each argument to two hours, and it took this course only after its indulgence toward counsel had been severely criticized in Congress. In the course of debate a senator said:

"It is quite familiar to us all that in a case which attracted some attention, one of the learned counsel occupied an entire day for the purpose of demonstrating this very difficult proposition in America, that the people are sovereign; and then pursued his argument on the second day by endeavoring to make out the very difficult conclusion from the first proposition that, being sovereign, they had a right to frame their own Constitution."

Wake and Shine

During a tedious trial held at the circuit court in Bloomington, Abraham Lincoln was defending a client on a warm summer afternoon, when glancing towards the bench, he thought that Judge Davis had fallen asleep. Although he was far from resting his case, Lincoln thought of a jest and raised his voice to a pitch loud enough to raise the soundest sleeper:

"If it please your Honor and the Court will wake up, we are ready to submit our cause for instructions to the jury on the pleadings and testimony."

Judge Davis, who had been listening attentively with his eyes closed, immediately straightened up in his chair and replied:

"The Court has been waiting on Counsel Lincoln for his argument on the part of the plaintiff for over an hour. This has not been made. If it had been, the Court could have reposed comfortably the whole time; but as the case is submitted without argument on the written pleadings and the testimony, the jury will find . . ." and the judge instructed the jury concerning the law involved in the case.

Lincoln lost on the joke, since he was deprived of his oral argument to the jury. But he recovered his wit by telling the judge:

"If it please your Honor, I will be pleased to make an argument any time, whenever it will bring comfort and repose to the Court."

Too Much Bard

When he was Chief Justice of Massachusetts, Oliver Wendell Holmes became so impatient with long-winded arguments that he once suggested that lawyers should learn the art of innuendo from risqué French novels of the period.

Although he was usually kind and gentle with lawyers before the Supreme Court, Holmes could become quite intolerant of his fellow judges. On one occasion, when one of the justices continually cross-examined counsel, thus delaying the argument, Chief Justice White moaned in a stage whisper: "I want to hear the argument." "So do I, damn him," Justice Holmes growled aloud.

James M. Beck, as Solicitor General of the United States in the early 1920s, argued many important cases before the Supreme Court. Beck was also a great lover of Shakespeare and something of an amateur scholar of his works. He loved to pepper liberally his erudite, literate, and often lengthy arguments with quotations from the Bard. After one such peroration, Justice Holmes leaned over to the chief justice and whispered quite audibly: "I hope to God Mrs. Beck likes Shakespeare."

Send-off

James Beck learned something from Justice Holmes. He was asked to pay tribute to the 91-year old justice before the Federal Bar Association. Getting hints from his restless audience, Beck finally ended his eulogy with a story that Justice Holmes had once told him about a clergyman in some New England village, who always welcomed guests within his house with lavish hospitality. But if the guest lingered too long and indefinitely, the minister would add to his usual blessing:

"O Lord, bless thy servant who is a guest within this home, and give him a safe and pleasant journey when he leaves tomorrow, on the eleven-ten train."

Bored to Death

Sir Thomas Davenport, an Englishman in the last century notorious for lengthy dull speeches, was retained on one occasion to argue a case on the Northern Circuit. The day was unusually hot and, as the case excited great interest, the court was full. Sir Thomas made a speech of three hours' duration, whose soporific influence, aided by the atmosphere of the court, was irresistible. Before the proceedings commenced, a boy had managed to climb up to a window sill at a considerable height from the floor, from which vantage point he watched for some time what was going on. At last the heat and the serjeant's dullness overcame him, and, nodding in his sleep, he lost his balance and tumbled down. He was reported at first to be dead. John Scott, therefore as Attorney General of the Northern Circuit—a jocular office on a court which generally held its sittings after mess—indicted the serjeant at the Circuit Court at Appleby for "manslaughter, perpetrated by a long dull instrument, of no value, to wit a speech." He was convicted and severely fined in bottles of wine.

Hot Air

A barrister was going on at unnecessary length in a court presided over by Mr. Justice Wills. He dwelled at length on some bags connected with the case: "They might have been full bags," he asserted pompously, "or they might have been half-filled bags, or they might even have been empty bags, or . . ."

"Or perhaps," the judge interpolated with some impatience, "they might have been wind-bags!"

Snoring

Jacob Hays was a crier at the New York Sessions in the early nineteenth century. Over many decades of service he became so used to crying, "Silence in the court!" that once when he fell asleep and was startled by a peal of thunder, Hays cried out: "Silence!"

Another time he dozed off, as was his wont in the late afternoon, when the courtroom got too warm. The recorder was charging the jury, when the snoring of the old man became quite audible. An officer went and whispered in his ear: "Uncle Jacob, someone is snoring and disturbing the court." Hays jumped up and cried out in his stentorian voice: "Silence! There must be no snoring in court!" He turned to the recorder and instructed him: "You may now proceed without interruption."

Taking Responsibility

In a Vancouver courtroom, as Canadian lawyer Peter Macdonald tells the story, counsel was droning on for several hours presenting his submission. The afternoon was hot and stuffy and the judge had fallen asleep. The lawyer was reasonably concerned that his thoroughly researched, closely reasoned argument was being wasted, and he stopped to whisper to Lou Mazur, the clerk-registrar of the court:

"Lou, wake up the judge!"

"You wake him up," Mazur hissed back, "you've put the bastard to sleep!"

Labyrinth

An eccentric serjeant-at-law in eighteenth-century London, named Hill, was also known as 'Serjeant Labyrinth' because of his circuitous arguments. Once in the middle of such an argument, which was so frequently perplexed with parentheses as to excite the laughter of the court, Lord Mansfield interrupted him with "Mr. Serjeant, Mr. Serjeant." The serjeant was rather deaf, and the words were repeated without effect. At length the counsel sitting beside him told him that Lord Mansfield spoke to him. This drew his attention to the bench, and Lord Mansfield, in his blandest tones, addressed him, "Mr. Serjeant, the court hopes your cold is better."

In one of the serjeant's abstracted moods he had forgotten to button up the front of his breeches. This was observed by some counsel near him during an argument of a very abstruse point, who whispered to him, "Your breeches are unbuttoned." The serjeant, thinking it some hint in connection with the cause, adopted it without consideration, and, in unaltered tone of voice, exclaimed, "My Lords, the plaintiff's breeches were unbuttoned." Nor was he aware of the inappropriateness of the introduction until informed by the same person of the hint having reference to his own breeches, not to the plaintiff's.

A Winker

Harry Deane Grady, a prominent lawyer in the early part of the nineteenth century, had a mischievous fund of Irish fun. One of his most efficient weapons was his right eye, which he constantly used to wink at the jury when he wished them to note some particular answer from an adverse witness. By mere dint of winking it seemed smaller than the left one. Appearing in court one morning in rather depressed spirits, which was very unusual with him, a sympathizing friend said:

"What's up, Harry? You are not as lively as usual."

"My dear fellow," Grady replied, "I'm ruined outright; my jury eye is out of order."

The Judge Smiled

In 1901, as a court reporter in the Chicago courts, Francis X. Busch attended the trial of a case titled People of the State of Illinois v. August M. Unger, Francis Wayland Brown and Frank H. Smiley. *The case involved the death of a young woman, Marie A. Defenbach, under mysterious circumstances, and the prosecution was trying to prove that the defendants had conspired to murder her and defraud the New York Life Insurance Company of $5,000.*

One thing fixing the case indelibly in my memory is that it was the first of many in which I saw Clarence Darrow in action. Bit by bit the sordid story was pieced together. Olson (one of the state prosecutors) was a master hand in the orderly and effective presentation of a criminal case. The burden of resisting his accumulation of incriminating facts fell almost entirely on Darrow. J. J. McDanold (an elderly lawyer more skilled in civil law than in criminal practice representing Unger) was old and ailing, and his few defense efforts were more often detrimental than helpful. Almost any lawyer other than Darrow would have taken advantage of the situation; he could have played a silent role and cross-examined only when specific testimony implicated his client. Darrow, however, as is well known, had his own peculiar ideas about criminals and the causes of crime and was sympathetic to almost any person charged with a criminal act.

This point of view and the obvious weakness of Unger's legal counsel prompted him to do what he could for Unger as well as his own client. Two instances lodged in my memory.

Darrow's drawling cross-examination was punctuated by the snap of his suspenders as he pulled them back and forth through the armholes of his vest. It developed that the witness, who had said so much about see-ing Marie leave the building with Unger hot on her heels, could not have seen anyone enter or leave unless he stood on the sidewalk outside the front door.

The trap laid, Darrow continued: "Mr. Peterson, aren't you commonly known in your neighborhood as a rubberneck?"

The embarrassed witness said he did not think so. Then, Darrow, increasing the tempo of his questioning, his voice resonant with sarcasm, asked, "But you are in the retail shoe business?"

"Yes."

"And you do sell shoes?"

"Yes."

"And rubbers?"

"Yes."

"Well," concluded Darrow, "I am going to assume those were for the feet, and not for the neck, and excuse you!"

Words cannot reproduce the shadings and the inflections of Darrow's voice or show the effect of this brief cross-examination. When it was suddenly ended, the astonished jury joined the crowded courtroom in a burst of unrestrained laughter. Austere Judge Tuley smiled.

The Old Math

A Hungarian judge in the early part of the century by the name of István Dusárdy would not tolerate laughter in his court. He believed that humor undermined and interfered with the proper administration of justice. One day Judge Dusárdy was hearing a routine case of petty larceny, and he asked a woman of a certain age in the witness box:

"How old are you, miss?"

"I was born in 1883," the woman replied, her face turning crimson.

The judge flashed his eyes at her, and repeated the ominous question:

"I asked how old you are."

"I was born in 1873," the woman replied barely audibly. The judge, grim at the best of times, now became enraged. He had a particular dislike of figures, which he thought of as a vocational skill for headwaiters and schoolteachers rather than useful for his own exalted profession. And now this woman expected him to work out her age?

"All right, you were born in 1873," he growled at his victim. "And you still haven't figured out your age in all this time?"

The court dissolved into pent-up laughter, and the judge who disliked humor, had a difficult time to restore solemn order.

Laughing on High

Charles Henry Butler as reporter of the U.S. Supreme Court at the turn of the century witnessed some amusing incidents even in those hallowed halls:

Once a young lawyer from Kansas argued an appeal in a *habeas corpus* proceeding. His client, who operated a drug store, had been arrested for selling liquor to an "allottee" Indian. The Government contended that the "allottee" did not become a full-fledged citizen of the United States under the particular statute involved, and therefore, still belonged to that class of Indians to which the sale of liquor was prohibited.

In the lower court the Judge had expressed the opinion that the United States still retained sufficient control over the Indian to curb his appetite for drink. The young attorney from Kansas, who appeared in a yellow tweed suit—no vest, flowing necktie, pink shirt and tan shoes—the most unique costume any lawyer ever wore during my time, paced up and down before the Bench gesticulating and arguing somewhat to this effect:

"In Kansas we don't think there's anything to the Indian except his appetite for drink. But we don't care what the law is. We want to know what he is. If this man is an actual citizen and we refuse to sell him liquor, he sues us under the State's Equal Civil Rights Law. If he isn't a citizen, the Federal Government sues us for selling him the liquor. Now please tell us just what he is."

Mr. Justice Brewer, who was the recognized authority on all Indian matters, interrupted the young Kansas lawyer to ask:

"Mr. Counselor, what do you think the status of an allottee is?"

The Kansas attorney stopped in front of Chief Justice Fuller and, spreading both his arms wide up in the air, exclaimed:

"If you fellows up there don't know, how do you think us fellows down here should know?"

The Court was stunned! Never before had it been described to its very face and in its own sacred precincts as "You fellows up there."

The shocked expression on the face of dear Chief Justice Fuller will never be forgotten. Justice Holmes, shaking with laughter, buried his face in his arms on the Bench to hide his amusement, and there was a sort of dazed expression on the features of the other members of the Court. After a brief breathing spell, argument was resumed.

Tension

In his days in the New York D.A.'s office, famed American attorney Arthur Train was once prosecuting a crooked New York lawyer named Victor Shanley, who had forged a client's name on a mortgage and pocketed the money:

During this trial an attractive young lady, who happened to be an important witness for the defense, became petrified when I arose to cross-examine her. Her evidence was essential to a conviction and she did not claim privilege. I tried her with all manner of questions without avail. Finally in despair I appealed to Judge Foster, whose efforts met with no better result. Apparently she was literally "speechless from terror." By this time the atmosphere in the courtroom had become tense, for it looked as if the defendant might escape conviction through the willful obstinacy of the witness.

"If your Honor please, I see nothing for it but to ask you to commit this witness for contempt," I said with some heat.

Judge Foster looked down at the girl sternly.

"Young woman, as you have willfully persisted in refusing to answer any questions I shall be obliged to commit you to the Tombs. Officer, take the witness into custody."

The court attendant started forward.

"I think the witness might be given a last chance," I interposed. "Look here, Miss————, isn't there anything you can say?"

"Why—yes!" she hesitated. "I can say:

Maud Muller on a summer's day,
Raked the meadows sweet with hay."

The courtrooom burst into a roar, the tension snapped, the young lady found her tongue, the situation was saved. I might add that the defendant was convicted.

Nothing to Wear
William Allen Butler, the nineteenth-century New York lawyer, was also something of a poet. He achieved considerable fame with a poem called "Nothing to Wear." He was once trying a case against another famous attorney, Bourke Cockran, in which it was necessary to prove the value of a stock which contained, among other things, fifty dozen fichus.

"Won't you explain to the jury," said Butler, "what a fichu is?"

"That's not necessary, Mr. Butler," Cockran came back. "Everybody knows that a fichu is an article that a lady puts on when she has *Nothing to Wear.*"

Soft Landing
When Sam Ervin was a superior court judge in North Carolina, he routinely asked any accused person not represented by counsel whether

the court should assign an attorney to him or her. On one such occasion in Lenoir County, a young man refused:

"Your Honor, I don't need a lawyer. I'm going to plead guilty and throw myself on the ignorance of the court."

Hard Choices

Judge George Stewart of the Provincial Court in British Columbia, Canada, was giving the man arraigned at the bar various options he could choose for his trial: "You have the right to be tried by a magistrate without a jury, or a judge without a jury, or a judge and jury. How do you wish to be tried?"

The man, who had no counsel representing him thought for a moment, chose a fourth option: "Trial without a judge."

As the laughter subsided in the courtroom, Judge Stewart remarked: "Young man, you're probably in the right place."

Truth Will Out

A witness was telling his story to a skeptical Martin Haley, presiding over a court in Dartmouth, Nova Scotia. According to Peter Macdonald, who tells the story in his book, *Court Jesters*, the man concluded his testimony by saying: "May God strike me with lightning, if I'm telling a lie!"

"Hit the deck!" the magistrate shouted, ducking under his desk.

Eight Is Enough

In another story, and another province, Saskatchewan judge H. Y. Macdonald was listening to a defense counsel asking for a lenient sentence for his client, who had seduced an employee and had fathered her child.

"He has no previous record, my lord," the lawyer began. "He's a family man, the father of seven children . . ."

"Eight," Justice Macdonald tersely interjected.

No Thanks, I Have My Own Tree

In the summer of 1986 the American Trial Lawyers Association and the Smithsonian Institution's Folklore program collaborated in a demonstration project on the Mall in Washington, D.C. Some of the best lawyers and judges from all over the United States displayed their courtroom skills in reenacting cases, and told stories from their rich experiences. At one of the story-telling sessions Chicago attorney Lorna Propes was remarking about the importance of knowing at least a few foreign words in our multilingual society:

"The only word of Spanish I know is *abogado*, which means lawyer, and it reminds me of the time when I was a young prosecutor in a high volume court in Chicago. Amid the big crunch of cases the sheriff once brought forward a Hispanic man. The presiding judge leaned forward, raised his voice, like we so often do when we think the other person does not understand English, and thundered, 'Sir, do you need an avocado?'"

LONG CIRCUITS

History

Judges' circuits apparently date back to the Old Testament. In the first book of Samuel (7:16) it is written: "And he [Samuel] went from year to year in circuit to Bethel and Gilgal and Mizpeh, and judged Israel in all those places."

In England, circuits were instituted by King Henry II, the one who had his friend Thomas à Becket dispatched from this world. In 1176 he divided his kingdom into six circuits, and commissioned his newly created "Justices in Eyre" (corrupted from the Latin *in itinere*, "on the journey") to administer justice and try writs of assize in the several counties. *Assize* was the name given the jury whom the sheriff was ordered to summon in such cases, usually involving tenancy and possession of land. Sometimes these justices were also called judges of assize.

Poor Shot

There was a very difficult judge on the Midland Circuit (wrote A. E. Bowker in 1961 about his lifetime of experiences with the law), who suffered from periodic attacks of gout. At such times he made things impossible for all around him. He would play merry hell with court officials especially, never missing an opportunity to give them a public dressing down.

One intolerably hot day in the Crown Court at Birmingham, when the tempers of all concerned in the trial were frayed, this judge sentenced an old lag to ten years for burglary—a sentence by no means excessive, in view of the prisoner's previous record. But the old lag took a different view.

He sprang to his feet in the dock and grabbed the stool on which he had been sitting, thrusting a prison officer contemptuously aside. He then accused the judge of being the son of unmarried parents, with comments on the disgrace and shame of such a condition in life. Then he threw the stool at the judge. It grazed his shoulder and displaced his wig.

In the moment's silence that followed, the clerk of assize, sitting beneath the judge, exclaimed in a whisper that could be heard in every part of the court:

"Good God! He missed him!"

Wild Wales

From the Recollections of a Deceased Welsh Judge, *we get this early nineteenth-century picture of how justice was dispensed in 'Wild Wales':*

In the old Welsh circuits the whole appearance of the court was different from an English court: the habits of the people, and even their dress, were distinct; and when, as in most cases, the witnesses could not talk English, and had to be examined by an interpreter, you might well fancy yourself in a foreign country. Indeed, in addressing the jury, whether by the bar or from the bench, it was but too obvious that the majority frequently understood but little of what was said to them. In the north, the dialect of the witnesses was occasionally puzzling enough. We used to hear people talk of the *house* or the *house-parts*—meaning the kitchen; of a *middenstead* for a dunghill; of a *stee* for a ladder; of *lating* for reckoning; and *laking* for playing; nay, of *darroch* for day's work, and a *tewthsin* for a three weeks since. But in Wales there was much less in common between the natives of the country and the professors of the law brought into the country to administer justice. This sometimes lead to some odd mistakes: take as an example, the jury who, after hearing a trial for sheep-stealing, in which the facts were that the sheep had been killed on the hill, and there skinned, the robber taking away the carcass, and leaving the skin for fear of detection—all this was proved in evidence, but the jury supposed it to relate not to the sheep but to a human being, and brought in, after some hesitation, what they considered a safe verdict of manslaughter!

The lawyers on these circuits were as comical in their way as the witnesses and juries. One of them, Clarke, all unintentionally to create a laugh, and not very fond of any such testimony to his powers, would now and then make his audience merry without meaning it. As when the opposite counsel had been pathetic on his orphan client's hard lot—"Gentlemen," said Clarke, "why, I am myself an orphan"—he was seventy-odd years old—"people's fathers and mothers cannot live forever." No one can doubt of the pathos raised before being suddenly dissipated by this unexpected sally, not of humour but of mere anger at any pathos having been imported into the cause. So when a witness whom he was pressing with his angry, and oftentimes scolding cross-examination, suddenly dropped down in a fit, and some said it was apoplectic, but privately Clarke heard it was epileptic: "My lord," said he, "it's only epilepsy, she must answer the question," as if the courts had taken a distinction between apoplexy and epilepsy.

The first time 'old Raine,' an ex-schoolmaster, sat in judgment, a man was tried before the sessions for robbing a hen-roost and acquitted for want of evidence against him. The chairman was ordering him to be discharged as a matter of course, but Raine said, though he fully agreed, yet he conceived it would be well to have him first whipped. The other justices repressed this ebullition of professional zeal, and explained the difference between justices and schoolmasters in respect of whipping.

The Handsome Plaintiff

On the Norfolk Circuit in England the famous Jack Lee was retained for the plaintiff in an action for breach of promise of marriage. When the brief was brought him he inquired whether the lady for whose injury he was to seek redress was good-looking.

"Very handsome, indeed, sir!" was the assurance of the woman's attorney.

"Then, sir," replied Lee, "I beg you will request her to be in the court and in a place where she can be seen."

The attorney promised compliance, and the lady, in accordance with Lee's wishes, took her seat in a conspicuous place. Lee, in addressing the jury, did not fail to insist with great warmth on the "abominable cruelty" that had been exercised toward "the lovely and confiding female" before them, and did not sit down until he had succeeded in working up their feelings to the desired point. The counsel on the other side, however, speedily broke the spell with which Lee had enchanted the jury, by observing that his learned friend in describing the graces and beauty of the plaintiff had not mentioned the fact that the lady had a wooden leg!

The court was convulsed with laughter, while Lee, who was ignorant of this circumstance, looked aghast; and the jury, ashamed of the influence that mere eloquence had had upon them, returned a verdict for the defendant.

Chacun à Son Goût

Baron Samuel Channell (1804-73) was a great eater, and at one o'clock precisely, whatever the state of the case being tried before him, the court adjourned for lunch, and an excellent lunch it was. When the Courts of Assizes are at any distance from the judges' lodgings, the judges' cook, who travels around the circuit with them, usually asks the judges before starting for the court in the sheriff's carriage in the morning what he shall send them down for lunch. Baron Channell and Justice B. were descending the stairs side by side, when the cook made the usual inquiry.

"Oh!" said Channell, who was senior judge, in the short clipping words and style peculiar to him, "send me my lunch at one punctually, mind. I'll have—let me see—I'll have a basin of clear mock turtle and a chicken, and some peas and potatoes, and an apple tart, and some sherry and seltzer; at one, mind, not later."

"Yes, my lud," replied the cook, and turning to Justice B., "What shall I send your lordship?"

"Oh, thank you, cook," was the reply in the slow, solemn, and almost mournful voice of the brother judge, "I'll have what I have at half-past one; then it won't disturb Baron Channell. I'll have, if you please, at half-past one, a piece of stale seed cake and some camomile tea."

Medium Rare

Justice Fletcher of the Common Pleas used to grow so ravenously hungry by about five o'clock every afternoon that country people agreed that he must have a wolf in his stomach. On one occasion, nearing that hour, a circuit counsel named French launched into a pompous cross-examination. The more contorted the judge's body shifted about the bench, the more pertinacious and long-winded did the attorney grow. At last the hour of six sounded. Flesh and blood could stand it no longer, at least not Fletcher's, and he made an outburst:

"Lord of heaven! Mr. French, do you mean to keep me here all night, like a bear tied to a stake?"

"Oh, no, my lord," French bowed reverentially, "not tied to a *steak*."

Gargoyle

J. A. Foote, who published his reminiscences of the Western Circuit in England in 1911, recalled

one judge whose hearing was somewhat impaired, had acquired the habit of repeating anything that he heard more distinctly than usual, often adding an involuntary expression of satisfaction. The result was sometimes a little embarrassing. "The prisoner called me an a-b-c-d, etc., my lord," said an old woman once at Dorchester. "An a-b-c-d—good!" said the judge with gusto, repeating the exact words as he wrote them down with every appearance of gratification. I am afraid some of the junior bar laughed, but fortunately he did not hear that.

Laughter in court is happily of rare occurrence, except at the witticisms of the Bench. I remember Mr. Justice Denman being much provoked by some manifestation of unseemly mirth at Bodmin. There was an old man there, well known to habitués of the place, whose face was permanently distorted into a ghastly grin. He was in fact a Cornish reproduction of Victor Hugo's "L'homme qui rit." Looking round for the offender, the judge saw this grotesque countenance leaning over the gallery. "You wicked old man," he said in stentorian tones; "I'll send you to prison!" The muscles of the supposed offender's face remained immovable; and the spectacle of this hideous grinning countenance looking down upon the judge upset the whole court. He was eventually removed by two policemen, apparently laughing still, but he evidently felt that he had been treated with injustice. I have seen him often since in the streets of Bodmin (still laughing); but he has been persuaded to discontinue his attendance at the Assize Court.

Sideshow

A famous old showman, John Robinson of the Robinson Circus, told the story in the early part of the century of arriving with his show in an American town that was all agog with a local murder trial. The population of the town and district for miles around stampeded the courthouse for admission, and so prospects for the afternoon show looked bad indeed. The parade took place nevertheless, and the route chosen for this procession led them past the court-house. The band blared its loudest as the cortege slowly passed. Gradually a few, then more, and finally the whole of the spectators of the murder trial came outside to look at the parade. The procession halted, the band played some particular popular tune of the moment, and the jury began to melt away . . . then some officers of the court . . . Finally the judge said:

"It's no good. This court cannot compete with the circus. The court is dismissed."

The sheriffs guarding the prisoner were human, and they too had to have a look at the lions and elephants. The man on trial was the only one who evinced no curiosity, for he seized his opportunity, bolted, and got safely away!

Not Waiting for Godot

One of the most famous plays of the modern theatre is Samuel Beckett's *Waiting For Godot*. It has been produced all over the world in all sorts of circumstances. In different places Godot is taken to symbolize God, or land reform, or whatever the audience has been vainly yearning for. One of the more unusual productions of the play took place in San Quentin Prison, in November 1957, under the auspices of the San Francisco Actors' Workshop. Alan Mandell, who was a member of the Workshop, told me that *Waiting For Godot* was done again recently at San Quentin by director Jan Jonson, who first produced the play in Sweden with Swedish inmates.

At first they only did the first of two acts, which was so well received that Jonson was encouraged by the prison authorities and Beckett himself to mount a full scale production and to take it on tour. Opening night was a gala event with all kinds of politicians and government people present. After the first act everybody was feeling very good about the show, but during intermission the entire cast managed to escape. Jan Jonson had to go on stage to explain why there would be no second act. When the director reported the episode to the author in Paris, Beckett said: "Ah, they didn't have the courage to wait."

The Literal Truth

The late Justice William Morrow was holding court in a small community hall somewhere in Canada's vast and empty Northwest Territories. According to Ontario lawyer Peter Macdonald, the accused, a native Inuit, had failed to show up. The judge asked the court clerk to summon the man by name in the usual manner. The servant of the court opened the door and cried out into the wilderness: "Wandering Spirit! Wandering Spirit! Wandering Spirit . . . !"

· 6 ·

THE PROOF OF THE PUDDING

BATTLES OF THE WILL

Sparring Partners

Sir Edward Marshall Hall's undiplomatic dealings made him many enemies and almost ruined his practice. His reckless courage once brought him to lock horns with Mr. Justice Hawkins, a notorious bully, who delighted in mistreating lawyers and especially in keeping them waiting around at court at his whim. Upon one occasion, after a long wait, Marshall Hall politely demanded bail for his client, adding by way of strengthening his argument that the police did not raise any objection.

"I don't care a farthing for the police," Hawkins yelled. "They are not superior to myself at present."

"Not even, I believe, in their own estimation," Hall drawled.

Injudicious Scrapes

Before his own elevation to the bench, and the lord chancellorship (1919), the brilliant and pugnacious F. E. Smith often dueled with judges. In an early case, Mr. Justice Ridley told him:

"Mr. Smith, I have read your pleadings, and I do not think much of your case."

"I am sorry to hear that, my lord," replied F. E. "But your lordship will find that the more you hear of it the more it will grow on you."

On another occasion, F. E. challenged the bench's ruling on a point of procedure and got no satisfaction. When he still persisted, the judge exclaimed in exasperation:

"What do you think I am on the bench for, Mr. Smith?"

"It is not for me," replied the barrister gravely, "to attempt to fathom the inscrutable workings of Providence."

But his worst fights were with Judge William Willis (1835-1911), a kindly but patronizing county court judge. F. E. was representing a tramway company that had been sued for damages arising from injuries to a boy who had been run over and had lost his sight.

"Poor boy, poor boy," said Willis. "Blind. Put him on a chair so that the jury can see him." The judge's unjudicial sympathy was clearly prejudicial to the case, so F. E. remarked:

"Perhaps Your Honour would like to have the boy passed round the jury box?"

"That is a most improper remark."

"It was provoked by a most improper suggestion."

One could cut the tension in court.

"Mr. Smith," Judge Willis went on ominously, "have you ever heard of a saying by Bacon, the great Bacon, that youth and discretion are ill-wed companions?"

"Indeed I have, Your Honour," F. E. came back, "and has Your Honour ever heard of a saying by Bacon, the great Bacon, that a much-talking judge is like an ill-tuned cymbal?"

"You are extremely offensive, young man," said judge Willis with great anger. But Smith had one more quiver to his arrow:

"As a matter of fact we both are; the difference between us is that I am trying to be, and you can't help it."

Stentorian

Chief Baron Thompson was once on the bench at York, when he heard a great noise at the other end of the hall, where the Crown cases were going on.

"Who's that man that's making such a noise, bailiff?" the judge asked. "Turn him out if he don't hold his tongue."

"Oh, my lord," Mr. Topping answered, "it's only Mr. Raine pleading at the other end of the Court."

No Collusion

When Lord Eldon was Chancellor, a well-known barrister at the Chancery Bar was attempting to deny that any collusion existed between him and the counsel who represented the other party:

"My lord, I assure you there is no understanding between us."

"I once heard," Lord Eldon reflected, "a squire in the House of Commons say of himself and another squire, 'We have never through life had one idea between us,' but I tremble for the suitors when I am told that two eminent practitioners have no understanding between them."

Getting Attention
Lord Clare, the Irish Chancellor (1749-1802), had a favorite dog that sometimes followed him to the bench. One day, while Curran was trying to make his argument, the Chancellor, in the spirit of habitual petulance that distinguished him, began to pet his dog instead of listening to the case. Counsel stopped suddenly in the middle of a sentence. The judge started. "I beg pardon," Curran said smoothly, "I thought your lordships had been in consultation; but as you have been pleased to resume your attention, allow me to impress upon your excellent understandings that . . ."

Fireworks
When John Curran was pleading a case before Lord Clare, the latter exclaimed at one of Curran's legal explanations: "Oh, if that be law, Mr. Curran, I may burn my law books!" "Better read them, my lord," was Curran's celebrated retort.

Brought to Book
Charles Russell (1832-1900) had easy manners, which rarely brought him into conflict with the bench. But once, when he was making a closely reasoned argument in court, the judge suddenly snapped at him:
"What is your authority for that statement?"
Russell turned with a gentle smile to an usher:
"Please bring his lordship a book on elementary law," he said.
There was a roar of laughter, and his lordship, turning red, ordered the court cleared. But he did not interrupt again.

Sarcasm
An eminent conveyancer, who prided himself on having answered thirty thousand cases, came express from the Court of Chancery to the King's Bench to argue a question of real property before Lord Ellenborough, known for his grave sarcasm. Taking for granted, rather too rashly, that common lawyers are little more acquainted with real property laws than

with the laws of China, the expert commenced his erudite harangue by observing than "an estate in fee simple was the highest estate known to the law of England."

"Stay, stay," interrupted the Chief Justice, with consummate gravity, "let me write that down." He wrote, then read slowly and deliberately, "An estate in fee-simple is the highest estate known to the law of England. The Court, sir, is indebted to you for this information."

There was only one person present who did not perceive the irony, and that was the learned counsel who incurred it. But though he was impervious to irony, it was impossible for him to avoid understanding the home thrust delivered by the judge at the conclusion of the harangue. Insensible alike to the grim repose of the bench and the yawning impatience of the ushers, the Conveyancer had exhausted the yearbooks and all the mysteries of the real property law in a sleepy oration that effectually cleared the court. When the clock struck four, and the judges started to their feet, he appealed to know when it would be their pleasure to hear the remainder of his argument. "Sir," replied the Chief Justice, "we are bound to hear you, and shall do so on Friday, but pleasure has long been out of the question."

Hardly an Encouraging Word
A young barrister began to recite a long speech before Lord Ellenborough, when his memory failed him. "My lord, the unfortunate client who appears by me—my lord, my unfortunate client . . ." The Lord Chief Justice intervened gruffly: "You may go on, sir; so far the court is quite with you."

How to Apologize
When John Clerk (1757-1832), afterward Lord Eldin, was at the Bar, he was remarkable for the *sang froid* with which he treated the judges. On one occasion a junior counsel, on hearing their lordships give judgment against his client, exclaimed that he was "surprised at such a decision." This was construed as contempt of court, and he was ordered to attend at the bar the next morning. Fearful of the consequences he consulted his friend, John Clerk, who told him to be perfectly at ease, for he would apologize for him in a way that would avert any unpleasant result. Accordingly, when the name of the delinquent was called, John Clerk rose and coolly addressed the assembled tribunal:

"I am very sorry, my lords, that my young friend had so forgotten himself as to treat your honourable bench with disrespect. He is extremely penitent, and you will kindly ascribe his unintentional insult to his ignorance. You must see at once that it did not originate in that. He said he was surprised at the decision of your lordships. Now, if he had not been very ignorant of what takes place in this court every day—had he known you but half so long as I have done—he would not be surprised at anything you did."

Another Interpretation

In the early part of our century, Matthew Carpenter was once vainly trying to argue before the U.S. Supreme Court that the justices should hear his case, but the chief justice said: "The Court does not care to hear the respondent." The opposing attorney was hard of hearing and missed the pronouncement.

"Matt, what did the chief justice say?" he whispered to Carpenter as he sat down. The displeased attorney's voice boomed out in the court:

"He said he would rather give you the damn case than hear you talk."

Distinction

Sir Frank Lockwood (1847-1897) was once cross-examining a man who claimed that a blow he had received on the head had caused him great physical and mental anguish:

"Were you really sick or did you only feel sick?" he demanded to know.

"Well, it's the same thing, isn't it?" said the witness.

"Oh, no it isn't," Lockwood glanced toward the barrister who opposed him in the case. "M'learned friend is sick with me, very sick, but I don't expect that he will throw up his brief."

Contempt

Vice-Chancellor Lord Cranworth (1790-1868), after hearing Sir Richard Bethell's argument in an appeal, said he "would turn the matter over in his mind." Sir Richard, turning to his junior partner with his usual bland calm utterance said: "Take note of that; His Honour says he will turn it over in what he is pleased to call his mind."

Mutual Contempt

Nineteenth-century British barrister and judge Sir Henry Hawkins was dining with Lord Watson at Gray's Inn when the latter told of the exchange between a famous advocate of the day and a very rude Scottish judge who never listened to arguments and liked to pooh-pooh whatever was said in court.

One day the advocate was arguing before him, when, to express his contempt, the cantankerous old curmudgeon pointed with one forefinger to one of his ears, and with the other to the opposite one.

"You see this, Mr. _____?"

"I do, my lord," said the advocate.

"Well, it just goes in here and comes out there!" and his lordship smiled with the hilarity of a judge who thinks he has actually said a good thing.

The advocate looked and smiled not likewise, but a good deal more wise. Then the expression of his face changed to one of contempt.

"I do not doubt it, my lord," said he. "What is there to prevent it?"

The learned judge sat immovable, commented Lord Watson, and looked like—a judicial wit.

Talking Rot

Australian Chief Justice Holroyd was presiding over a case, when in the middle of counsel's speech a portion of the ceiling fell, scattering plaster all over the court. The barrister paused in his speech and advanced the following suggestion:

"Dry rot has probably been the cause of that, my lord."

"I am quite of your opinion, sir," the judge observed with matching dryness.

Learning from His Mistake

Justice Van Brunt of the appelate court once interrupted a young lawyer in the middle of his long quotations from authorities: "I suggest that you get down to the merits of your own case."

"Presently, Your Honor, presently," the young lawyer responded, but he continued to expound the law earnestly as he saw it.

"Let me suggest to you," Justice Van Brunt interrupted him again, "that you get down to the merits of your case, and take for granted that the court is familiar with the elementary principles of law."

"No, Your Honor," dissented the sincere young man, "that was a mistake I made when I argued this case in lower court."

Procrastination

Lawyers are well known for their ability to stretch out cases through a succession of postponements and adjournments. One such typical procrastinator was a nineteenth-century lawyer in New York by the name of George Wilson. Never ready for trial, he was constantly asking the bench to put off a case. His standard plea was that he had been up all night nursing a sick child. On one occasion he was nonplussed before Judge John T. Irving of the New York Common Pleas, when his honor insisted in proceeding with Wilson's case.

Wilson went out of court for a moment and was told there of the death of Francis Arden, a well-known lawyer of the previous generation, but who had not been professionally active for twenty years. Wilson returned to court, and drawing as long a face as his square features would allow, claimed silence. He began by stating the great loss the bar had sustained by the death of Mr. Arden, eulogized the deceased and moved that the court adjourn. The mild-mannered judge echoed all that Wilson had said in praise, and then stopped.

"Then Your Honor will forthwith adjourn?" Wilson asked wistfully.

"No, Mr. Wilson, not forthwith; we will adjourn after your cause is tried."

The Procrastinator Trapped

Abraham Crist, a nineteenth-century lawyer who later met his death on a burning steamboat on the Hudson river, used to tell how he once got the better of George Wilson. Crist had brought an action in which Wilson was retained for the defendant. The trial, from his opponent's procrastinating disposition, had been repeatedly postponed, and Crist was determined to bring the case on when it was next called. At the opening of court on the day when it was on the calendar, he went to Wilson, assuming an air of concern, and asked him to allow the case to be postponed because of the absence of a material witness. This would have been a god-sent opportunity for Wilson, but he was wrestling with a different emotion. He could not resist the opportunity of driving an antagonist into a corner. So with many professions of regard for Mr. Crist, and of his personal readiness to oblige, he stated that his client was in attendance with witnesses, ready for trial, and so he regretted that he had to insist on going on whenever the case was called; he ended by declaring he should strenuously oppose its being put off in case his adversary should make an attempt to do so. Crist heard all this with well-acted vexation. Shortly afterward the case was called, and Wilson promptly answered "ready." To his chagrin Crist answered likewise, and Wilson was trapped into defending his case.

Too Much Hope

In an address to the Canadian Bar Association in 1947, Lord Norman Birkett told the story of a barrister friend who had made application to the bench to postpone the case for three weeks. The judge exclaimed in mock horror:

"But, sir, in three weeks all the judges of the King's Bench Division might be dead!"

To which Lord Birkett's friend replied:

"Oh, my lord, that would be too much to hope for!"

Surprise

Earlier in our century, John T. Bevins, an archetypal country lawyer from Pearsall, Texas, was pleading for a continuance of his case, because he was missing two witnesses.

"I think, Mr. Bevins," the judge interrupted, "that your witnesses have just entered the courtroom."

"Then Your Honor, may I still apply for a continuance?"

"Oh what grounds?" asked the judge.

"On the grounds of surprise," Bevins drawled. "Both of these rascals promised me that they wouldn't appear."

Too Clever by Half

William McKinley, later President of the United States, was pleading for mitigation of sentence on behalf of a client in a Canton, Ohio court, when the judge interrupted him:

"You cannot tell me that two blacks make a white, Mr. McKinley."

"They may sometimes, Your Honor."

"How is that? Please explain, sir."

"A pair of black Spanish fowls may be the parents of a white egg," said McKinley.

The court dissolved into laughter.

The same story has been attributed to Sir Henry Hawkins.

Why We Have Appeals Courts

Chief Justice Melville W. Fuller (1833-1910) was still practicing law in Chicago and pleading a case in the Superior Court before Judge Arthur McArthur, in which he argued that his client's ignorance of the law should be considered in extenuating his offense. The judge said:

"Every man is presumed to know the law, Mr. Fuller."

"I am aware of that, Your Honor," Fuller replied. "Every shoemaker, tailor, mechanic, and illiterate laborer is presumed to know the law. Every man is presumed to know it, except judges of the Superior Court, and we have a Court of Appeals to correct their mistakes."

Bacon and Egg

The English Court of Chancery is not, as a rule, a very amusing resort, but according to a story from the turn of the century, Vice-Chancellor Sir Richard Malins was always able to command a fairly good house whenever he had the opportunity. At one time when Vice-Chancellor Bacon was one of his colleagues, Malins had before him a case in which one of the parties was of that species particularly obnoxious to the legal mind, namely, a cranky litigant.

In delivering judgment, the Vice-Chancellor felt constrained to take a view adverse to the claims set up by this individual, who determined to avenge himself for what he chose to call a miscarriage of justice. The morning after the judgment, he presented himself in court, and taking aim from amid the bystanders hurled a rather ancient egg at the head of the judge. Vice-Chancellor Malins, by adroitly ducking, managed to avoid the missile, which discharged itself malodorously at a safe distance from its target. "I think," observed Sir Richard Malins, almost grateful in spite of the *lèse majesté* for so apt an opportunity of exercising his judicial wit, "I think that egg must have been intended for my brother Bacon."

Dressing Down

Judge Gary of Chicago was once trying a case when he was disturbed by a young man who was moving about in the rear of the court room, lifting chairs and searching under things. "Young man," the judge called out, "you are making a great deal of unnecessary noise. What are you about?" "I have lost my overcoat, Your Honor," the young man replied, "and I am trying to find it." "Well," said the venerable jurist, "people often lose whole suits in here without making all that disturbance."

A Change of Profession

Eli Perkins (the *nom de plume* of the nineteenth-century American humorist Melville D. Landon) tells the story of a disturbance in Judge Brady's courtroom. The prosecution was cross-examining a pale, consumptive-looking man, who was continually coughing. The judge's patience gave out after a while, and he said petulantly:

"Here, just stop that coughing, now: stop it!"

There was a short, painful silence, during which the pale cougher struggled with himself, and then coughed again and continued it for several minutes.

"I'm bound to stop that coughing," exclaimed Judge Brady. "I fine you ten dollars. That'll stop it, I guess."

"Jedge," said the cadaverous man, "I'd be willing to pay twenty dollars to have that cough stopped. If you can stop it for ten dollars you'd better get right off of that bench and go to practicing medicine. There's money in it, Jedge—money in it!"

Insulting the Audience

Judge White, an Australian judge about fifty years ago, was once listening to the testimony of the chief witness in a case, a fifteen-year-old girl, who was hesitant and frequently glancing toward the public gallery.

"Speak up, my girl," said the judge, directing a withering look toward the public. "I know you do not like speaking about such things in this crowded court, but you must. Most of us have business here, while others are listening because of their beastly minds."

In another case, Judge White suddenly addressed the gallery:

"This is not the kind of case for women to hear," and he paused expectantly. Nobody moved. So the judge added: "Old women may stay and listen if they like, but I insist now that young girls must go out."

Every female, irrespective of her age, got up and trooped out, the grandmothers leading.

No Fun

Frank M. Johnson, Jr., federal judge in Alabama, has done as much as anyone to make that state one of the most progressive in the Union. He invalidated the poll tax, silenced the Ku Klux Klan and desegregated schools and public facilities. Governor George C. Wallace, a law school classmate of Johnson's, would regularly refer to him as that "integratin', scallywaggin', carpetbaggin', baldface lyin' federal judge." Robert F. Kennedy, Jr., spent a year in Alabama and wrote a biography of Judge Johnson, in which he describes some of the clashes that took place in his court.

There is much to be said for the allegations that Frank M. Johnson, Jr., is no fun. He won't go to parties. He won't play in the local ball game. He is tough enough to make others play by his rules. Even those close to him were sometimes astounded by how harsh Johnson could be in the courtroom. "Sometimes when I see him dress down a lawyer in a crowded courtroom, it makes my skin shiver. I feel so bad for the guy," a friend said.

Johnson's court was once invaded by a Philadelphia lawyer who was convinced he knew more about how to try a civil rights case than the court. Johnson dressed him down, heard his stunned apology, then ordered him to pack his briefcase and get back to Pennsylvania.

In 1964 a Selma policeman entered the courtroom, having forgotten to remove his gun. According to a witness, "All hell broke loose. Johnson stood up and berated the man for daring to enter his courtroom while wearing the weapon. The poor policeman ran out of the courtroom like he was runnin' for his life."

Another time a young Justice Department lawyer, who had caught wind of Johnson's reputation for severity with those who entered his courtroom unprepared, fainted dead away with fear as he approached the judge. Johnson signaled the bailiff, and the man was carried out with no comment from the bench.

Judge John C. Godbold, one of the younger judges on the U.S. Court of Appeals for the Fifth Circuit, had argued in front of Johnson, and he recalled the "tight ship" that was Johnson's courtroom. "I may have been the only lawyer in history who was threatened with contempt because of the expression on his face."

ART AND TECHNIQUE

The Rest Is Up to You

Francis L. Wellman, the British judge who wrote *The Art of Cross Examination*, was once asked what he considered necessary to win a court case. "First you need a good case," he replied, "then you need good evidence, then you need good witnesses, then you need a good jury, and then you need good luck."

Too Literal

Baron Alderson (1781-1857) once remarked to a counsel who was notorious for the personal nature of the questions he addressed to witnesses: "Really, you seem to think the art of cross-examining is to examine crossly."

From Both Sides of the Mouth

Pylaeus was a celebrated Italian lawyer around 1170. A native of Milan, he practiced in Bologna. An early liability case of his is reported in a medieval legal textbook:

Some workmen, on the point of hurling a stone from a high place, called out to persons passing beneath that they should take care. A man passing by, and neglecting the caution given, was wounded by a stone. He summoned the masons into a court of law and demanded damages. The workmen went to Pylaeus to hire him as their counselor. On examining the story, the lawyer found that it would be impossible to find witnesses that his clients had called out to the passers by. He made use of the following stratagem on their behalf. Leading the workmen into the court, they were interrogated by the judge why they had hurled down the stone so carelessly. As their counsel advised them, they kept silent. The judge was astonished, but Pylaeus informed him that his clients were deaf and dumb.

"Nay, I heard these very men call out to everybody to take care."

"Then they should be acquitted," Pylaeus said to the judge.

Citations

Jacob Le Duchat, a French lawyer exiled to Berlin at the end of the seventeenth century, collected anas, as anecdotes are sometimes called. In his collection is to be found the story of Jason Magnus and Bartholomeus Socinus, two eminent Italian lawyers of Pisa in the fifteenth century. They frequently argued over matters of the law. One day Jason found himself driven hard by his adversary, and cited a law that he had that moment forged, which made him win his argument. Socinus, no less quick than his opponent, served him the same trick. Jason, who had never heard of that law, called upon Socinus to quote the passage.

"It stands on the same page that you had just cited," Socinus replied with great gravity.

Rattling the Witness

Sir James Scarlett (1769-1844), later Lord Abinger, had to examine a witness whose evidence would be somewhat dangerous unless he could be thrown off guard and "rattled." The witness in question was an influential man whose vulnerable point was said to be his self-esteem. He was ushered into the box, a portly, overdressed person beaming with self-assurance. After looking him over for a few minutes without saying a word, Sir James opened fire:

"Mr. Tompkins, I believe?"

"Yes."

"You are a stockbroker, I believe, are you not?"

"I ham," said the witness, somewhat pompously aspirating the word. Pausing for a few seconds and making an attentive survey of him, Sir James remarked sententiously:

"And a very fine and well-dressed ham you are, sir."

In another case, involving a breach of promise, Scarlett appeared for the defendant, who was supposed to have been cajoled into the engagement by the plaintiff's mother, a titled lady. The mother, as a witness, completely baffled the defendant's clever counsel when under cross-examination, but by one of his happiest strokes of advocacy, Scarlett turned his failure into success:

"You saw, gentlemen of the jury, that I was but a child in her hands. *What must my client have been?*"

Trapped

In an action brought for assault by a priest of the Church of Rome against late eighteenth-century Irish statesman Lord Doneraile at the Cork Assizes, John Curran had to cross-examine Mr. St. Ledger, brother to the defendant, and, as it was his object to depreciate his evidence, he had described him in very gross and insulting language in his speech. In doing so, however, he had not mentioned his name. When Mr. St. Ledger came to the table and took the Testament in his hand, the plaintiff's counsel, in a tone of affected respect, addressed him, saying:

"Oh, Mr. St. Ledger, the jury will, I am sure, believe you without the ceremony of swearing you; your character will justify us from insisting on your oath." The witness, described by this mild and complimentary language (his irritation evidently diverted his attention from the very palpable trap laid for him), replied, with mingled surprise and vexation:

"I am happy, sir, to see you have changed the opinion you entertained of me when you were describing me a while ago."

"What, sir! then you confess it was a description of yourself! Gentlemen, act as you please; but I leave it to you to say, whether a thousand oaths could bind the conscience of the man I have just described."

Horse Play

John Curran was preeminent in the art of cross-examining a witness. In a case involving a horse, he asked the jockey's servant his master's age, to which the man retorted, with a ready gibe: "I never put my hand into his mouth to try." The laugh was against Curran until he made the bitter reply: "You did perfectly right, friend, for your master is said to be a great bite."

Thomas Erskine displayed similar readiness in a case of breach of warranty. The horse taken on trial had become dead lame, but the witness to prove it said the horse had a cataract in his eye. "A singular proof of lameness," suggested the court. "It is cause and effect," remarked Erskine, "for what is a cataract but a fall?"

Louder than Words

The great F. E. Smith, later Lord Birkenhead, was once cross-examining a boy whose right arm, the prosecution alleged, had been crippled through the negligence of the defendant, a bus company.

"Will you show me," F. E. asked with great sympathy toward the boy, "just how high you can lift your arm?"

His face exhibiting great pain, the boy could barely bring his arm in line with his shoulder.

"Thank you," said F. E., "and now will you show me how high you could lift it before the accident?"

The boy's arm immediately shot up in the air, and the defense had no further questions.

Lethal

Sir Edward Carson was one of the most lethal cross-examiners. In one of the classic stories about him, he pointed his long index finger at a red-nosed witness:

"I believe you're a heavy drinker?" he asked in his brogue.

"That's my business!"

"And have you any other business?" Carson asked and sat down.

In another case, Carson was cross-examining a certain Captain Scott, a private detective, who had changed his name several times during a long and checkered career.

"Why did you change your name to Scott?"

"No particular reason."

"And why Captain?" Carson pressed him.

"At the office they called me the Boss, the Captain or Governor; I liked Captain best."

"I suppose," said Carson, "it means Captain of the detective corps. But why Scott? Was it because it reminded you of Great Scott?"

But on one occasion a witness got the better of Carson. The case involved the purchase of cattle at a fair.

"Have you got a receipt for the money?" he demanded.

The Irishman appealed to the bench:

"Yer Honour, I wonder if the man was ever at a fair, or did he ever sell cattle?"

Method In His Madness

Lord Chancellor Loughborough once ordered to be brought to him a man against whom his heirs wished to take out a statute of lunacy. He examined him very attentively and put various questions to him, to all of which the man made the most pertinent and apposite answers. "This man mad!" thought he, "verily, he is one of the ablest men I ever met with." Toward the end of his examination, however, a little scrap of paper, torn from a letter, was put into Lord Loughborough's hand, on which was written a single word: "Ezekiel." This was enough for such a shrewd man as the Chancellor, who forthwith took his cue. "What fine poetry," said his lordship, "is in Isaiah!" "Very fine," replied the man, "especially when read in the original Hebrew." "And how well Jeremiah wrote!" "Surely," said the man. "What a genius, too, was Ezekiel!" "Do you like him?" said the man, drawing closer confidentially: "I'll tell you a secret—I am Ezekiel!"

The Long and the Thick of It

Thomas Erskine, who later became Lord Chancellor, almost cast a spell over juries when he was practicing at the Bar. "Juries have declared," wrote Lord Brougham, "that they have felt it impossible to remove their looks from him when he had riveted, and as it were fascinated them by his first glance. Then hear his voice, of surpassing sweetness, clear, flexible, strong, exquisitely fitted to strains of serious earnestness."

Though he did not rely on wit, humor, or sarcasm in addressing a jury, he could use them to effect in cross-examination. "You were born and bred in Manchester, I perceive," he said to a witness. "Yes." "I knew it," said Erskine carelessly, "from the absurd tie of your neckcloth." The witness's presence of mind was gone, and he was made to unsay the greater part of his evidence. Another witness confounded "thick" whalebone with "long" whalebone, and was unable to distinguish the difference after counsel's explanation, causing Erskine to exclaim, "Why, man, you do not seem to know the difference between what is thick and what is long! Now I tell you the difference. You are thick-headed, and you are not long-headed."

Browbeaten

American humorist Eli Perkins wrote in the late nineteenth century one of the classic satires on the browbeating lawyer during cross-examination:

I used to have a strong contempt for lawyers. I thought their long cross-examinations were brainless dialogues for no purpose. But ever since Lawyer Johnson had me as a witness in a wood case, I have had a better opinion of the lawyer's skill. In my direct testimony I had sworn truthfully that John Hall had cut ten cords of wood in three days. Then Johnson sharpened his pencil and commenced examining me.

"Now, Mr. Perkins," he began, "how much wood do you say was cut by Mr. Hall?"

"Just ten cords, sir," I answered boldly. "I measured it."

"That's your impression?"

"Yes, sir."

"Well, we don't want impressions, sir. What we want is facts before this jury—f-a-c-t-s, sir; facts!"

"The witness will please state facts hereafter," said the judge, while the crimson came to my face.

"Now, sir," continued Johnson, pointing his finger at me, "will you swear that it was more than nine cords?"

"Yes, sir. It was ten cords—just . . ."

"There! never mind," interrupted Johnson.

"Now, how much less than twelve cords were there?"

"Two cords, sir."

"How do you know there were just two cords less, sir? Did you measure these two cords, sir?" asked Johnson savagely.

"No, sir; I . . ."

"There, that will do! You did not measure it. Just as I expected. All guess-work. Now didn't you swear a moment ago that you measured this wood?"

"Yes, sir; but . . ."

"Stop, sir! The jury will note this discrepancy."

"Now, sir," continued Johnson slowly, as he pointed his finger almost down my throat; "now, sir, on your oath, will you swear that there were not ten cords and a half?"

"Yes, sir," I answered meekly.

"Well, now, Mr. Perkins, I demand a straight answer—a truthful answer, sir. How much wood was there?"

"T-t-ten c-c-c-ords," I answered hesitatingly.

"You swear it?"

"I d-d-do."

"Now," continued Johnson, as he smiled satirically, "do you know the penalty of perjury, sir?"

"Yes, sir; I think . . ."

"On your oath, on your s-o-l-e-m-n oath, with no evasion, are you willing to perjure yourself by solemnly swearing that there were more than nine cords of wood?"

"Yes, sir; I . . ."

"Aha! Yes, sir. You are willing to perjure yourself, then? Just as I thought" [turning to the judge] "you see, your Honor, that this witness is prevaricating. He is not willing to swear that there were more than nine cords of wood. It is infamous, gentlemen of the jury, such testimony as this." The jury nodded assent and smiled sarcastically at me.

"Now," said Johnson, "I will ask this perjured witness just one more question."

"I ask you, sir,—do you know—do you realize, sir, what an awful—a-w-f-u-l thing it is to tell a lie?"

"Yes, sir," I said, my voice trembling.

"And, knowing this, you swear on your solemn oath that there were about nine cords of wood?"

"No, sir; I don't do anything of . . ."

"Hold on, sir! Now, how do you know there were just nine cords?"

"I don't know any such thing, sir! I . . ."

"Aha! you don't know then? Just as I expected. And yet you swore you did know. Swore you measured it. Infamous! Gentlemen of the jury, what shall we do with this perjurer?"

"But . . ."

"Not a word, sir—hush! This jury shall not be insulted by a perjurer! Call the next witness!"

Revenge

Sometimes, the browbeaten witness will get back at his tormentor. In his day, Rufus Choate (1799-1859) was one of the shrewdest cross-examiners of the Massachusetts Bar. Once, trying to impeach the veracity of a witness, he had been toying with the man on the stand for some time without getting any damaging admissions, and finally he made up his mind to go at him plump and force him to the wall.

"Now," he said, eyeing the witness savagely, "you know what robbery is, don't you?"

"Yes, sir."

"Well, you look like it. Now, sir, I ask you plainly and categorically, were you ever engaged in a bank robbery?"

The witness hesitated.

"I repeat, sir—did you not once rob a bank? Come, no evasion."

"I was never indicted for bank robbery. I—"

"Never mind that; answer my question. Were you ever engaged in a bank robbery? Speak up."

"Judge, must I answer this question?" said the witness, appealing to the Court.

"Yes, you will have to answer it."

"Well, what is the question?"

"I give it to you again, sir. Did you not once rob a bank? Speak up, sir; no equivocation. Did you?"

"No, sir," said the witness, smiling broadly, while the whole court screamed with laughter.

Getting the Worst of It

Rufus Choate was examining the chief mate of the ship *Challenge*, one Dick Barton. Choate had already been grilling the sailor for over an hour, hurling questions with the speed of a rapid-fire gun. And when victory seemed in sight, came this exchange:

"Was there a moon that night?"

"Yes, sir."

"Did you see it?"

"No, sir."

"Then how did you know there was a moon?"

"The *Nautical Almanac* said so, and I'll believe that sooner than any lawyer in the world."

"Be civil, sir. And now tell me in what latitude and longitude you crossed the equator."

"Ah, you are joking."

"No, sir, I'm in earnest and I desire an answer."

"That's more than I can give."

"Indeed. You a chief mate and unable to answer so simple a question?"

"Yes, the simplest question I was ever asked. I thought even a fool of a lawyer knew there's no latitude at the equator."

Contest of Wills

Daniel Webster and Rufus Choate were on opposite sides of an inheritance case in Springfield, Massachusetts, with Choate trying to break the will and Webster defending it. Choate alleged inequalities in the will and especially anathemized the power of the "dead hand." In his closing address, he said, "Gentlemen of the jury, look here upon the living, with all the hopes, fears, anxieties and tribulations of the living—think of them, and the dark auguries of their future—while John Smith is dead—dead—DEAD!"

Silence reigned in the courtroom and everybody supposed that the case would be settled in favor of the plaintiffs. But then Webster arose, and in a quick, rather haughty tone, he summed up: "Gentlemen of the jury, this is an attempt to break the last will and testament of John Smith of Hampden County, yeoman. And when he made this will he wasn't dead—dead—DEAD!"

The last three words uttered rapidly and with a half-suppressed sneer brought the whole room to the verge of laughter. The jury promptly sustained the will.

Dead Files

William Allen Butler, well-known American lawyer of the nineteenth century, was at one time opening a case to the jury growing out of the failure of a merchant who had been engaged in the East India trade. His failure was caused by the fall in price of a large quantity of manila hemp he had ordered. Butler, after stating the facts, said that this firm, like certain other unfortunate persons, was finally suspended by too much hemp.

On another occasion Butler began the argument of an appeal in this way: "May it please the court. This action was begun about thirty years ago; the original plaintiff is dead, the substituted plaintiff is dead; the original defendant is dead; all of the counsel originally connected with the case are dead; and the principal question upon this appeal is whether the cause of action survives."

Brain Dead

John Tierney, Minneapolis prosecutor, gives the following example of how badgering of an expert witness in a Chicago homicide case backfired on counsel:

Defence: Doctor, do I understand you correctly that you didn't conduct the autopsy yourself?

Witness: That's right, counsel.

Defence: And you didn't know Jimmy Spence when he was alive, did you?

Witness: No, counsel.

Counsel: And you certainly didn't know him after he was dead, did you doctor?

Witness: No, counsel.

Counsel (pouncing): Then isn't it a fact that you don't know, from your personal knowledge that is, whether Jimmy Spence is alive or dead?

Witness (with a leisurely drawl): Well, I suppose you could say that, counsel, were it not for the fact that I have his brain in a jar in my office. Of course, I suppose he could be wandering about the streets of Chicago, practicing law . . .

Exaggeration

A good lawyer never denies a true statement before the jury; it is much easier to exaggerate that statement and make the jury laugh it out of court. Robert Ingersoll, a famous agnostic and one of the great orators of the last century, often squelched the opposing counsel by a blast of ridicule. One day in Peoria, Illinois, they were trying a patent churn case. The opposing counsel used many scientific terms. He talked about the workings of the machine and how his client had made a valuable contribution to science.

"Science!" yelled Colonel Ingersoll. "The opposing counsel is always talking about science, and see—" as he looked over at the opposing counsel's brief—"he spells it with a y—with a y, sir! C-y-e-n-c-e!"

Absurdity

Another one of Robert Ingersoll's favorite forms of arguing was *reductio ad absurdum*, which the famous agnostic particularly enjoyed using in baiting gentlemen of the cloth. Once when Connecticut's blue laws, forbidding certain activities on Sunday, were a matter of public debate, Ingersoll was talking with Charles Horace Talmage, one of the great preachers of the day, about the laws enforcing Sunday observance:

"Would you like to live in a community, Mr. Talmage, where not one cigar could be smoked and not one drop of spirituous liquor could be sold or drunk?"

"Certainly," said Talmage, "that would be a social heaven."

"And you would like to live where no one could play on the Sabbath day; where no one could laugh out loud and enjoy a frolic?"

"Certainly."

"And where everyone had to go to church?"

"Yes, sir; that would suit me. It would be paradise to live in a community where everyone was compelled to go to church every Sunday, where no one could drink a drop, where no one could swear, and where the law would make every man good. There the law would make every man's deportment absolutely correct."

"And you think such a man would be a good Christian—a better man than I am?"

"Why, of course, Colonel."

"Then," said Mr. Ingersoll, "I advise you to go right to the penitentiary. At Sing Sing there is a commmunity of 1500 men and women governed in precisely that manner. They are all good by law."

The Wrong Question

Michael Donaldson, Los Angeles-based entertainment lawyer, whom I am happy and proud to have as my attorney, told me of a lesson he learned when he was starting out in the late 1960s. He had just left the D.A.'s office in Los Angeles, and was appointed by the court as private counsel to represent a man who stood accused of theft he was alleged to have committed with a partner. Donaldson had spent much of his time in court trying to disassociate his client from this partner, whose guilt was more or less established. The case was going well; Donaldson felt that Judge Broady was sympathetic to his client and was even trying to help with his strategy in the case. At one point when Donaldson's client tried to interrupt, the judge warned him not to speak except through his attorney. Unfortunately, his attorney was less mindful of this advice, and instead of quickly ending the cross-examination of his client and dismissing him from the witness box, Donaldson asked one last question:

"Is there anything you wish to add?"

The accused, oblivious of his counsel's strategy to make the jury forget that he ever had an associate, blurted out:

"Yeah, I just want to say that I and my partner really didn't do it."

This compelled the judge to ask who the man's partner was, and of course they were both convicted.

And Michael Donaldson says he learned an important lesson: "Never ask a question to which you don't already know the answer."

Knowing When to Stop

Charles Garry, a great cross-examiner and the well-known defense attorney of Huey Newton, Bobby Seale, and other Black Panthers, is fond of repeating an old story about a man who was charged with biting off his neighbor's ear.

The sole eyewitness was asked on the stand if he saw the man bite off the ear. He answered no. The district attorney said, "You didn't see him do anything to the ear?" The witness replied, "I didn't see him bite anything at all." Turning to the judge, the prosecutor said, "Well, I guess I have no case, Your Honor." The defense counsel, a pompous ass, chose to cross-examine instead of asking for dismissal. "Sir, if you didn't see this happen, why have you had the gall to come into this court and testify against my client?" The witness responded, "Well, I didn't see him bite off the ear, but I did see him spit it out."

A wise lawyer does his fishing before the trial starts, not during cross-examination. Sometimes prosecutors also don't know enough to quit when ahead.

During an actual trial in San Francisco, a man charged with forcible rape produced a local priest as a character witness. The woman who brought the charge had been the prosecutor's chief witness. Knowing that the same priest had interviewed the woman right after the alleged incident, the prosecutor brought out on cross-examination that she had told exactly the same story to the priest as on the witness stand. Not satisfied with corroboration by a defense witness, he then asked, "And when she told you that story you believed her to be sincere, did you not?" The priest answered, "I believe her to be a liar and a common prostitute." The man was acquitted.

English

As a self-taught man, Charles Garry has waged a lifelong battle with the English language. Some of his Garryisms are as well-known in the legal profession as Goldwynisms are in Hollywood. Jessica Mitford, in the preface to Garry's book *Streetfighter in the Courtroom*, mentions a couple:

Garry once asked a witness: "Did you by chance or otherwise shoot and kill Officer Frey?"

And one of his classic statements: "And then the client proceeded to die."

Garry himself remembers the time he told a reporter about a client being "arrested in the dead of late evening."

Latin

A lawyer opposing Abraham Lincoln in a suit used a Latin maxim to impress the court with his erudition. Then he turned suddenly to Lincoln and asked him:

"Is not that so?"

"If that is Latin," replied Lincoln, "I think you had better call another witness."

Steamrolled

Abraham Lincoln was once opposed by a lawyer who was, as described by Senator Daniel Voorhees, a glib courtroom orator but a shallow thinker given to reckless and irresponsible statements.

"My friend on the other side," Lincoln told the jury, "is all right, or would be all right if it were not for a physico-mental peculiarity which I am about to explain. His habit—of which you have witnessed a very painful specimen in his argument to you in this case—of reckless assertion without grounds, need not be imputed to him as a moral fault or blemish. He can't help it. The oratory of the gentleman completely suspends all action of his mind.

"I never knew of but one thing which compared with my friend in this particular. That was a steamboat. Back in the days when I performed my part as a keel boatman, I made the acquaintance of a trifling little steamboat which used to bustle and puff and wheeze about in the Sangamon River. It had a five-foot boiler and a seven-foot whistle, and every time it whistled the boat stopped."

Delicate Simile

Thomas Erskine was winding down a passionate peroration, with the following words: "Gentlemen of the jury, the reputation of a cheesemonger in the City of London is like the bloom upon a peach. Breathe upon it, and it is gone forever."

Mixed Metaphors

The English jurist Sir Henry Hawkins collected a number of verbal twisters in his entertaining recollections published in the early part of the century:

I must tell you of a distinguished judge who had to sentence a dishonest butler for robbing his master of some silver spoons. He considered it his duty to say a few words to the prisoner in passing sentence, in order to show the enormity of the crime of a servant in his position robbing his master, and by way of warning to others who might be tempted to follow his example.

"You, prisoner," said his lordship, "have been found guilty, by a jury of your country, of stealing these articles from your employer—mark that—your employer! Now, it aggravates your offence that he is your employer, because he employs you to look after his property. You did look after it, but not in the way that a butler should—mark that!" The judge here hemmed and coughed, as if somewhat exhausted with his exemplary speech; and then resumed his address, which was ethical and judicial: "You, prisoner, have no excuse for your conduct. You had a most excellent situation, and a kind master to whom you owed a debt of the deepest gratitude and your allegiance as a faithful servant, instead of which you paid him by *feathering your nest with his silver spoons*; therefore you must be transported for the term of seven years!"

The metaphor was equal to that employed by an attorney general who at a certain time in the history of the Home Rule agitation, addressing his constituents, told them that Mr. Gladstone had *sent up a balloon to see which way the cat jumped with regard to Ireland.* He was soon appointed a judge of the High Court.

Irish Bull

The British Parliament, toward the end of the nineteenth century, was having one of its innumerable debates on the Irish question, when Baron Dowse, one of the Irish judges, made the following comment: "I do not know the cause, but it is fact that many people are dying this year who have never died before."

The Clinching Argument

Governor Samuel R. McKelvie of Nebraska (1919-1923) told the story of a man who came before the State Board of Pardons. He was serving time in the penitentiary, having been party to stealing an automobile. He came from a small community and from a poor, respectable family. His counsel was not particularly distinguished or known for having a large practice at the bar, and he directed his principal arguments at impressing the board with the humanitarian aspects of the case. Wanting substance, he gave full vent to his feelings, and flights of eloquence were liberally employed.

Finally, after reciting that the applicant had been incarcerated for an unusual length of time, that his parents were poor and needed his support, and that he had previously appeared before the Board, he dramatically closed his arguments with this statement: "And gentlemen of your honorable board, you must bear in mind that there comes a time in every man's life when he should not be in the penitentiary."

Brevity

The English philanthropist Sir Thomas Buxton (1786-1845) relates that he once asked Lord Abinger what was the secret of his preeminent success as an advocate. He replied that he took care to press home the one principal point of the case, without paying much attention to others. He also said that he knew the secret of being brief. "I find," he said, "that when I exceed half an hour I am always doing mischief to my client; if I drive into the heads of the jury important matter, I drive out matter more important that I had previously lodged there."

Parry and Thrust

William M. Evarts was once opposed in a case by future New York governor David B. Hill, who was just beginning his career and was in fact delivering to the court his maiden speech. Like many young lawyers, he was florid, rhetorical, scattering, and weary. For four tedious hours he talked at the court and at the jury, until everybody felt like lynching him. When he got through, Evarts rose deliberately, looked sweetly at the judge, and said:

"Your Honor, I will follow the example of the distinguished but youthful counsel on the other side and submit the case *without argument.*"

Then he sat down and an awful silence took possession of the courtroom.

Extremely Concise

In the Recollections of a Deceased Welsh Judge, *there is a portrait of a colleague, George Wood, nicknamed the Wood Demon (after a melodrama in vogue in the early nineteenth century). Wood was*

a lawyer greatly quizzed for his ugliness, and highly esteemed for his profound knowledge of special pleading, accurate understanding, sound judgment and inflexible honesty. He was famous for the extreme conciseness of his style, which followed him to the bench; and his brother judge gives us a specimen, a story which, it may be well said, "he used to tell," for I believe he never told any other, and that one he was constantly called upon to tell at the circuit table, and always told it in the same words, and always with the same unbounded applause. It was as follows, for having so often heard it, we knew it by heart:

"A man having stolen a fish, one saw him carrying it away, half under his coat, and said, 'Friend, when next you steal, take a shorter fish, or wear a longer coat.'"

In this narrative—which certainly represents the scene perfectly, and gives an epigrammatic speech—there are not quite thirty words, particles included.

Stylist

Oliver Wendell Holmes astonished and overawed some of his colleagues on the Supreme Court by the clarity of his thinking and the force of his writing. Justice Cardozo said in 1931 that "one almost writhes at the futility, too painfully apparent, of imitation or approach." One of Melville Fuller's secretaries reported that whenever a new opinion by Holmes was brought to the chief justice, he would stop what he was doing and read it aloud with exclamations of pleasure and admiration: "Isn't that marvelous? Doesn't he write superbly?"

Justice Holmes wrote many of his opinions in his library at a high desk, which he had inherited from his grandfather, Judge Jackson. Often he wrote them while standing. Being asked once why he did so, Holmes replied:

"If I sit down, I write a long opinion and don't come to the point as quickly as I could. If I stand up I write as long as my knees hold out. When they don't, I know it's time to stop."

However, neither the brevity nor the clarity came easily. Reading one of his draft opinions, a secretary pointed out a passage that did not seem clear. Holmes replied:

"Well, if you don't understand it, there may be some other damn fool who won't. So I had better change it."

And when another objected that there wasn't a man in a thousand who would understand a particular sentence, the justice snapped back:

"That's the man I am writing for."

Music

Chief Justice Harlan Fiske Stone was very fond of music and was a great devotee of the Washington municipal orchestra. After a concert by Yehudi Menuhin, then a teenager, Stone dropped in on his old friend, the ninety-two-year-old Oliver Wendell Holmes. He told the retired justice how this awkward adolescent had held three thousand people spellbound.

"Ah," said Holmes, "what a triumph! Sometimes I think I would give ten years of my life to be able to play like that."

"And some of us," replied Justice Stone, "would give ten years of our lives to be able to write opinions like yours."

Justice Holmes's twinkling eyes betrayed that he enjoyed the praise as he said to Stone, who was then 62:

"My boy, God sees through all this modesty."

Research

Josiah Quincy, mayor of Boston in the 1840s, records an anecdote Daniel Webster told him at dinner:

The conversation was running upon the importance of doing small things thoroughly and with the full measure of one's ability. This Webster illustrated by an account of some petty insurance case that was brought to him when a young lawyer in Portsmouth. Only a small amount was involved, and a twenty-dollar fee was all that was promised. He saw that, to do his clients full justice, a journey to Boston, to consult the Law Library, would be desirable. He would be out of pocket by such an expedition, and for his time he would receive no adequate compensation. After a little hesitation, he determined to do his very best, cost what it might. He accordingly went to Boston, looked up the authorities, and gained the case. Years after this, Webster, then famous, was passing through New York. An important insurance case was to be tried the day after his arrival, and one of the counsel had been suddenly taken ill. Money was no object, and Webster was begged to name his terms and conduct the case.

"I told them," said Mr. Webster, "that it was preposterous to expect me to prepare a legal argument at a few hours' notice. They insisted, however, that I should look at the papers; and this, after some demur, I consented to do. Well, it was my old twenty-dollar case over again, and, as I never forget anything, I had all the authorities at my fingers' ends. The court knew that I had no time to prepare, and were astonished at the range of my acquirements. So, you see, I was handsomely paid both in fame and money for that journey to Boston; and the moral is, that good work is rewarded in the end, though, to be sure, one's own self-approval should be enough."

Just the Facts

Wrote U.S. Solicitor General James Beck:

It was probably true of Webster, as it was said of Erskine, that his statement of facts was worth another man's argument. No barrister ever made so deep and permanent impression as Judah P. Benjamin [Secretary of State for the Confederacy] upon the English bar, and I once asked Lord Halsbury, a former Lord Chancellor, the secret of his power, and he replied that it was his convincing statement of fact. He instanced a case that he had heard Benjamin argue, where the Court was opposed to his contention as developed by his junior. When Benjamin arose the Court was impatient of further discussion. In an aggressive voice the great advocate said: "If your Lordships please, if you will listen to me for ten minutes I will convince you that my contention is correct." Lord Halsbury added that Benjamin in ten minutes completely changed the opinion of the Court.

Persuasion

A. E. Bowker was Norman (later Lord) Birkett's assistant from the 1930s. He wrote that:

Norman Birkett's astonishingly rapid rise at the Bar, and his later distinguished career on the Bench, are only to be explained by his remarkable powers as an advocate and lawyer . . . I have seen juries who were like putty in his hands. Once at London Sessions, where he defended a little Swiss nurse-maid charged with shoplifting, he cast such a spell over the jury that they acquitted her without leaving the box, although the prosecution had quite a strong case. He wound up a wonderful speech with a quotation, the last line of which ran, "As all seems yellow to the jaundiced eye." It was like the final stroke of a hammer that drives home a nail.

After the case, our solicitor client remarked as we were walking from the Court: "Do you know, this man could convince me that a box of matches was a coach and four."

Eloquence

The poor crippled widow of a revolutionary soldier had been defrauded of her government pension by a man named Wright, who had secured her four hundred dollars and then kept half the award. Her appeals to the government had produced no results, and she came to Abraham Lincoln for help. As soon as the old woman left his office, Lincoln walked to the pension agent's office and demanded the rest of her money. Wright refused, and Lincoln immediately brought suit against him.

The day before the trial, Lincoln asked his junior associate, William Herndon, to get him a history of the Revolutionary War, which he carefully read that night. The next morning he produced only one witness—the crippled old widow, who retold her story in a most moving manner. Then Lincoln rose to make his case. He began by painting the scene at Valley Forge, describing the barefoot patriots leaving a trail of blood across the ice. Then he went back to the time when the plaintiff's husband had kissed her and her baby farewell before departing to war.

"Time rolls by," Lincoln continued in a sad, subdued voice, "the heroes of '76 have passed away and are encamped on the other shore. The soldier has gone to rest, and now, crippled, blinded and broken, his widow comes to you and to me, gentlemen of the jury, to right her wrongs. She was not always thus. She was once a beautiful woman. Her step was as elastic, her face as fair, and her voice as sweet as any that rang in the mountains of Virginia. But now she is poor and defenseless. Out here on the prairies of Illinois, many hundreds of miles away from the scenes of her childhood, she appeals to us who enjoy the privileges achieved for us by the patriots of the Revolution, for our sympathetic aid and manly protection. All I ask," Lincoln concluded by stretching his long arms in supplication towards the jury, "shall we befriend her?"

The speech made the desired impression on the jury. Half of them were in tears, while the defendant sat in the courtroom, drawn up and writhing under the fire of Lincoln's invective. "The jury returned a verdict in our favor," Herndon recalls, "and Lincoln was so much interested in the old lady that he became her surety for costs, paid her way home, and her hotel bill while she was in Springfield. When the judgment was paid, we remitted the proceeds to her and made no charge for our services."

Herndon also preserved Lincoln's notes for his brief, which reads: "No contract—No professional services—Unreasonable charge—Money retained by defendant not given by plaintiff—Revolutionary War—

describe Valley Forge privations—ice—Soldiers' bleeding feet—Plaintiff's husband, soldier leaving home for army—Skin defendant! Close!"

The Cigar Trick

Sometimes, when Clarence Darrow felt that his defense was a bit shaky, he would take out a long cigar and light it just as the prosecution began summing up. Leaning forward, seemingly lost in his opponent's argument, Darrow would let the ash on his cigar grow longer and longer. The jury's attention usually became fixed on the ash, waiting for it to fall, while the prosecution's carefully wrought arguments were ignored. It was part of the Darrow legend that he had his cigars specially constructed with a wire inside to sustain the ash.

Advocacy 101

The British author Somerset Maugham cites, in *A Writer's Notebook*, advice that a law professor gave his students:

"If you have the facts on your side, hammer them into your jury. If you have the law on your side, hammer it into the judge."

"And what if you have neither?" asked one of professor's students.

"Then hammer on the table," he replied.

It's All in the Mind

If all the world's a stage, as Shakespeare once wrote, then the courtroom is only more so. Trial lawyers who know how to project their words and personalities, to keep cool under pressure, and to hypnotize the jury with a compelling story, will maintain an edge over their opponents. Attorneys have been turning increasingly to drama coaches to develop or polish their theatrical skills. One firm specializing in such coaching is Applied Theatre Techniques in Los Angeles, started by my friend Joshua Karton and his partner Katherine James. They have wide acting and teaching experience in the theater; the problem is with their clients, who often lack the extrovert personality and aggressive self-confidence that most aspirants for the stage possess.

On one occasion, Karton and James were trying to help a female attorney who was afraid of going to pieces under the constant barrage of sexist comments from opposing counsel. "We noticed a ceramic pair of ballet slippers on her desk," Katherine James told *Los Angeles* magazine, "and we got her to imagine the man as the hippo in Fantasia wearing toe shoes and a tutu."

Their client went on to win her case.

ON THE EVIDENCE

Explanation
Justice William Maule (1788-1858), summing up for the jury, once reached into his ample store of irony:

"Gentlemen—the learned counsel is perfectly right in his law, there is *some* evidence upon that point, but he's a lawyer, and you're not, and you don't know what he means by *some* evidence, so I'll tell you. Suppose there was an action on a bill of exchange, and six people swore that they saw the defendant accept it, and six others swore they heard him say he should have to pay it, and six others knew him intimately, and swore to his handwriting; and suppose, on the other side, they called a poor old man, who had been at school with the defendant forty years before, and had not seen him since, and he said he rather thought the acceptance was not his writing, why there'd by *some* evidence that it was not, and that's what learned counsel means in this case."

That Is the Question
A witness once said to Justice Maule:

"You may believe me or not, but I have stated not a word that is false, for I have been wedded to truth from infancy."

"Yes, sir," said the judge drily, "but the question is how long have you been a widower?"

Court Reporter
English solicitor E. S. P. Haynes recorded his great-grandfather, who was Chief Baron of the Exchequer, saying of Lespinasse, the law reporter:

"He heard only half of what went on in Court and reported *the other half.*"

Dressing Down
Lord Ellenborough was once strangely posed by a witness, a laboring bricklayer, who came to be sworn.

"Really, witness," said the Lord Chief Justice, "when you have to appear before this court, it is your bounden duty to be more clean and decent in your appearance."

"Upon my life," said the witness, "if your lordship come to that, I am every bit as well dressed as your lordship."

"How do you mean, sir?" demanded his lordship angrily.

"Why, faith," said the laborer, "you come here in your working clothes, and I'm come in mine."

On another occasion, a witness dressed in a fantastical manner gave very rambling and discreditable evidence. Asked by cross-examining counsel what he was, the witness replied:

"I employ myself as a surgeon."

Chief Justice Ellenborough interjected:

"But does anyone else employ you as a surgeon?"

Disguise

A Quaker came into the witness box at Guildhall rather smartly dressed and without a broadbrim or dittoes. The crier put the Bible into his hand and was about to administer the oath, when he asked to be examined on his affirmation. Lord Ellenborough asked him if he was really a Quaker, and being answered in the affirmative, exclaimed:

"Do you really mean to impose upon the court by appearing here in the disguise of a reasonable being?"

Taking the Oath Literally

Chief Justice Melville Fuller used to relate an incident from his lawyering days in Chicago, in the last century, when two witnesses had to be sworn, the Reverend Dr. Thomas, a conscientious clergyman, and broker Hutchinson, sometimes called "Old Hutch." The probate judge was a very dignified man, and allowed witnesses to swear or affirm according to the dictates of conscience. Addressing Dr. Thomas he said:

"Now, Doctor, will you affirm, or take the regular oath?"

"The Bible says 'swear not at all,' Judge," said the man of the cloth, "so I prefer to affirm."

After the doctor had solemnly affirmed, the judge asked Mr. Hutchinson:

"Which do you prefer, the affirmation or the oath?"

"I don't care a damned which," said "Old Hutch"; then smiling at the judge he added: "You see the Bible says swear not at all, and I don't swear at all; I only swear at my particular friends."

Bully

George Jeffreys (1648-89), as Chief Justice and Chancellor, was known as perhaps the most cruel judge in English legal history. He gained practice when he was counsel, bullying witnesses. He was once retained on a trial in the course of which he had to cross-examine a sturdy countryman. Finding the evidence of this witness telling against his client, Jeffreys was determined to disconcert him. So he exclaimed in his own bluff manner:

"You fellow in the leathern doublet, what have you been paid for swearing?" The man looked steadily at him, and replied:

"Truly, sir, if you have no more for lying than I have for swearing, you might wear a leathern doublet as well as I."

In another case, Jeffreys was cross-examining a gentleman who in the course of his evidence had made frequent use of the terms lessor, lessee, assignor, assignee.

"There," said Jeffreys, "you have been with your assignor and assignee, lessor and lessee; do you know what a lessor or lessee is? I question if you do, with all your formal evidence."

"Yes, I do," returned the witness, "and I will give you an instance—if you nod to me you are the nodder; and if I nod to you, you are the noddee."

Terminology

Lord Chief Justice Mansfield (1705-93) was trying an action that arose from the collision of two ships at sea. A sailor, giving testimony about the accident, said: "At the time, I was standing abaft the binnacle." Lord Mansfield asked: "Where's abaft the binnacle?" Upon which the witness, who had taken a large share of grog before coming into court, exclaimed, loud enough to be heard by all present: "A pretty fellow to be a judge, who does not where abaft the binnacle is!"

Lord Mansfield, instead of threatening to commit him for his contempt, looked indulgently at his inebriated state and said: "Well, my friend, fit me for my office by telling me where abaft the binnacle is; you have already shown me the meaning of half seas over."

Stitches

In his journals Josiah Quincy relates another story he had heard at a Washington dinner party told by Daniel Webster:

One of the party mentioned that a president of one of the Boston banks had that morning redeemed a counterfeit bill for fifty dollars, never doubting that his signature upon it was genuine. This incident led to a discussion of the value of expert testimony in regard to writing, the majority of our company holding it in little esteem. Mr. Webster then came to the defence of this sort of testimony, saying that he had found it of much value, although experts were like children who saw more than they were able to explain to others.

"And this reminds me," he said, "of my story of the tailor. It was a capital case that was being tried, and the tailor's testimony was very important. He had been called to prove that he made a certain coat for the criminal; and he swore to the fact stoutly. Upon cross-examination he was asked how he knew that the coat was his work.

"'Why, I know it by my stitches, of course.'

"'Are your stitches longer than those of other tailors?'

"'Oh, no!'

"'Well, than, are they shorter?'

"'Not a bit shorter.'

"'Anything peculiar about them?'

"'Well, I don't believe there is.'

"'Then how do you dare to come here and swear that they are yours?'

"This seemed to be a poser, but the witness met it triumphantly. Casting a look of contempt upon his examiner, the tailor raised both hands to heaven and exclaimed:

"'Good lord! as if I didn't know my own stitches!'

"The jury believed him, and they were right in doing so. The fact is, we continually build our judgment upon details too fine for distinct cognizance. And these nice shades of sensibility are trustworthy, although we can give no good account of them. We can swear to our stitches, notwithstanding they seem to be neither longer nor shorter than those of other people."

Sitting Ducks

Judge Monroe of Louisville, Kentucky liked to tell the following story, as an example of how a browbeaten witness will sometimes retaliate upon an overbearing lawyer. The plaintiff was a farmer accusing a neighbor of stealing his ducks.

"Do you know that these are your ducks?" asked the defendant's lawyer in his most severe manner.

"Yes, I should know them anywhere," the farmer affirmed confidently and proceeded to give in detail the various points and marks by which his birds might be identified.

"But these ducks you describe are no different from any other ducks," the lawyer objected, "I have a good many in my yard at home just like them. What have you to say to that, sir?"

The farmer uncrossed his legs, crossed them again, expectorated, and finally remarked in his inimitable drawl:

"That's not unlikely. These are not the only ducks I have had stolen in recent weeks!"

The smart lawyer took his seat amid a roar of laughter in the court.

Music

Tom Cooke, a well-known actor and musician in the early nineteenth century, was cross-examined as a witness by Sir James Scarlett, who was rarely bested. The examination culminated in this exchange:

Scarlett: Sir, you say that the melodies are the same, but different; now what do you mean by that, sir?

Cooke: I said that the notes in the two copies are alike, but with a different accent.

Scarlett: What is a musical accent?

Cooke: My terms are nine guineas a quarter, sir.

Scarlett (ruffled): Never mind your terms here. I ask you what is a musical accent? Can you see it?

Cooke: No.

Scarlett: Can you feel it?

Cooke: A musician can.

Scarlett (angrily): Now, sir, don't beat about the bush, but explain to his lordship and the jury, who are expected to know nothing about music, the meaning of what you call accent.

Cooke: Accent in music is a certain stress laid upon a particular note, in the same manner as you would lay stress upon a given word, for the purpose of being better understood. For instance, if I were to say, "You are an *ass*," it rests on *ass*, but if I were to say, "*You* are an ass," it rests on you, Sir James.

The judge, with as much gravity as he could assume, then asked the crestfallen counsel:

"Are you satisfied, Sir James?"

"The witness may step down," was counsel's reply.

Manners

James T. Brady, a prominent American lawyer of the nineteenth century, was of Irish origin. He was once examining an unwilling witness who persistently called him Mr. O'Brady. At length, the attorney's proverbial good nature became ruffled, and he said to the witness somewhat brusquely:

"You need not call me Mr. O'Brady. I've mended my name since I came here and dropped the O."

"Have ye, now? 'Pon my sowl it's a pity ye didn't mend yer manners at the same time."

Where Angels Fear to Tread

Daniel Webster told a story that happened to his friend Jeremiah Mason, when he was defending E. K. Avery, a Methodist minister accused of murdering Mrs. Cornell at Fall River, Massachusetts. The Methodists, feeling that the reputation of their denomination was at stake, raised a large subscription and employed Mason to defend the Rev. Avery. The trial was a long and tedious one; Jeremiah Mason was much perplexed and harassed by the constant stream of impertinent inquiry and suggestion that came from the prisoner's friends. A great deal of testimony was taken at the trial, which lasted for three weeks; and, as Mason was then old and about to give up his profession, he wanted a quiet night to prepare himself physically for engaging in the final arguments. He knew by experience that he must take precautions to avoid being roused from his sleep by some of these meddling friends. So he told the barkeeper at his hotel that he was going to bed early and that he did not wish to be, and would not be, disturbed after he had retired to his room. About eleven o'clock, a ministerial-looking person came in and said to the barkeeper:

"I want to see Mr. Mason."

"You can't see him tonight. He is very tired and gave orders that he should not be disturbed."

"But I must see him. If I should not see him tonight and if tomorrow the case should go wrong, I never should forgive myself."

"Well," returned the barkeeper, "I'll show you his room."

This he did. Mr. Mason rose up in bed and exclaimed to the barkeeper:

"What did I tell you, sir?"

"Well," replied he, "the man must explain."

Mr. Mason thought the best way to get out of the difficulty was to hear what the intruder had to say, and he told him, rather roughly, to begin.

"I had retired to rest about an hour ago," said the man, "after having commended this case, Brother Avery, and everybody connected with it to the Throne of Grace, in fervent prayer that the truth might be elicited; and I do not know how long I had slept, when I was awakened by an audible voice. I saw an angel standing right at the foot of the bed, just as distinctly as I see you, and in a very distinct tone of voice, it said: 'Mr. Avery is innocent of this crime,' and immediately vanished. Of this, sir, I am ready to take my oath."

Mr. Mason looked at him with an expression of mixed indignation and contempt, but he was so much struck, after a moment, by the ludicrousness of the scene that he began to question the man.

"You yourself saw this angel?"

"Yes."

"And he immediately vanished?"

"He did."

"Do you think there is any possibility of seeing him again?"

"It may be."

"Well, if you should happen to see him, you just ask him how he could prove it!"

Discovery

Ferenc Molnár, the Hungarian playwright and coffeehouse wit in the early part of the century, rarely got out of bed before the afternoon. To his great distress, he was once summoned as a witness, which involved getting to court by nine o'clock. As soon as he left his house, blinking in Budapest's early light, he noticed vast numbers of people hurrying along the street. "Good heavens," Molnár exclaimed with genuine astonishment, "are they all witnesses, too?"

Ghost Stories

In 1831 Sir Walter Scott wrote a brief essay on ghosts giving evidence in court. Among the cases he quotes is a summary from Howell's State Trials *(1692):*

A gentleman named Harrison had been accused of beguiling a Dr. Clenche into a hackney coach, on pretence of taking him to see a patient. There were two men in the coach, besides the doctor. They sent the coachman on an errand, and when he came back he found the men fled and Clenche murdered. He had been strangled with a handkerchief. On evidence which was chiefly circumstantial, Harrison was found guilty, and died protesting his innocence. Later a Mrs. Milward declared that her husband, before his death, confessed to her that he and a man named Cole were the murderers of Dr. Clenche. The ghost of her husband persecuted her, she said, till Cole was arrested. Mr. Justice Dolben asked her in court for the story, but feared that the jury would laugh at her. She asserted the truth of her story, but if she gave any details, they are not reported. Cole was acquitted and the motives of Mrs. Milward remained obscure.

Later, during a murder trial in Warwick, England, the defense set up a line of reasoning that the crime must have been committed by a ghost. After the summing up, the judge instructed the jury:

"I think, gentlemen, you seem inclined to lay more stress upon an apparition than it will bear. I cannot say I give much credit to those kinds of stories; but be that as it will, we have no right to follow our own private opinion here. We are now in a court of law, and must determine to it; and I know not of any law now in being which will admit the testimony of an apparition; nor yet if it did, doth the ghost appear to give evidence. Crier," the judge asked, "call the ghost!"—which was thrice done to no manner of purpose.

Mistaken Identity

One of the most popular French plays of the nineteenth century was *The Lyons Mail*, based on a true story of mistaken identity. Sir Henry Irving made it famous in English, and part of its success lay in providing the actor with the possibility of playing the dual roles of Lesurques and Duboscq, something few stars can resist.

During the French Revolution, Lesurques was positively identified as the man who had traveled by the mail coach, and he was in due course convicted. Yet, at the eleventh hour a woman came into court and declared his innocence, swearing that the witnesses had mistaken him for another, Duboscq, whom he greatly resembled. She was the confidante of one of the gang who had planned and carried out the robbery. But her testimony, although corroborated by other confederates, was rejected, and Lesurques received sentence of death. Still, there were grave doubts, and the matter was brought before the Revolutionary legislature by the Directory, who called for a reprieve. But the Five Hundred refused on the extraordinary ground that to annul a sentence that had been legally pronounced "would subvert all ideas of justice and equality before the law."

Lesurques died protesting his innocence to the last. "Truth has not been heard," he wrote a friend; "I shall die the victim of a mistake." He also published a letter in the papers addressed to Duboscq: "You, in whose place I am to die, be satisfied with the sacrifice of my life. If you are ever brought to justice, think of my three children, covered with shame, and of their mother's despair, and do not prolong the misfortunes of so fatal a resemblance." On the scaffold he said: "I pardon my judges and the witnesses whose mistake has murdered me. I die protesting my innocence."

Four years elapsed before Duboscq was captured. When, after a couple of escapes and many delays, he was finally tried, the judge ordered him to wear a fair wig, such as Lesurques had worn, and the strange likeness between them was immediately apparent. He denied his guilt but was convicted and guillotined. Thus two men suffered for one offense.

French justice was very tardy in atoning for its error. The rehabilitation of Lesurques's family was not decreed until after repeated applications under several regimes—the Directory, the Consulate, the Empire, and the Restoration. In the reign of Louis XVIII the sequestrated property was restored, but there was no revision of the sentence, although the case was repeatedly revived.

Happy End

Another case of mistaken identity on a lighter note and with a happier ending took place in an American city in 1804. A man was indicted for bigamy, the allegation being that he was a certain James Hoag. The man himself said that he was Thomas Parker. At the trial, Mrs. Hoag, the wife, and many relatives with other respectable witnesses, swore positively that he was James Hoag. On the other hand, Thomas Parker's wife, and an equal number of credible witnesses, swore that he was Thomas Parker.

Then the court recalled the first set of witnesses, who maintained their opinion and were satisfied that he was James Hoag, his stature, shape, gestures, complexion, looks, voice, and speech leaving no doubt on the subject. They even described a particular scar on his forehead, underneath his hair, and when this was turned back, there, sure enough, was the scar. Yet the Parker witnesses declared that Thomas Parker had lived among them, worked with them, and was with them on the very day he was supposed to have contracted his alleged marriage with Mrs. Hoag. Now Mrs. Hoag played her last card, and said that her husband had a peculiar mark on the sole of his foot; Mrs. Parker admitted that her husband had no such mark. So the court ordered the prisoner to take off his shoes and stockings and show the soles of his feet; there was no mark on either of them. Mrs. Parker now claimed him with great insistence, but Mrs. Hoag would not give up her husband, and there was a very violent discussion in court. At last a justice of the peace from Parker's village entered the court and gave evidence to the effect that he had known him from a child as Thomas Parker, and had often given him employment. So Mrs. Parker carried off her husband in triumph.

Open and Shut

One of Abraham Lincoln's favorite stories concerned a case he had won but which, in his own words, "beat me badly, more than any I ever had." As his partner William Herndon relates it, a man of Coles County, Illinois was indicted for stealing hogs but claimed to be too poor to employ counsel for his defense.

"In that case, I will appoint one," the judge offered. "Have you any preferences among the members of the bar?"

"I'll take that tall man sitting there," the hog thief pointed to Lincoln.

Lincoln took his client into a private room.

"What is your defense—what are the facts of the case?" he asked his client.

"I have no facts to tell you, Mr. Lincoln," the man confessed. "The truth is we'll jump in and fight 'em on general principles and clear me as I know you can."

"This is curious. Here are half a dozen witnesses on the back of this indictment who will swear that you stole the hogs."

"Well, I can't help that." The man remained calm and he had a peculiar quiz on his face, something that showed confidence in his acquittal.

They returned to the court and pleaded not guilty. The witnesses came and swore that the defendant stole the hogs and sold them to various persons. The prosecuting attorney said it was a plain case of hog-stealing. As he concluded, the accused leaned over to Lincoln and urged him:

"Pitch in, go it on general principles with a whoop and a yell. I'll be cleared, you bet."

Lincoln ran over the evidence quickly. He noticed that the jury, which had paid no attention to the prosecutor's speech, now hung upon every word he spoke. In summing up, Lincoln asked that the jury acquit his client on account of reasonable doubt based on all the evidence.

The jury retired, deliberated on the case for about an hour and came back with a verdict of not guilty. Lincoln followed his client out of the courthouse and when they were out of anybody's earshot, he said:

"I do not understand this case at all, but I would like to know all the facts from top to bottom."

"Well, Lincoln, I'll tell you," said the man. "I did steal the hogs and more of 'em than I was indicted for, many more, and sold 'em to my neighbors, the jury. They knew that if I was convicted that they would have to pay for the hogs that I sold them. Now, Lincoln, do you see where the joke comes in?"

Instructions

Chauncey Depew, a towering figure in nineteenth-century American public life, repeated a famous story by Abraham Lincoln, about a court trial he visited soon after his admission to the bar in 1837. In Lincoln's own words:

The court, I remember, was held in a small town in the Eighth Judicial District of Illinois. On account of the absence of a courthouse, the town school, much to the joy of the scholars, was brought into use. The circuit judge, an elderly and portly man, had had a touch of the gout, and the master's hard wooden chair in which he sat became decidedly uncomfortable as a long, uninteresting case dragged through the hot afternoon. Finally the opposing lawyer finished and he arose for the final address.

"Gentlemen of the jury," he began, savagely brushing a pair of hungry flies from his shiny bald head, "you have heard all the evidence. If you believe what the counsel for the plaintiff has told you, your verdict will be for the plaintiff. But, if on the other hand, you believe what the defendant's counsel has told you, then you will give a verdict for the defendant. But if you are like me, and don't believe what either of them said, then I'll be hanged if I know what you will do."

Alibi

Sir Frank Lockwood, a well-known British barrister in the late nineteenth century, usually undertook to defend cases where he could honestly assume the prisoner's innocence. After one such case, when he had gained acquittal for his client by pleading an alibi, he met the judge, who congratulated him:

"Well, Lockwood, that was a very good alibi."

"Yes, my lord, I had three suggested to me, and I think I selected the best one."

Knowing Ways

In the 1930s, the Ontario Court of Appeals in Canada heard the case of a woman convicted of keeping a common bawdy house. The defense was attacking the evidence of a police informer who had testified that he had been admitted by the accused and taken to the second floor, where he had enjoyed the favors of a certain girl, then paid her two dollars and left.

"How could anyone possibly believe a witness like that?" Justice W. T. Henderson exclaimed. "Everybody knows that you pay downstairs!"

THE JURY IS OUT

The Jury System

Early in his career, Clarence Darrow was in some small town, presenting a suit for damages in a civil proceeding. Looking at the jury, he worried whether these simple people would understand the legal niceties of the case. But there was one man who seemed just by his looks to be more intelligent than the rest, and assuming that he would probably be elected foreman, Darrow concentrated all his oratory on this man. The case went to the jury, which, after a long wait, filed back into the courtroom. Darrow was pleased to see his hunch confirmed and that the intelligent-looking man was indeed leading the jury.

"Gentlemen of the jury," asked the judge, "have you reached a decision?"

"No, Your Honor," the foreman replied, "we came back for further information. Two words have been used constantly throughout the trial that we don't know the meaning of."

"What are they?"

"One word is plaintiff, and the other is defendant."

Scratch a Judge

Lord Justice Bramwell (1808-92) once asserted in court that one-third of every judge was a common juror, if you got beneath the ermine.

Stubborn as a Mule

Judge Jim Corrigan of Denver, Colorado, strongly believes that America has kept its freedom primarily through two little boxes: the ballot box and the jury box. One of his favorite stories about the contrary ways of juries comes from a small town in the Old West where a man had stolen his neighbor's mule. The evidence was pretty well conclusive against the defendant but the jury knew him to be fundamentally an honest man who had a great need for a short time. So ten minutes after the judge had sent the jury away with his instructions, they came back with a typically wise jury verdict:

"The defendant is not guilty, but he has to return the mule."

The judge knew that the law could not tolerate such an inconsistent verdict, so he sent the jury away again with instructions to come back with a consistent verdict.

After another ten minutes, the jury returned the new verdict:

"The defendent is not guilty, and he can keep the mule."

Don't Feed the Animals

From a report of an English case heard in the Court of Common Pleas in 1588:

In tresspass by Mounson against West, the jury was charged and evidence given, and the jurors being retired into a house for to consider of their evidence, they remained there a long time without concluding anything; and the officers of the Court who attended them seeing their delay searched the jurors if they had anything about them to eat, upon which search it was found that some of them had figs and other pippins, for which the next day the matter was moved to the court and the jurors were examined upon it upon oath.

And two of them did confess that they had eaten figs before they had agreed of their verdict: and three others of them confessed that they had pippins, but did not eat of them, and that they did it without the knowledge or will of any of the parties. And afterwards the Court set a fine of five pounds upon each of them which had eaten and upon the others who had not eaten, forty shillings, and they would advise, if the verdict was good or not, for the jury found for the plaintiff.

And afterwards, at another day, the matter was moved, and Anderson was of opinion that notwithstanding the said misdemeanor of the jury, the verdict was good enough for these victuals were not given to them by any of the parties to the action, nor by their means or procurement. Rhodes thought the contrary because some of the jurors had eaten and some not, contrary if all of them had eaten.

And upon great advice and deliberation, and conference with other judges, the verdict was holden to be good notwithstanding the misdemeanor aforesaid. The eating and drinking by the jury at their own costs is but fineable, but if it be at the cost of the parties, the verdict is void.

Inducement

In the trial of the seven bishops under James II, Judge Jeffreys, who was known by the epithet "Bloody," had the jury locked up all night without fire or candle. They could not agree on a verdict, owing to the obstinacy of Arnold, the king's brewer. Their treatment is described in a letter to the Archbishop of Canterbury, dated June 30th, 1688, which suggests bribery as the best way to break the deadlock:

MAY IT PLEASE YOUR GRACE—We have watched the jury carefully all night, attending without the door on the stair-head. They have, by order, been kept all night without fire or candle, save only some basins of water and towels this morning about four. I am informed by my servant and Mr. Granges that about midnight they were very loud one among another, and that the like happened about three this morning, which makes me collect they are not yet agreed. They beg for a candle to light their pipes, but are denied. In case a verdict pass for us, which God grant in His own best time, the present consideration will be how the jury shall be treated. The course is, usually, each man so many guineas, and a common dinner for them all. The quantum is at Your Grace's and my lord's desire. But it seems to my poor understanding that the dinner might be spared, lest our watchful enemies should interpret it against us. It may be ordered thus: To each man ———— guineas for his trouble, and each man a guinea over for his own desire.

My lord, Your Grace's most humble servant,

John Ince.

N.B. There must be 150 to 200 guineas provided.

My Time Is Not Your Time

Judge John Sloss Hobart, one of the early Supreme Court judges of the State of New York (from 1777 to 1798) insisted that jurymen attend on the call of the panel exactly at ten o'clock each morning, and he would always fine anyone who did not attend or was late. Just a day or two after he had handed out one such fine to a tardy juror, the judge himself was late. After he took his seat on the bench, the delinquent juryman was bold enough to address his honor. He politely expressed the hope that the fine imposed on him would be now withdrawn, seeing that even the presiding officer could fall behind time, as the present example indicated. Judge Hobart was unfazed:

"I desire the jury, and this juryman in particular, to understand," he thundered with emphasis, "that it is not ten o'clock until the judge reaches the bench."

Peers

Henry W. Paine, a brilliant American jurist of the nineteenth century, undertook at the end of his career, for no fee, the defense of a retarded boy of fifteen who had been charged with arson. Paine offered conclusive evidence that his client was mentally incompetent and could not be held responsible for his actions. The jury, after listening to a charge from the judge that was virtually an order for acquittal, nevertheless brought in a verdict of guilty. The judge then addressed Paine:

"You will move for a new trial, I presume, Mr. Paine?" The lawyer rose, and, with an air that was painful in its solemnity, replied:

"I thank Your Honor for your suggestion, but I am oppressed with the gravest doubts as to whether I have the right to move for a new trial in this case. Your Honor, I have already asked for and have received for my idiot client the most precious heritage of our American and English common law—a trial by a jury of his peers."

The judge ordered the verdict to be set aside.

Juries Are Not Always Right

When a stupid jury returns an obviously wrong verdict the judge faces a delicate situation. On one such occasion, Sir William Maule got himself extricated in the following manner:

"Prisoner, your counsel thinks you innocent, the prosecution thinks you innocent, and I think you innocent. But a jury of your own fellow-countrymen, in the exercise of such common sense as they possess, have found you guilty, and it remains that I should pass sentence on you. You will be imprisoned for one day, and as that day was yesterday, you are free to go about your business."

Ask Not the Reason Why

Sir Henry Hawkins cites a curious reason a British jury once gave for not finding a murderer guilty:

This man had been tried for the murder of his father and mother, and the evidence was too clear to leave a doubt as to his guilt. The jury retired to consider their verdict and were away so long that the judge sent for them and asked if there was any point upon which he could enlighten them. They answered no and thought they understood the case perfectly well.

After a great deal of further consideration they brought in a verdict of not guilty.

The judge was angry at so outrageous a violation of their plain duty and did what he ought not to have done—namely, asked the reason they brought in such a verdict, when they knew the culprit was guilty and ought to have been hanged.

"That's just it, my lord," said the foreman of this distinguished body. "I assure you we had no doubt about the prisoner's guilt, but we thought there had been deaths in the family lately and so gave him the benefit of the doubt!"

Should Auld Acquaintance Be Forgot

The following coroner's inquest was reported by The Times *in London, June 9th, 1831.*

A coroner's inquest was held yesterday afternoon at the Duke of Wellington Tavern, Brighton Street, Brunswick Square, touching the death of a female infant only five years old.

A juror stated to the Coroner that the present was a disgraceful transaction. The reputed father of the deceased child was the son of a celebrated deceased Scotch poet, and was holding a situation in a Government office at a salary of £400 per annum. He resided contiguous to the above neighbourhood, and it was his constant boast that he had 52 children by various females, and it was a known fact that there were several pregnant by him at that moment.

Another juror: "You make a mistake, it is not 52, but 32" (a laugh).

Elizabeth Brooks, with whom the mother of the child lodged, gave evidence of the birth and death of the infant. Witness remonstrated with the mother on the impropriety of not burying it; but she was told that she had a right to keep 'her own' above ground as long as she pleased. Fearing that a contagious fever might be the consequence of delaying the interment longer, witness called in an officer.

Mr. Edmondson, of Judd Street, surgeon, deposed that the child died a natural death.

The mother was brought into the jury room at the desire of the jury. She is a poor squalid wretched-looking woman, apparently worn down by disease and poverty: her appearance excited sympathy.

The Coroner asked her if she could think of leaving her own child in the state it was found? It was not only indecent, but dangerous to the health and safety of the inhabitants: a fever might be the result of her conduct.

She replied that her ill state of health and her distress had prevented her burying the child.

Coroner: "You ought to have appealed to your parish and they could have assisted you."

She said she did not wish to do so; she could keep herself and children by hard work; she took in washing and ironing; if she had done wrong it was through ignorance; they might suspect her but she knew she did not murder her child, and she defied them to prove it.

Juror: "How many children have you got?"

"I have eight, but only two alive."

Juror: "Who was the father of the deceased?"

"I would rather decline answering the question."

Juror: "You have a right to answer it. Your conduct is unnatural and unmotherly, and we condemn you altogether. You have had several children by several men (or one) and you ought to answer the question, if it is only for the sake of your offspring."

She burst into tears, saying that her poverty and ignorance had caused her not to bury her child, but she would not divulge who the father was. She had received two shillings from him which would have buried it, had she not parted with the money. She thought she was privileged in keeping the child above ground, as she knew a woman who kept her son twelve months.

Several of the jurymen pressed her to mention the name of the father, but she tenaciously refused to do so.

The jury returned a verdict that the deceased died by the visitation of God, the jury being of opinion that the mother was reprehensible in not having the child buried previous to putrefaction.

The person above alluded to is the son of Robert Burns, the poet, and lives in Queen Square.

Holdout

Abraham Lincoln was hired once to defend a gentle and refined woman in a divorce case. She was married to a gross, fault-finding, and abusive man who appeared completely unfitted to be the husband of such a woman. Lincoln was able to prove that the man had used very offensive and vulgar epithets to describe his wife, and had committed all sorts of other annoyances, but no acts of such personal violence that the statute required to justify a divorce. So he appealed to the jury to have compassion on the woman and not bind her to suffer such a life with such a man.

In their deliberations the jury were clearly inclined to take the same view but could find no evidence to justify a verdict in her favor. So they drew up a verdict for the husband which they all signed except for one, who, when he was asked to sign, said:

"Gentlemen, I am going to lie down to sleep and when you get ready to give verdict for that woman, wake me up, for before I will give a verdict against her I will lie here until I rot, and the pismires carry me out through the keyhole."

Looking for a Few Good Men

In early nineteenth-century America, jurors were as difficult to be caught and brought into court as a fish was to be hooked and brought to market. In thinly populated regions the court was often forced to adjourn, from day to day, for the lack of a complete panel. Finally, in one of these small communities, things came to a crisis. The judge had fixed a day beyond which no further forbearance could be exercised. When that day arrived, the enthusiastic sheriff rushed into the courtroom and exclaimed: "It's all right, your honor: we'll have the jury by twelve o'clock. I've got eleven of them locked up in a barn and we are running the twelfth with dogs."

Difficulties

The difficulty of empanelling a jury in a high criminal case in New York was never more apparent than in the case of Polly Bodine, indicted for murder in 1847. The court, with Judge Edmonds presiding, was laboriously engaged for two and a half weeks to empanel a jury. Between five and six thousand had been summoned and called as talesmen, and upward of four thousand of those were personally examined by the court either as to their fitness for jurors or concerning their excuses. Many who were summoned took the precaution, before being called, to remark to a bystander: "I think Polly Bodine ought to be hanged," and then, when his name was announced, he truthfully confessed that he had expressed an opinion—and was duly excused. All this resulted in the dismissal of the few jurors empanelled, and finally the trial had to be moved from New York County (Manhattan).

In the summer of 1844, Polly Bodine was tried in Richmond County (Staten Island). The jury could not reach a verdict. Eleven of them were for conviction, but one would not come out either for acquittal or for conviction. After the jury had been discharged, Clinton DeWitt, one of the counsels for her defense, asked the twelfth juror on what grounds he

had refused to join the eleven? The man replied that in his view this was a case of circumstantial evidence and he could never convict on such testimony unless it was in the fourth degree. Then DeWitt asked:
"What do you mean by circumstantial evidence in the fourth degree?"
"Why, four eyewitnesses who swear they saw the act committed."
After this hung jury, the case was moved back to New York, where finally a jury was empanelled and Polly Bodine was convicted. But the Supreme Court granted a new trial, and this took place up the Hudson River in Newburgh, New York. After two weeks, she was acquitted. During the progress of the case, the counsel for the defense heaped abuse on the city of New York. They spoke of its corruptions and iniquities, while at the same time they took great pains to set forth the great purity of the country. They had come, they said, to the peaceful shores of the Hudson to get justice for their client, which was denied her in the wicked city of New York. James R. Whiting, the prosecutor, resented the abuse that New York lawyers had cast upon the city where they themselves resided:
"Why is it, that the city of New York is such a vile place, when we find that the counsel, Mr. Jordan, had left his practice on 'the peaceful shores of the Hudson' and taken up his abode there?"
"Oh, sir," interrupted John W. Brown, a fellow counsel, "Mr. Jordan went to New York as a missionary."

Excuses, Excuses

In a New York court in 1861 (writes Charles Edwards in his book *Pleasantries about Courts and Lawyers of the State of New York*), incidents occurred reminiscent of the Biblical parable of the man who had made a great supper. There was a panel of one hundred jurors summoned, but only twenty-two answered to their names, and of these eighteen presented excuses for not serving. Number one had rheumatism. Number two, a bad cold. As to number three, his wife, poor thing, was sick. Numbers four and five were suffering from neuralgia. Number six had served on the grand jury the month before. Number seven was taking medicine which unfitted him for jury duty. Number eight (he must have been a poet) had been overworked with mental labor. Number nine had served in the superior court. As to numbers ten and eleven, it would greatly inconvenience their business (probably shad fishing). Number twelve had been summoned three times during the last year and had served once. Number thirteen could not possibly be on a jury on account of (as he put it) "urgent business." Number fourteen was very ill indeed;

number fifteen, of course, could not stay in a court of law, being in the court of Hymen [Greek god of marriage], about to be married. Number sixteen, another happy man, had that morning been pronounced a father. Meanwhile numbers seventeen and eighteen informed the court by proxy that they were under the physician's hand and could not come under the operations of a court.

Deaf, Not Dumb

Judge Hand of the New York Supreme Court once delivered an elaborate charge to a grand jury, going over all possible matters that could come before them. After this a man came forward to excuse himself from jury duty, holding his hand up to his ear.

"What is your excuse?" asked the judge.

"I am very deaf, Your Honor."

"Did you not hear my charge?"

"Well, yes, I did: but I assure Your Honor I could not make either head or tail of it."

In England, Lord Alderson once released a juryman who confessed of being deaf in one ear, with these words:

"Leave the box before the trial begins; it is necessary that the jurymen should hear both sides."

His Own Funeral

Only once was British judge Lord Hannen known to be hoaxed. It was when a juryman, dressed in deep mourning and downcast in expression, stood up and claimed exemption from service on that day as he was, he told the official, deeply interested in the funeral of a gentleman at which it was his desire to be present.

"Oh! Certainly," was the courteous reply of the judge, and the sad, melancholic-looking man left the court. "My lord," his faithful clerk, Mr. G. J. Widdicombe quietly interposed as soon as the ex-juryman had gone, "Do you know who that man is that you exempted?" "No!" "He is the undertaker!"

Should Have Known

Judge William Kent, presiding over circuit court in mid-nineteenth-century New York, tried to solve the problem of not having enough jurors, by pressing several lawyers attending the court into the jury box to serve as talesmen. Although the case being heard was straightforward and with no real defense, the lawyers who had been forced on the jury against their wishes now began to act as lawyers do. Asking one question after another from the witnesses, they made various suggestions and managed to intimate legal doubts, occupying the court for several hours. Judge Kent vowed that he would never again put lawyers on a jury.

The Ideal Juror

Melville D. Landon, who under the nom de plume of Eli Perkins was one of America's greatest humorists in the nineteenth century, had a sharp eye and tongue for all humbug, especially of the judiciary kind. Here is one of his many stories, which he called slight exaggerations:

A Chicago lawyer was visiting New York for the first time. Meeting a man on the crowded street, he said:

"Here, my friend, I want you to tell me something about this city."

"I don't know anything about it," said the hurrying business man, with a faraway look.

"What street is it?"

"I don't know," said the busy man, with his mind occupied and staring at vacancy.

"What city is it?"

"Can't tell; I am busy."

"Is it London or New York?"

"Don't know anything about it."

"You don't?"

"No."

"Well, by heavens, sir, you're the very man I'm looking for. I've been looking for you for years."

"What do you want me for?"

"I want you to go to Chicago and sit on a jury."

Puritan Justice

Eli Perkins once told this story to Bret Harte, and the author came back with his own recollection of the early California jury system:

It was over in the Mariposa Gulch in '50; they had never had a jury trial there. If a man stole a horse they lynched him, and that settled it. But the people, many of whom came from Massachusetts, began to tire of lynch law and sigh for the good old Puritan jury trial of the East. So one day, when Bill Stevens had jumped a poor man's claim, the Massachusetts fellows resolved to give him a good old-fashioned jury trial. They took Bill into the back end of the board post-office, selected a jury, and the trial commenced.

Dozens of witnesses were called, and finally the jury retired to agree upon a verdict. When they had been out about twenty minutes, and about concluded that Bill was innocent, the boys outside came banging at the door.

"What do you fellows want?" asked the foreman through the keyhole.

"We want to know if you hain't about agreed on the verdict. If you hain't you'll have to get out. We want this room to lay out the corpse in."

Wild West

A coroner's jury in Leadville, Colorado, investigating a murder case in 1870, brought in this verdict:

"We find that Jack Smith came to his death from heart disease. We find two bullet holes and a dirk knife in that organ, and we recommend that Bill Younger be lynched to prevent the spreading of the disease."

Buying the Jury

In the late nineteenth century, when Senator Daniel Voorhees was a hard-working lawyer in Terre Haute, Indiana, he had occasion to defend a gambler for killing a man. There were some doubts about the case—whether it was murder or manslaughter. Voorhees made a superb plea, but still the gambler's friends were afraid he would be convicted. They had plenty of money and had raised $5,000 to influence a juryman, someone whom they picked as weak enough to take a bribe. They offered him the money, if he would "hang the jury."

The man seemed to have earned his money, because sure enough, the jury could not reach agreement. The next day there was a meeting of Daniel Voorhees and the friends to thank the juryman for his services. After he pocketed the money, the man related how he kept the jury out for two days:

"I wouldn't give them a wink of sleep till they agreed with me in a verdict of manslaughter, and they knew it."

"How did they stand when they first went out?" asked Voorhees.

"Well," said the bribed juryman expansively, "there were eleven of them for acquittal—but I brought 'em round!"

Doubtful Compliment

F. W. Ahrens filled many functions, including (judge) magistrate, in the administration of justice in South Africa, during the early part of the century:

During the hearing of a civil case before Sir Percival Maitland-Lawrence and a special jury, and after a lengthy trial and prolonged addresses by counsel for the parties concerned, the learned judge remarked: "Gentlemen of the jury, much sand has been thrown into your eyes and it is now up to me to supply some boracic acid in order to clear your vision."

Another rather amusing incident occurred when the judge, who was of a sarcastic disposition, charged the jury, his remarks pointing in one direction only, which was that the accused should be found guilty, and added that if they felt that there was justification for adding a rider asking for leniency, he would consider it. After due deliberation the jury returned a unanimous verdict of "not guilty." The judge promptly ordered the accused to stand up, and addressed him: "The jury have paid you the somewhat doubtful compliment of not believing your own words. You may go."

Jury to the Rescue

Sometimes, when the heat between the bench and bar becomes unbearable, the jury takes on the responsibility of deciding who is right. Peter Macdonald, Canadian lawyer and author, tells this story in Court Jesters, *his first book of legal anecdotes:*

The late Arthur Maloney, Q.C., of Toronto, one of the finest jury lawyers Canada has ever produced, loved to tell about his first jury case, which he said was his most satisfying.

His client was charged with embezzlement, and the evidence against him was so overwhelming that Maloney urged him to plead guilty and throw himself on the mercy of the court. The client wouldn't hear of it.

"I've paid you a good retainer and I want you to defend the case vigorously," he told the young lawyer. "What's more, I want a jury trial."

"A jury will crucify you," Maloney warned.

"No matter! Do what I say! Give it everything you've got!"

Maloney said he would, but he was far from optimistic.

The trial judge was notorious for badgering and bullying young counsel; he felt it was part of their education. Maloney was well aware of this. He prepared his case thoroughly and resolved that the nasty judge wouldn't get his goat. The judge was on Maloney's back from start to finish, interrupting him constantly and treating him like dirt, but counsel managed to keep his cool.

Arthur told the jurors it was his first jury trial, and he noted in passing that he would never be able to make that statement again. He said everything he could in favor of his client, then sat down, heavy-hearted. He felt there was only one possible verdict—guilty. He was positive of this when the jury returned after only ten minutes of deliberation.

They found the accused not guilty. The judge exploded with anger. He called the jurors irresponsible and said their verdict was a disgrace.

An hour or so later, the foreman and several members of the jury were drinking in the beverage room of the hotel where Maloney had been staying. The foreman noticed Arthur checking out and invited him to join the group.

"Well, young fellow, how'd you like our verdict?" the foreman asked.

"I loved it," Maloney said, "but I think you were dead wrong."

"Oh, yeah, we knew it was the wrong verdict," the man said, "but we were determined to teach that old bastard a lesson for tormenting you all through the trial."

· 7 ·

JUSTICE AND INJUSTICE

SENTENCING

How It Works

In sentencing a man convicted of bigamy Sir William Maule also gave him a quick course about the justice system:

Prisoner, you have been convicted of the serious offence of bigamy. You plead mitigation that your wife was a drunkard, was a curse to your household, and finally deserted you, but I cannot recognize any such plea. You say that when she left you, you were left with several young children who required a woman's care, but the law makes no allowance for bigamists with large families. Had you taken another woman to live with you as your concubine, the law would never have interfered, but you insisted—in your own language—on making an honest woman of her—and that is a criminal offence.

Another of your irrational excuses is that your wife had committed adultery, but the law has provided a process by which you could have rid yourself of the woman who dishonored you; this, however, you did not see fit to adopt. I will tell you what that process is. You ought first to have brought an action against your wife's seducer, if you could discover him; that might have cost you money, and you say you are a poor working man, but that is not the fault of the law. You would then be obliged to prove by evidence your wife's criminality in a court of justice, and thus obtain a verdict with damages against the defendant, who was not likely to turn out a pauper. But, so jealous is the law of the sanctity of the marriage tie, that, in accomplishing this you would have only fulfilled the lighter portion of your duty. You must then have gone with your verdict in your hand, and petitioned the House of Lords for a divorce. It would have cost you perhaps five or six hundred pounds and you do not seem to be worth as many pence. But it is the boast of the law that it is impartial, and makes no difference between rich and poor. The wealthiest man in the kingdom would have to pay no less a sum for the same luxury; so that you would have no reason to complain. You would have to prove your case over again, and at the end of a year, or possibly two, you might have obtained a decree which would have enabled you to do legally what you have thought proper to do without it. You have thus wilfully rejected the boon the Legislature offered you, and it is my duty to pass upon you such a sentence as I think your offence deserves, and that sentence is that you be imprisoned for one day; and inasmuch as the present assize is three days old, the result is that you will be immediately discharged.

Judging

John Hogarth, law professor at the University of British Columbia, is an authority on sentencing:

After finishing my Ph.D. at Cambridge, in England, I undertook my first large research project in Toronto. I was trying to figure out how judges made their decisions on sentencing: what aspects of their own personality and background affected these decisions. It seemed important to determine how they dealt with information, and whether being conservative or liberal, rigid or tolerant, or exhibiting other strong personality traits, could place their judgments into predictable categories. The first step in gathering data was to set up three-hour interviews with judges in the Province of Ontario, who had agreed to co-operate. Then I was going to compare what they said with the decisions they actually made.

In the early 1960s, judges of the Provincial Court Bench were working under awful conditions in Toronto, many being forced to share offices. I was trying to interview a young judge who happened to share with a much older and highly controversial colleague, who was notorious, among other things, for arresting people on the highway for speeding or cutting in on him. He then held summary court on the roadside, collected fines on the spot which he deposited next day in court. He was the most talked-about judge in the province, and he also greatly enjoyed expressing his opinions.

When I asked the young judge what use he made of the pre-sentence report prepared by a probation officer, the other judge interrupted from across the office: "Never listen to a probation officer! They're a bunch of transvestites!" Later, when I asked about psychiatric reports, he had further advice: "Don't use psychiatric reports. I got one once and I didn't know whom to commit—the accused or the psychiatrist!"

I was trying to get into detail with my interviewee on the subject, but the older judge was now unstoppable:

"I can find out more about an accused than any psychiatrist or social worker just by asking two questions."

It was pointless to carry on, but I was bold enough to ask his honor to share his secret with his brother and sister judges in Ontario:

"Could we for the moment suppose," I ventured, "that I am a 22-year-old convicted of breaking and entering a house. I have had one previous conviction, and your honor knows nothing else about me. What two questions would your honor ask?"

The man drew himself up with such dignity and authority that I suddenly felt myself that young offender. And he asked, in a very august voice, the first of his two questions:

"Where do you live?" I thought for a moment and said:

"Your honor, a typical answer to your question would be, 'I used to live with my parents, but I don't get on very well with them anymore; I'm now staying with a friend.'" Then he asked his other question:

"Are you a homosexual?"

"No, m'lord, I'm not."

"You wouldn't be staying with him if you weren't," he retorted triumphantly.

"I forgot to tell you," I said, "it was a female friend."

The judge didn't blink an eye. He came back at me at once:

"I knew you were some kind of pervert!"

Double Entendre

The time I spent in British Columbia coincided with the last years of Les Bewley on the Provincial Court. This colorful and self-willed judge was notorious for having his foot most of the time firmly lodged in his mouth. At one time he was about to pronounce sentence on a Vancouver prostitute, when he addressed her: "Strange as this may sound, coming from a man, but will you please stand up?"

Whole Hog

During the reign of Queen Elizabeth I, Sir Nicholas Bacon had sentenced a man named Hog to death. The felon appealed for a remission of his sentence on the ground that he was related to his lordship. "Nay, my friend," replied the judge, "you and I cannot be kindred unless you be hanged, for hog is not bacon until it be well hung."

Unmitigating Boast

Henry Hunt, radical British reformer (1773-1835), was brought before Lord Ellenborough to receive sentence upon a conviction for holding a seditious meeting. The well-known demagogue began his address in mitigation of punishment by complaining of certain persons who had accused him of "stirring up the people by dangerous eloquence." The Chief Justice interjected in a very mild tone: "My impartiality as a judge calls upon me to say, sir, that in accusing you of that they do you a great injustice."

Courtesy

Justice Graham was said to be the most polite judge that ever adorned the bench. To one found guilty of burglary, or a similar offense, he would say, "My honest friend, you are found guilty of felony, for which it is my painful duty to sentence you," etc. On one occasion he had hastily condemned a man, who had been capitally convicted, to transportation, when the clerk of the court in a whisper set him right. "Oh," he exclaimed to the criminal, "I beg your pardon, come back," and putting on his black cap, he courteously apologized for his mistake, and consigned the prisoner to the gallows, to be hanged by the neck until he was dead.

A Master of Bathos

In pronouncing sentence of death, Lord Eskgrove would console a prisoner by assuring him that "whatever you religi-ous persua-shon may be, or even if, as I suppose, you be of no persua-shon at all, there are plenty of rever-end gentlemen who will be most happy to show you the way to eternal life."

In condemning two or three persons to die for burglary and violence, after reminding them that they attacked the house and the persons within it, and robbed them, he came to this climax: "All this you did, and, God preserve us! joost when they were sitten doon to their denner!"

And in sentencing a tailor to death for murdering a soldier by stabbing him, the judge aggravated the offense thus: "And not only did you murder him, whereby he was berea-ved of his life, but you did thrust, or push, or pierce, or project, or propel the let-thall weapon through the belly-band of his regimen-tal breeches, which were his Majes-ty's!"

Checkmate

Lord Kames, a Scottish judge described by Lord Cockburn in *Memorials of His Time* as "an indefatigable and speculative but coarse man," tried Matthew Hay, with whom he used to play chess, for murder in September 1780. When the verdict of guilty was returned, his Lordship exclaimed: "That's checkmate for you, Matthew!"

The Soul of Wit

Justice Harold H. Burton once gave one of the shortest oral opinions on record. A defendant who had been convicted of murder was before the court for sentencing. As usual, the judge asked if he had anything to say before the sentence was pronounced. The defendant said:

"As God is my judge, I didn't do it. I'm not guilty." To which the judge replied:

"He isn't, I am. You did. You are."

One of the shortest written opinions was handed down by the Supreme Court of California in 1855. It involved an action for damages sustained by the plaintiff in falling into an unguarded hole, dug in the sidewalk in front of the defendant's premises. The defense was contributory negligence, since there was evidence that the plaintiff was drunk at the time. The trial judge instructed the jury that it was proper for them to consider this fact in determining whether the plaintiff was in fact negligent. The jury found for the defendant and the plaintiff appealed. Here is the *entire* opinion of the court:

> The court below erred in giving the third, fourth, and fifth instructions. If the defendants were at fault in leaving an unguarded hole in the sidewalk of a public street, the intoxication of the plaintiff cannot excuse such gross negligence. A drunken man is as much entitled to a safe street as a sober one, and much more in need of it.
> The judgement is reversed and the cause is remanded.

Comeback

Famous British judge Justice Hawkins was about to sentence a prisoner who had been found guilty of forgery, when the prisoner asked permission to say a few words. The judge gave his permission, and the prisoner said: "It is absurd to say that I am guilty of forgery, my lord. I cannot even sign my own name." Sir Henry was equal to the occasion: "That may well be, but you are not charged with signing your own name."

Reduced Sentence

Baron Samuel Martin (1801-83) was a good-natured Irish judge. In sentencing a man of a petty theft, he said to him:

"Look, I hardly know what to do with you, but you can take six months."

"I can't take that, my lord," said the prisoner, "it's too much. I can't take it; your lordship sees I did not steal very much after all."

The baron indulged in one of his characteristic chuckling laughs, and said:

"Well, that's vera true; ye didn't steal much. Well then, ye can tak' four. Will that do—four months?"

"No, my lord, but I can't take that neither."

"Then take three."

"That's nearer the mark, my lord," replied the prisoner, "but I'd rather you'd make it two, if you'll be so kind."

"Very well then, tak' two," said the judge; "and don't come here again. If you do, I'll give you—well, it'll all depend."

Change of Mind

Judge Walton, an English dispenser of justice in the last century, once sentenced a man for seven years for a grave offense. Counsel asked for mitigation of the sentence, on the ground that the prisoner's health was very poor.

"Your lordship," he argued, "I am satisfied that my client cannot live out half of that term, and I beg you to change the sentence."

"Very well," Judge Walton obliged, "under those circumstances I will change the sentence; I will make it for life, instead of seven years." At that point, the respondent agreed to abide by the original sentence.

Haggling

Austin H. Kerin collected some amusing legal cases from Vermont in his 1937 book, Yankees in Court:

Judge Howe was holding an arraignment session at Burlington, Vermont, in the time of the "Great Drouth" [i.e., Prohibition]. Some sixty-odd violators of the liquor laws were awaiting the call of their cases.

Most of them had been arrested while transporting liquor they had previously smuggled into the United States from Canada. Among the attorneys present was Squire Steele, a good friend of the judge. The two often had fun one with the other. As the smuggling cases were called in succession and each defendant pleaded guilty, Judge Howe dispensed his usual fine of five hundred dollars, which was on top of having both the liquor and the automobile in which it had been transported seized. When Steele's client was called and pleaded guilty, the judge remarked:

"Well, Squire, is there any reason why your client should not pay five hundred dollars?"

The Squire rose to his feet.

"Yes, Your Honor, there is a reason. I have observed in each of the cases Your Honor has already disposed of that the automobile was an old or second hand of little value and that in no case was a very large quantity of liquor being smuggled. Now, of course, each of those defendants has lost his liquor and lost his car but the loss to any one of them is trivial when compared to the loss my client suffered. My client had a truck—a new Speedway truck for which he had paid fifteen hundred dollars—cash. He has lost that."

The Squire paused and scrutinized his friend on the bench in an effort to learn if his argument was making any impression.

"Yes, Mr. Steele, go on," Judge Howe said, showing interest. "How much liquor did your client have?"

"He had fifteen hundred bottles of ale. That ale cost him seven hundred and fifty dollars—cash."

"Isn't that quite a lot of money for ale, Squire?"

"They were quart bottles, Your Honor."

"Well then, that's twenty-two hundred and fifty dollars. Has your client suffered any other losses?"

"Yes, Your Honor. He has paid me and has been put to the expense of coming here to Burlington from Albany to attend court."

"Now, Squire, let me understand you correctly. You claim that because your client lost a high-priced truck he should not be fined so much?"

"Yes, Your Honor."

"And that because he was hauling a large load of liquor he should not be fined so much?"

"That's right."

"Carry that line of reasoning a little further, Squire," and the judge's eyes twinkled. "If your client had a freight car load, do you think the government would owe him something?"

Mitigating Circumstances
Another story from Judge Howe's court:

Judge Howe had been assigned to hold a term of court at Utica in the Northern District of New York. It was the first day of the term and a large number of defendants were to be arraigned for violations of the National Prohibition Act. The District Attorney had let it become known that he would recommend a fine of one hundred dollars in each case in which the defendant pleaded guilty. Such a recommendation was, if followed by the judge, considered 'easy terms,' and the courtroom and corridors overflowed with defendants and lawyers.

The defendant in the first case pleaded guilty. The D.A. recommended the imposition of a fine of one hundred dollars. THe judge turned to the defendant's lawyer and asked:

"Have you got anything to say?"

"Yes, indeed, Your Honor. The imposition of a fine of a hundred dollars in this case would be a grave injustice. As Your Honor can see my client is poorly dressed. He is also out of work and has been for the past two years, ever since the railroad repair shops closed. He is not a liquor dealer. It is true he sold some small quantities of liquor on one or two occasions. But such sales were made merely in an attempt to provide food for his hungry children. He has a wife and five small children. He has been evicted twice in the past year because he could not pay his rent. He . . ."

Judge Howe interrupted:

"Maybe I should send him to jail and let the city take care of his family."

"No. No, Your Honor. Such a course would be ruinous for him. His family would suffer disgrace and it would be a great deal more difficult for him to obtain work when he was released from prison."

"Well, how much of a fine can he pay?"

"Your Honor, he has been around among his friends and has borrowed ten dollars. I feel that a fine in that amount would be for him a substantial punishment."

"Very well. The sentence of this court is that the defendant pay a fine of ten dollars without costs."

The defendant stepped to the clerk's desk to pay his fine. The clerk was an elderly man and at the time had no one assisting him. Several moments passed during which much low-voiced conversation took place between the clerk and the defendant. Finally the clerk addressed the judge:

"Your Honor, I must ask you to suspend for a few minutes while I get some change. The smallest piece of money this man has is a hundred dollar bill."

Neighborhood Justice

Sam Mandelbaum, whom F.D.R. appointed to New York's Southern District in 1936, dispensed justice in a somewhat rabbinical manner over his congregation in the "Neighborhood," as the then largely Jewish Lower East Side of Manhattan was known. Raphael P. Koenig, a young barrister from the Neighborhood and later a judge himself, had not been prepared by law school for the informal patriarchal ways of Judge Mandelbaum, as described in Milton Gould's hilarious book, The Witness Who Spoke With God and Other Tales from the Courthouse:

In the late 1930s, Koenig found himself before Judge Mandlebaum, representing a notorious securities swindler, Walter Gutterson, who was tried with some other confidence men, all charged with bilking the widows and orphans of New York (including some from the sacred Neighborhood) in violation of the Securities Act of 1933. While the jury was working its way toward the inevitable verdict of "guilty," Mandelbaum called Koenig into the robing room. "Raphie," said the judge, "you and I know from the Neighborhood that Gutterson is a thief and a rascal. Him I will sentence immediately. The others can wait. Now, Raphie, if you are Sam Mandelbaum, knowing what a terrible crook Gutterson is, what would you give him?"

Koening wriggled in discomfort. "Judge, I am his lawyer; how can you ask me what his sentence should be?"

"Raphie", said the judge, "you better think it over, because I am going to ask you the same question when the jury comes back!"

The jury returned with the expected verdict of "guilty." Mandelbaum wasted no time. "Stand up, Gutterson," he said. "Stand up and listen. Okay, Mr. Prosecutor, what does the government recommend for this man?"

The youthful prosecutor, flushed with victory and virtue, recited all the details of Gutterson's sordid career, and finished with a ringing recommendation that Gutterson be removed from society for a period of seven years.

"All right, Mr. Raphie Koenig," said the judge, "you have heard the recommendation of the government. Now, if you were Sam Mandelbaum, what would you do with this bum?"

Koenig made some appropriate professional noises about his duty to the client.

"Never mind all that," said the judge. "Raphie, I ask you again, if you were Sam Mandelbaum, what would you give him?"

Koening thought hard. He knew that Gutterson had a gruesome record of convictions, that previous exposure to the rehabilitative processes of Lewisburg had been futile; most of all, he knew that the government's recommendation of seven years made it certain that Mandelbaum would have to impose a substantial penitentiary sentence.

He swallowed hard. "Your Honor," he said, "knowing the defendant's background and history, I think if I were the sentencing judge I would impose a sentence of *three* years."

The judge fixed his severest glance on the unregenerate rogue who stood before him. "Gutterson," he intoned, "you are a thief and a scoundrel. You are a disgrace to your family! The government recommends that I put you away for seven years. Your own lawyer recommends three years in the penitentiary. But I am going to show you that Sam Mandelbaum has a bigger heart even than your own lawyer. The sentence is two years in the penitentiary. Bail is canceled. The motion for a stay is denied." Hurriedly the judge left the bench, choking back the tears of anguish that flowed always when the law required him to sentence another human being to penal servitude—especially when the miscreant came from his own milieu.

The ungrateful Gutterson stood stunned both by the sentence and by its immediacy. He felt the hand of the marshal on his shoulder. He turned to Koenig. "You dumb bastard," he shouted, "why didn't you recommend a year and a day? He might have given me a suspended sentence!"

CRUEL AND TOO USUAL

Honor Thy Parents—Or Else

In ancient Jewish law, children who cursed or struck their parents were condemned to death.

According to the *Lex Pompeia* of the Romans, parricides were to be put into a sack, with a dog, a cock, a viper, and an ape, and then thrown into the sea.

Every Man Has His Price

The Saxons were particularly curious in fixing pecuniary compensation for injuries of all kinds, without leaving it to the discretion of the judge to proportion the amends to the degree of injury suffered. Cutting off an ear involved a penalty of thirty shillings; if the hearing was lost, sixty shillings. Striking out the front tooth was punished with a fine of eight shillings; the canine tooth, four shillings; the grinders, sixteen shillings. If a common person was bound with chains, the amends were ten shillings; if beaten, twenty shillings; if hung up, thirty shillings. A man who mutilated an ox's horn was to pay a fine of tenpence; but if it was a cow, the fine was only twopence. To fight or make a brawl in the court or yard of a common person was punished with a fine of six shillings; to draw a sword in the same place, even though there was no fighting, was a fine of three shillings; if the party in whose yard or court this happened was worth six hundred shillings, the amends were treble.

The notion of compensation ran through the whole criminal law of the Anglo-Saxons, who allowed a sum of money as a recompense for every kind of crime, not excepting murder. Every man's life had its value, called a *were*, or *capitis estimatis*. This had varied at different periods; therefore in the time of King Athelstan a law was made to settle the *were* of every order of persons in the state. The king, who on this occasion was only distinguished as a superior personage, was rated at thirty thousand thrymsae; an archbishop or earl at fifteen thousand; a bishop or alderman at eight thousand; *Belli imperator* or *summus praefectus* [supreme commander] at four thousand; a priest or thane at two thousand; and a common person at two hundred sixty-seven thrymsae.

How to Cure Practically Anything

Seneca informs us that some quartan fevers have been cured by blows, and a learned commentator conjectured that this arose from the viscid bilious humor being warmed by the strokes and dissipated by motion. Another author held that the rod is a capital specific for tertian fever and gave a story of a lawyer, who had suffered from it and was cured when he was forced to run the gauntlet by a gentleman he had ridiculed: "He ran the course, and was dismissed black and blue, bruised and bleeding, to return to his family, a sadder and a wiser man; but he was so fortunate as to derive one advantage from the flaggellation bestowed upon him—he was cured of his tertian fever!"

In medieval England, the regular remuneration to the executioner for inflicting a whipping was fourpence a head. In the corporation records of a town in Huntingdonshire there is an entry of eight shillings and sixpence, billed for taking up a distracted woman, watching, and whipping her next day, and there is a further charge of two shillings to pay a nurse for her. The legal authorities of this town thought the lash a sort of universal panacea, for they paid eightpence to Thomas Hawkins for whipping two people with small-pox. In a village hard by they paid fourpence "to a woman for whipping ye said Ellen Shaw," and then, to prevent any disastrous consequences, expended threepence "for beare for her after she was whipped."

Not Sparing the Rod

In 1803 there were 391 children in Newgate prison. In 1833 the death sentence was passed on a child of nine who had poked a stick through a patched-up pane of glass in a shop window, and, thrusting his little hand through the aperture, had stolen fifteen pieces of paint, worth twopence. The lawyers construed this into "house breaking," the principal witness being another child of nine, who told because he had not had his share of the paint.

Lucky Coin

There used to be a special coin in England called a "thirteener" worth thirteen pence and a half, which the state paid the hangman for cropping people's ears off.

Manicure

A medieval Scotsman named Fian, supposed to be a male wizard, was put to a severe and cruel torture called the "boots." As he would not confess after three strokes, the king's judges commanded him to have a most strange torment, which was done in the following manner. His nails upon all his fingers were riven and pulled off with an instrument called in Scottish a *turkas*, or in England a pair of pincers, and under every nail there was thrust in two needles up to the heads. At all of which torments the victim of the law reportedly never shrank a whit.

The Good Old Days

Alice Earle Morse writes in her fascinating book, Curious Punishment of Bygone Days *(1896), about the punitive instruments that the colonists brought to America:*

The ducking stool seems to have been placed on the lowest and most contempt-bearing stage among English instruments of punishment. The pillory and stocks, the gibbet, and even the whipping-post, have seen many a noble victim, many a martyr. But I cannot think any save the most ignoble criminals ever sat in a ducking stool. It was an engine of punishment specially assigned to scolding women; though sometimes kindred offenders, such as slanderers, "makebayts," "chyderers," brawlers, railers, and women of light carriage also suffered through it.

We read in Blackstone's *Commentaries*:

"A common scold may be indicted, and if convicted shall be sentenced to be placed in a certain engine of correction called the trebucket, castigatory, or ducking-stool."

At the time of the colonization of America the ducking-stool was at the height of its English reign; and apparently the amiability of the lower classes was equally at ebb. The colonists brought their tempers to the new land, and they brought their ducking-stools. Many minor and some great historians of this country have called the ducking-stool a Puritan punishment. I have never found in the hundreds of pages of court records that I have examined a single entry of an execution of ducking in any Puritan community; while in the "cavalier colonies," so called, in Virginia and the Carolinas, and in Quaker Pennsylvania, many duckings took place, and in law survived as long as similar punishments in England.

In the Statute Books of Virginia many laws may be found designed to silence idle tongues by ducking.

"Whereas oftentimes many brabling women often slander and scandalize their neighbours, for which their poor husbands are often brought into chargeable and vexatious suits and cast in great damages, be it enacted that all women found guilty be sentenced to ducking."

Others dated 1662 are most explicit.

"The court in every county shall cause to be set up near a Court House a Pillory, a pair of Stocks, a Whipping Post and a Ducking-Stool in such place as they think convenient, which not being set up within six months after the date of this act the said Court shall be fined 5,000 lbs. of Tobacco.

"In actions of slander caused by a man's wife, after judgment past for damages, the woman shall be punished by Ducking, and if the slander be such as the damages shall be adjudged as above 500 lbs. of Tobacco, then the woman shall have ducking for every 500 lbs. of Tobacco adjudged against the husband if he refuse to pay the Tobacco."

One of the latest, and certainly the most notorious sentences to ducking was that of Mrs. Anne Royall, of Washington, D.C. This extraordinary woman had lived through an eventful career in love and adventure; she had been stolen by the Indians when a child, and kept by them fifteen years; then she was married to Captain Royall, and taught to read and write. She traveled much and wrote several vituperatively amusing books. She settled down upon Washington society as editor of a newspaper called the "Washington Paul Pry" and of another, "The Huntress"; and she soon terrorized the place. No one in public office was spared, either in personal or printed abuse, if any offense or neglect was given to her. A persistent lobbyist, she was shunned like the plague by all congressmen. John Quincy Adams called her an itinerant virago. She was arraigned as a common scold before Judge William Cranch, and he sentenced her to be ducked in the Potomac River. She was, however, released with a fine, and appears to us to-day [i.e., 1896] to have been insane—possibly through over-humored temper.

Red Hannah

The whipping post remained on the books until recent times, notably in Delaware. Despite continuous efforts to abolish a form of punishment that was reminiscent of slavery and was applied much more to black prisoners than white, in 1945 there were still twenty-four crimes that were punishable with public whippings. For example, burning down ''a court house or office where public records are kept,'' was a felony requiring a fine of one thousand dollars, sixty lashes, and imprisonment for not more than twenty years. Embezzlement by a cashier or clerk, on the other hand, drew no fine, but up to twenty lashes, and imprisonment for up to ten years. Wilmington's Journal Every Evening, *published on August 2nd, 1938, a historical note on this relic of the good old days:*

Here is a little penological history which may be of interest to Delawareans and others who are cursed with pilfering fingers and who live in constant danger of being punished at our much discussed and much abused whipping post. In days gone by, the whipping post in Kent County stood out brazenly in the open courtyard of the county jail not far from the old state house. It looked like an old-time octagonal pump without a handle. It had a slit near the top of it in which the equally old-time pillory boards might be inserted when needed for punitive use. There also were iron shackles for holding the prisoners while they were being whipped. That whipping post was painted red from top to bottom. Negro residents bestowed upon it the name of "Red Hannah." Of any prisoner who had been whipped at the post it was said, "He has hugged Red Hannah!"

Since those days the pillory has gone out of use in Delaware and for several years all the whipping was done at the New Castle County Workhouse at Greenbank. Those old days are recalled by the fact that last Friday each of four prisoners who had pleaded guilty in the Court of General Sessions here [Wilmington] was sentenced to imprisonment and also to receive ten lashes. It is safe to assert that none of the four prisoners whipped under the sentences imposed will care to pass through the ordeal again.

Dissenter

Daniel Defoe, the author of *Robinson Crusoe*, was by birth and belief a Dissenter, and he wrote an anonymous satire against the Church party, entitled *The Shortest Way with the Dissenters*. The pamphlet, so ironically and with such apparent soberness reduced the argument of the intolerant to an absurdity, that for a short time it was welcomed and praised by zealous church-folk, who turned on Defoe with redoubled hatred when they finally perceived the satire. It was termed a scandalous and seditious pamphlet, and fifty pounds reward was offered for him. He was arrested, tried, pilloried in three places, and imprisoned for a year; but Queen Anne paid the fine for his release from prison, and his pillory was hung with garlands of flowers, and his health was drunk, and scraps of his vigorous doggerel from his *Hymn to the Pillory* passed from lip to lip:

Men that are men in thee can feel no pain
And all thy insignificants disdain
   Contempt that false new word for shame
   Is, without crime, an empty name.

   The first intent of laws
Was to correct the effect and check the cause
   And all the ends of punishment
Were only future mischiefs to prevent.

But Justice is inverted when
   Those engines of the law
Instead of pinching vicious men
   Keep honest ones in awe.

Lucky To Be Alive

Until about one hundred fifty years ago the most common punishments in civilized England, short of the death penalty, were branding, mutilation, dismemberment, whipping, and degrading public exposure. Vagabonds were branded with the letter *V*, idlers and masterless men with the letter *S*, because they were condemned to slavery; any church brawler lost his ears, and for a second offense might be branded with the letter *F* as a fray maker or fighter. Sometimes the penalty was to bore a one-inch-diameter hole through the gristle of the right ear.

Tar and Feathers

Tarring and feathering became a popular phrase in New England shortly before the Revolution, but the origin of the practice goes back much further. Richard the Lionheart included in the regulations for the English Navy, drawn up in 1189: "A thief or felon that hath stolen, being lawfully convicted, shall have his head shorn, and boiling pitch poured upon his head, and feathers or down strewn upon the same, whereby he may be known, and so at the first landing place they shall come to, there to be cast up." Raphael Holinshed, one of Shakespeare's major historical sources, quotes the same law for sailors in 1578, and in 1623 it seems to have been ordered to punish "a party of incontinent friars and nuns."

On November 5th, or Guy Fawkes Day, celebrations of which in England match some of the antics of today's American Halloween, boys would dress up as the Devil's Imps, wearing clothes covered with tar and feathers. The anti-papist Puritans of New England adopted these to celebrate Pope's Day, and then turned it against their British oppressors with a vengeance. In October 1769, George Geyer was exposed as an informant to the customs officials; he was stripped, tarred and feathered, and exhibited around Boston. The following year the same was done to Owen Richards, another informer. By 1773, "Committees on Tarring and Feathering" were founded in Rhode Island and Massachusetts. On the night of January 25, 1774, a lynch mob went after a customs official named John Malcomb. Tarred and feathered, he was dragged through the streets of Boston and then flogged and roughed up. But a week later, someone signing himself as "Joyce, junr., Chairman of the Committee on Tarring and Feathering," disclaimed any responsibility in a printed handbill:

Brethren and fellow citizens:
this is to certify that the modern
punishment lately inflicted on the ignoble John Malcomb was not

done by our order. We reserve that method for bringing villains of greater consequence to a sense of guilt and infamy.

As for the wretched Malcomb, who had apparently suffered similar ignominy elsewhere in the colonies, he decided to call it quits. He sent a piece of his own skin, showing the tar and feathers, to his employers in London, and the British government granted him a pension in return.

Now They Just Charge Interest

In 1758 Dr. Samuel Johnson calculated that the total number of people imprisoned for debt in England stood at around twenty thousand, or about one three-hundredth of a population of six million. Reckoning that every sufferer had at least two dependents injured by his confinement, Johnson estimated that the distress affected about one percent of the whole community. Computing next that one in four debtors died every year, this amounted to half a million people during a century. "The misery of jails is not half the evil," the good doctor commented, "they are filled with every corruption which poverty and wickedness can generate between them; with all the shameless and profligate enormities that can be produced by the impotence of ignominy, the rage of want, and the malignity of despair."

One of the great innovations of the American system of law was to abolish the compulsory process for the recovery of debts. In Spain, someone in debt was stoned every year: he was dunned, persecuted, and ultimately harassed to death by the perpetual visitation of his creditors. In England, many were driven to the Bedlam mental hospital, or to suicide, by financial embarrassment. An English statesman in the early nineteenth century urged the adoption of the American example with these words:

"It would not only root out a fruitful source of litigation and inconsiderate speculation, but abolish a gross anomaly in our jurisprudence. To give the arbitrary power of imprisonment to a creditor is to identify the prosecutor with the judge, and to make a man amenable not to fixed laws, but to the passions and caprice of incensed individuals. A hog upon trust grunts till he is paid for."

It Isn't Over Till It's Over

Until the last century, debt was considered such a serious crime that one could be arrested and detained for it even after death. According to the register in the English parish of Sparsholt, Berkshire, the corpse of John Matthews "was stopt on the church-way for debt, August 27, 1689. And having lain there four days, was, by Justices' warrant, buried in the place to prevent annoyances—but about six weeks after, by an Order of Sessions, taken up and buried in the churchyard by the wife of the deceased."

In Prussia arresting corpses was regular practice until Frederick the Great reformed the legal code in the eighteenth century. But in England, there were rumors, when Richard Brinsley Sheridan died in 1816, that the body of the great playwright and politician would be detained for his notorious debts; however, his funeral went smoothly. Five years earlier, there was a case that ended up in court.

A man named John Elliott, at the time of his death, on October 3rd, 1811, was indebted to Baker, a bricklayer, and Heasman, a carpenter, a small sum for work done. These two men, with two sheriffs' officers, proceeded on Monday, October 7th, to the house where Elliott lay dead, and were met by the son of the deceased. He stated that his father was dead. The officers informed him that they had a warrant to arrest the deceased and asked where the body lay. The son pointed out the room, saying that the door was locked, and his mother had gone out and taken the key, but was expected every minute. After waiting a few minutes, one of the men kicked the door open and entered the room where the body lay in the coffin. The body was identified, and possession taken of it.

The interment was fixed by the family for the following Wednesday, and at four o'clock on that day the undertaker and his man arrived for the purpose of removing the body to Shoreditch Church for burial, but Baker and Heasman and the sheriff's men entered the house with a shell, and took it into the room where the corpse lay. After asking the son to pay the debt and prevent his father's body being taken away, and he replying that he was unable to discharge it, Baker and Heasman crammed the naked body into the shell, and put it into a cart before the house, where it remained over half-an-hour, attracting to the place a large number of people who behaved in a riotous manner. The body was then removed to Heasman's house, and placed in a cellar until October 11th, when it was conveyed by him and others to Bethnal Green, and left in a burial vault.

Such were the details given to the judge who tried the men who committed this outrageous public indecency. The jury, after retiring for a few minutes, returned, and awarded the Elliott family damages of £200.

One-Stop Shopping

In recent years there has been a trend in the United States to contract to private, profit-making companies what used to be public services. The collecting of garbage is one example, and the maintenance of prisons another. But there is little that is new under the sun, and private prisons were common in eighteenth-century England. The great prison reformer John Howard pointed his finger at the Dukes of Portland (who ran a modest jail with a cellar in Chesterfield), of Devonshire, Norfolk and Leeds; the Marquis of Carnarvon; the Lords Salisbury, Exeter, Arundel, and Derby. There was healthy competition in the prison industry from the Bishops of Salisbury, Durham and the Dean and Chapter of Westminster Abbey. One disgraceful prison, according to Howard, was owned by the Bishop of Ely. Unlike the entrepreneurs of today, these lords and bishops also sat in the House of Lords as the supreme lawmakers in the court of last resort.

Pressing Engagement

At the Kilkenny Assizes, in 1740, one Matthew Ryan was tried for highway robbery. When he was apprehended, he pretended to be a lunatic, stripped himself in the jail, threw away his clothes, and could not be prevailed on to put them on again, but went as he was to the court to take his trial. He then affected to be dumb, and would not plead, on which the judges ordered a jury to be impanneled, to inquire and give their opinion whether he was mute and lunatic by the hand of God, or willfully so.

The jury returned in a short time and brought in a verdict of "wilful and affected dumbness and lunacy." The judges desired the prisoner to plead, but he still pretended to be insensible to all that was said to him. The law now called for the *peine forte et dure*, but the judges compassionately deferred awarding it until a future day, in the hope that he might in the meantime acquire a juster sense of his situation. When again brought up, however, the criminal persisted in his refusal to plead: and the court at last pronounced the dreadful sentence, that he should be *pressed to death*.

This sentence was accordingly executed upon him two days later in the public marketplace of Kilkenny. As the weights were being heaped on the wretched man, he earnestly supplicated to be hanged, but it was beyond the power of the sheriff to deviate from the mode of punishment prescribed in the sentence, and even this indulgence could no longer be granted him.

New and Improved

The gallows formerly consisted of three posts over which were laid three transverse beams. This clumsy instrument of legal coercion gave way in the progressive nineteenth century to an elegant contrivance called "The New Drop," in which a hinged board, resembling the leaf of a table, was propped up, then allowed to fall. Hence the phrase "to go off with the fall of the leaf."

The Wages of Sin

According to the *Newgate Calendar*, the Reverend Peter Vine, a minister of the Holy Gospel, was hanged at Exeter, on October 5th, 1753, for paying too boisterous attentions to a young woman who did not appreciate them.

I Sing the Chair Electric

Martin Stone, an early television personality, also enjoyed a successful career as a lawyer. An example of his quick-wittedness circulating in New York had one of his clients phoning Stone from the death house at Sing Sing with the desperate news that he was about to be taken to the electric chair in a few minutes.

"You're my lawyer. Tell me what to do." In a flash, his attorney replied: "Don't sit down."

Do It Yourself

In the old days in Sweden, serious crime was relatively uncommon and there were many towns without an executioner. In one such place, some time during the last century, a criminal was sentenced to be hanged. This caused some embarrassment, as it obliged the town to bring a hangman from a distance at considerable expense, besides paying him the customary fee of two crowns. During a debate at the City Council, a young businessman offered the following solution: "I think, gentlemen, we had best give the malefactor the two crowns, and let him go and be hanged where he pleases."

THE HIGHER LAW

Justice

Early in the fifteenth century a band of Highland robbers, headed by one Macdonald of Rosse, took two cows from a poor woman, and she vowed that she would wear no shoes till she had complained to the king. The savages, in ridicule of her oath, nailed horseshoes to the soles of her feet.

When her wounds were healed, she proceeded to the royal presence, told her story, and showed her scars.

The just monarch instantly dispatched an armed force to secure Macdonald, who was brought to Perth, along with twelve of his associates. The king caused them all to be shod in the same manner as they had done by the poor woman; and after they had been for three days exhibited through the streets of the town as a public spectacle, Macdonald was beheaded and his companions hanged.

As God Was Her Witness

Although Joan of Arc was tried in ecclesiastical court for magic and witchcraft, hers was in fact a political show trial. Joan was a prisoner of the English, who were determined to do away with her one way or another, because the eighteen-year-old girl had become the symbol of resurgent nationalism in France. Having revealed that various saints spoke to her, Joan was closely questioned about these voices she claimed were giving her instructions. Asked if St. Margaret spoke to her in English, she replied:

"Why would she speak English, when she is not on their side?" And when one of the curious clerics asked if St. Michael appeared to her in the nude, the Maid of Orleans shot back:

"Do you think that the Almighty has not wherewithal to clothe him?"

And That's Why We Have Pennsylvania

It is typical of human society that people who renounce violence provoke even greater violence against them. Gandhi and Martin Luther King, Jr., were assassinated; Christ and many early Christians were martyred; and pacifists have been thrown in jail. As the peaceful Bahai sect has been singled out for recent persecution in Iran, so the Quakers encountered great hostility in the seventeenth century. William Penn, before he came to the New World, was arrested on August 15, 1670, during a prayer meeting in London's Gracechurch Street, and then tried with an associate named Mead at the Old Bailey. Reports of the trial have been preserved:

Penn and his friend, according to the custom of their sect, entered the court with their hats on, and when one of the officers pulled them off, the lord mayor exclaimed, "Sirrah, who bid you put off their hats? Put on their hats again."

The recorder then asked the prisoners: "Do you know where you are? Do you know it is the king's court?"

Penn: "I know it to be a court, and I suppose it to be the king's court."
Recorder: "Do you know that there is respect due to the court? And why do you not pull off your hats?"
Penn: "Because I do not believe that to be any respect."
Recorder: "Well, the court sets forty marks a piece upon your heads, as a fine for your contempt of the court."
Penn: "I desire it may be observed, that we came into the court with our hats off, and if they have been put on since, it was by order of the bench, and therefore not we, but the bench should be fined."

After the witnesses for the prosecution had been examined and the prisoners were called upon for their defense, Penn demanded to know upon what law the indictment was grounded.
Recorder: "Upon the common law."
Penn: "Where is that common law?"
Recorder: "You must not think that I am able to run up so many years, and ever so many adjudged cases, which we call common law, to answer your curiosity."
Penn: "This answer, I am sure, is very short of my question; for if it be common, it should not be so hard to produce."
Recorder: "Sir, will you plead to your indictment?"

Penn reiterated his demand to know on what law that indictment was founded.
Recorder: "You are a saucy, impertinent fellow; will you teach the court what law is? It is *lex non scripta* [the unwritten law], that which many have studied thirty or forty years to know, and would you have me tell you in a moment?"
Penn: "Certainly, if the common law is so hard to be understood, it is far from being common; but if Lord Coke, in his Institutes, be of any consideration, he tells us that common law is common right, and that common right is the greater charter of privileges. I design no affront to the court, but to be heard in my just plea, and I must plainly tell you, that if you will deny me oyer [hearing] of the law which you say I have broken, you do at once deny me an acknowledged right; and evidence to the whole world, your resolution to sacrifice the privileges of Englishmen to your sinister and arbitrary designs."
Recorder: "Take him away."
Lord Mayor: "Take him away, take him away; turn him in the bail dock."

Penn was now dragged into the bail dock.

Mead being then called on, a scene exactly similar to the preceding took place, and he also was thrust into the bail dock.

The recorder charged the jury to bring in a verdict of guilty.

Penn (with a loud voice from the bail dock): "I appeal to the jury, who are my judges, and this great assembly, whether the proceedings of the court are not most arbitrary, and void of all law. I have not been heard, neither you of the jury legally depart the court before I have been *fully* heard."

Recorder: "Pull the fellow down, pull him down."

The jury were now desired to go upstairs, in order to agree upon a verdict, and the prisoners remained in the bail dock. After an hour and a half's time, eight came down agreed, but four remained above until sent for. The bench used many threats to the four that dissented, and the recorder, addressing himself to one of them of the name of Bushel, said, "Sir, you are the cause of this disturbance, and manifestly show yourself an abettor of faction; I shall set a mark upon you, sir."

Then Alderman Sir J. Robinson, Lieutenant of the Tower, said, "Mr. Bushel, I have known you near these fourteen years; you have never thrust yourself upon this jury."

Alderman Bludworth: "Mr. Bushel, we know what you are."

Lord Mayor: "Sirrah, you are an impudent fellow; I will put a mark upon you."

The jury being then sent back to consider their verdict, remained for some time, and on their return, the clerk having asked in the usual manner, "Is William Penn guilty of the matter wherein he stands indicted, or not guilty?" the foreman replied, "Guilty of speaking in Gracechurch Street."

Court: "Is that all?"

Foreman: "That is all I have in commission."

Recorder: "You had as good say nothing."

The jury were ordered to go and consider their verdict once more. They declared that they had given their verdict, and could deliver no other.

Recorder: "Gentlemen, you shall not be dismissed till we have a verdict that the court will accept, and you shall be locked up without meat, drink, fire, or tobacco; you shall not think thus to abuse the court; we will have a verdict by the help of God, or you shall starve for it."

Penn: "My jury, who are my judges, ought not to be thus menaced; I do desire that justice may be done me, and that the arbitrary resolves of the bench may not be made the measure of my jury's verdict."

Recorder: "Stop that prating fellow."

Penn: "The agreement of twelve men is a verdict in law, and such a one being given by the jury, I require the clerk of the peace to record it, as he will answer at his peril. And if the jury bring in another verdict contradictory to this, I affirm they are perjured men in law." Then looking toward them, he emphatically added: "You are Englishmen: mind your privilege, give not away your right."

The court now swore several of its officers to keep the jury all night without meat, drink, fire, etc., and adjourned.

Next morning, which happened to be Sunday, the jury were again brought up; when having persevered in their verdict, much abuse was heaped upon them, particularly on the 'factious fellow' Bushel.

Bushel observed that he had acted conscientiously. The expression called forth some very pleasant jeers from the court; who, being still determined not to yield the point, sent back the jury a third time. The jury were, however, inflexible; a third time they returned with the same verdict.

The recorder, greatly incensed and perplexed at this, threatened Bushel with the weight of his vengeance. "While we had anything to do with the city, he would have an eye upon him." The lord mayor termed him, 'a pitiful fellow,' and added, "I will cut his nose for this."

Penn: "It is intolerable that my jury should be thus menaced."

Lord Mayor: "Stop his mouth, jailor; bring him fetters, and stake him to the ground."

Penn: "Do your pleasure. I matter not your fetters."

The court determined to try once more the firmness of the jury. The foreman remonstrated in vain that any other verdict "would be a force on them to save their lives," and the jury refused to go out of court until obliged by the sheriff.

The court sat again next morning at seven o'clock, when the prisoners and the jury were brought up for the fourth time.

The Clerk: "Is William Penn guilty or not?"

Foreman: "Not guilty."

Clerk: "Is William Mead guilty or not guilty?"

Foreman: "Not guilty."

Recorder: "I am sorry, gentlemen, you have followed your own judgments and opinions, rather than the good and wholesome advice that was given you. God keep my life out of your hands! But for this the court fines you forty marks a man, and commands imprisonment till paid."

Both jury and prisoners were forced together into the bail-dock, for nonpayment of their fines, whence they were carried to Newgate.

Mr. Bushel immediately sued out a writ of *habeas corpus*, and the cause having come to be heard, at length, before the twelve judges, they decided that the fining and imprisonment were contrary to law.

The jury were accordingly discharged; upon which they respectively brought actions against the lord mayor, aldermen, and recorder, and obtained exemplary verdicts.

The Great Emancipator

Abraham Lincoln was not originally in favor of the abolition of slavery. But, as Harriet Beecher Stowe wrote: "In politics and in law alike, both the strength of his conscientiousness and the kind of yearning after a rounded wholeness of view which was an intellectual instinct with him, forced him habitually to consider all sides of any question." In the fifteen years before his election to the presidency, "he grew slowly, as public opinion grew," according to a contemporary biographer, "and, as an anti-slavery man, was a gradual convert." He subscribed regularly to *The Richmond Enquirer* and *The Charleston Mercury*, and "while Rhett and Wise with slavery in full feather, wrote every day of the inviolateness of secession and the divinity of bondage, these two Illinois lawyers (Lincoln and his partner Herndon), in their little square office, read every vaunting cruel word, paid to read it, and educated themselves out of their mutual indignations."

The author of *Uncle Tom's Cabin* recounts how, during the period, it was considered an unpopular and politically dangerous business for a lawyer to defend any fugitive slave on trial, and even the brave Colonel Barker, in those days also practicing there, on one occasion directly refused to defend such a case, saying that as a political man he could not afford it. The luckless applicant, having consulted with an abolitionist friend, went next to Lincoln, and got him. "He's not afraid of an unpopular case," said the friend; "when I go for a lawyer to defend an arrested fugitive slave, other lawyers will refuse me; but if Mr. Lincoln is at home, he will always take up my case."

In 1841 Lincoln argued before the Supreme Court of Illinois the case of Nance, a black girl who had been sold within the state. A note had been given in payment for her, and the suit was brought to recover upon this note. Mr. Lincoln, defending, proved that Nance was free, and that therefore nothing had been sold, and so the note was void. The Appeals Court had sustained the note, but the Supreme Court, in accordance with Mr. Lincoln's argument, reversed this judgment. The decision set Nance free and put a stop to sales of human beings in Illinois.

He Is All Yours

In the year 1785 an Indian murdered a Mr. Evans at Pittsburgh. When, after a confinement of several months, his trial was to begin, the chiefs of his nation (the Delaware), were invited to be present at the proceedings, and see how the trial would be conducted, as well as to speak on behalf of the accused, if they chose. These chiefs, however, instead of attending, sent to the civil officers the following laconic answer: "Brethren, you inform us that N.N. who murdered one of your men in Pittsburg is shortly to be tried by the laws of your country, at which trial you request that some of us may be present. Brethren! knowing N.N. to have been always a very bad man, we do not wish to see him. We advise you to try him by your laws, and to hang him, so that he may never return to us again."

Justice Can Wait

In December 1902, after Oliver Wendell Holmes had been appointed and confirmed as associate justice of the U.S. Supreme Court, the Middlesex Bar Association in his home state of Massachusetts honored him with a send-off banquet. At the end of the festivities, one of his supporters said:

"Finally, justice will be done in Washington."

"Don't be too sure," replied Justice Holmes. "I am going there to administer the laws."

Playing the Game

Justice Oliver Wendell Holmes was not an activist in his judicial philosophy. Judge Learned Hand said about him:

He was to me the master craftsman certainly of our time; and he said: "I hate justice"; which he didn't quite mean. What he did mean was this. I remember once I was with him; it was a Saturday when the Court was to confer. It was before we had a motor car, and we jogged along in an old coupe. When we got down to the Capitol, I wanted to provoke a response, so as he walked off, I said to him: "Well, sir, goodbye. Do justice!" He turned quite sharply and he said: "Come here. Come here." I answered: "Oh, I know, I know." He replied: "That's not my job. My job is to play the game according to the rules."

According to John W. Davis, Solicitor General of the United States (1913-1918), Justice Holmes did not have to believe personally in a law to uphold it. Following one of Davis's arguments in an antitrust case, Holmes asked him:

"How many more of these economic policy cases have you got?"

"Quite a basketful," Davis replied.

"Well, bring 'em on and we'll decide them. Of course I know, and every other sensible man knows, that the Sherman [antitrust] law is damned nonsense, but if my country wants to go to hell, I am here to help it."

Echoing Justice Holmes' sentiments, his younger colleague, Harlan Fiske Stone said about the New Dealers: "If the damn fools want to go to hell, it's not our duty to stop them if that's what they want to do."

Final Appeal

During the last, desperate days to save Nicola Sacco and Bartolomeo Vanzetti from execution in 1927, Arthur D. Hill, one of their many successive counsels, appealed to the governor of Massachusetts for a stay of execution pending a final appeal to the full bench of the supreme judicial court. The governor called a special meeting of his council. He asked seven of the eight living attorneys general in Massachusetts help him consider the request for a respite.

While these meetings were in progress in the State House, Hill sped to the home of Supreme Court Justice Oliver Wendell Holmes at Beverly Farms, thirty miles away. The justice held he could not stay the execution as he had no jurisdiction in the case.

A second appeal was made to Justice Holmes. Those who undertook the mission were Mr. Thompson and John Finerty, a Washington lawyer. They talked to him on the porch of his Beverly Farms home. The jurist was deeply moved by the lawyers' recital and told them that there was nothing he would rather do than to grant their request, but he saw no legal way in which he could act.

"You don't have to convince me that the atmosphere in which these men were tried precluded a fair trial," said Justice Holmes. "But that is not enough to give me, as a federal judge, jurisdiction. If I listened to you any more I would do it. I must not do it."

He turned on his heel and went into the house.

Adds Louis Stark, who reported the case for the *New York Times*: "To Justice Holmes preservation of the fabric of Federal-State relations was a principle higher than life. It was what he had fought for as a lad in the Civil War."

Dissent

Justice Pierce Butler was the lone dissenter from the Supreme Court's decision in the 1930s that upheld a Virginia statute providing for the sterilization of the mentally retarded. As a Catholic, Butler wrestled with his conscience. Justice Oliver Wendell Holmes, reading the majority decision which he had crafted, remarked: "Three generations of imbeciles are enough." Professor Lewis [later Justice] Powell read the opinion to his Harvard class, and added: "Mr. Justice Butler dissenting."

· 8 ·

THE RULE OF LAW

UP FROM THE JUNGLE

Through Fire and Water

One of the most ancient forms of settling disputes and clearing one's name was the ordeal, whether by fire, water, poison or other bizzarre means. It was practiced during the dark ages of mankind as well as in the bright sunlight of Greece; traces of it survive among primitive tribes, not to mention present-day Los Angeles, where an ex-salesman has been inspiring some bored and fashionable people in search of thrills to pay him for the privilege of walking on hot coals.

"I will go through fire and water for my friend," was a common expression in the Middle Ages, when it could be meant more literally than today. The water ordeal was more for bondsmen and rustics, and boiling water was preferred. The accused person was required to take a stone from a pan of boiling water, to insert the hand and wrist into the liquid, and in case of the triple ordeal, to plunge the arm in up to the elbow.

When cold water was employed, as generally in cases of witchcraft, the suspect was flung into a river or pond. If he floated without appearance of swimming, he was pronounced innocent; if he sank, he was condemned as guilty—rather a superfluous proceeding, considering that the man was in all probability already drowned.

The ordeal of fire was practiced by the Greeks in the time of Sophocles. The Guard in *Antigone* offers to Kreon that he would be willing to handle hot coals and walk over fire to prove his innocence. But on the whole this distinction was reserved for persons of high rank. The accused was required to carry a red-hot iron for some distance in his hand, or to walk nine feet, bare-footed and blindfolded, over red-hot ploughshares. The hands and feet were immediately bound up and inspected three days afterwards. If, on examination, no injury was visible, the accused was considered innocent; if traces of the burning remained, he was reckoned guilty and received punishment commensurate with his offense, without any discount for the harm he had already suffered.

Curiously, this ancient practice survived Christianity, and a famous instance involved Queen Emma, the mother of Edward the Confessor. She was accused of a criminal intrigue with Alwyn, Bishop of Winchester, and condemned to the ordeal of fire, which, on this particular occasion, took the form of nine red-hot ploughshares, laid lengthwise at irregular intervals, over which she was required to walk with bandaged eyes. She passed successfully through the severe trial and at the conclusion innocently asked when the ordeal would begin. Thus the Queen's innocence was established more substantially to the popular mind than would have been possible in any existing court of law.

Take Two And Call Me in the Morning

Wrote Ernest Rann in an 1897 essay on Trials in Superstitious Ages:

In Africa especially the ordeal is well known. During his travels among the tribes north of the Zambesi, Dr. Livingstone encountered the curious practice of the "mauvi," which consisted of making all the women of a tribe drink an infusion of "goho," for the purpose of ascertaining which of them had bewitched a particular man. The accused women were drawn up in a row before the hut of the king, and the draught administered to them. Those who were unable to retain the horrible decoction and vomited were considered innocent of the charge; those who were purged were adjudged guilty, and put to death by burning.

The Calabar bean is also used by the natives of Africa in the form of an emulsion as an ordeal for persons accused of witchcraft, proof of innocence consisting of ability to throw off the poison by vomiting. Among the Dyak tribes lumps of salt are thrown into a bowl of water by the accuser and the accused, and judgment is given against the owner whose lump disappears first. Another method adopted by the Dyaks is for each of the two parties to choose a mollusc, and to squeeze over it a few drops of lime-juice; the owner of the mollusc which moves first under the acid stimulant losing his case.

Among the Malay tribes ordeals by fire, ducking, pulling a ring out of boiling water, or licking red-hot iron are still frequent. Where the ordeal fails to produce the desired result, wager of battle, in reality another form of ordeal, is resorted to. Among the Tagals it is usual to light a consecrated candle, and to consider the person guilty of the crime under consideration to whom the candle flame is blown during the performance of the ceremony.

The Igorrotes have a more painful method of fixing guilt. The accuser and the accused are placed together; the backs of their heads are scratched with a sharply pointed bamboo stick, and the man who loses most blood also loses his case.

In Hawaii ordeals are administered by priests, the suspected person being compelled to hold his hands over consecrated water, and adjudged guilty if the liquid trembles in the vessel while the priest looks at him. The Siamese have a form of ordeal which consists of making the two parties to a suit swallow consecrated purgative pills; the man who retains them for the greater length of time winning the case.

Different Strokes for Different Folks

The ancient Phoenicians, in taking a legal oath, held a lamb in one hand and a stone in the other, to intimate their wishes that God might strike them dead, as they were ready to do to the lamb, if they swore not according to the truth. The old Romans, upon a like occasion, took a pastern, and cast it from them, imprecating to themselves that God might cast them away, if there was any falsity in what they swore.

The ancient Jews, in taking or administering an oath, slew a calf, and cut it up, and the person who was to swear walked through the dissected parts, to convince the spectators that he wished God, in like manner, might cut him asunder, in case he falsified his oath. Lifting up the hands to heaven, as an act of swearing, is practiced among the angels themselves both in the Old and New Testaments. (*Daniel 7:7*, and *Revelation 10:5*).

Where It Hurts

The word *testify* has its origin in the ancient custom of a man placing a hand over his testicles ('testes' in Latin) when swearing a solemn oath. The implication was that he would risk becoming impotent if he lied under oath. Robert Hendrickson, in his recent *Encyclopedia of Word and Phrase Origins*, quotes a letter to *Ms. Magazine*, in which a feminist wrote: "I protest the use of the word 'testimony' when referring to a woman's statements, because its root is 'testes,' which has nothing to do with being female." Unfortunately the lady who thus protested ought to have avoided also the word 'protest,' which has the same, very masculine root.

Ah, Chivalry

By the law of Gondebaldus, king of the Burgundians, passed in the year 501, proof by combat was allowed in all legal proceedings in lieu of swearing. In the time of Charlemagne, the Burgundian practice had spread over the empire of the Franks, and not only the suitors for justice, but the witnesses, and even the judges, were obliged to defend their cause, their evidence, or their decision at the point of the sword. Louis the Debonnaire, his successor, endeavored to remedy the growing evil by permitting the duel only in appeals of felony, in civil cases, or issue joined in a writ of right, and in cases of the court of chivalry, or attacks upon a man's knighthood. None were exempt from these trials except women, the sick and the maimed, and persons under fifteen or above sixty years of age. Ecclesiastics were allowed to produce champions to fight for their cause in their stead. In the course of time, this practice extended to all trial of civil and criminal cases, which had to be decided by battle.

When an Englishman named Abraham Thornton, on November 6th, 1817 wanted to avail himself of trial by wager of battle, Lord Ellensborough was forced to extend this ancient privilege to him. An outraged contemporary jurist wrote:

> The folly of admitting that "right should follow might" must be obvious to all; besides there are other ridiculous points that make it unpalatable to an enlightened age. For instance, if the appellant be a widow of the murdered person, and in just indignation should proceed against the murderer, yet if she should marry before the appeal comes into court, then she can have no redress against the slayer of her first husband, because, in the eyes of our old legislators, one man was as good as another; and as she was thus supposed to have taken compensation into her own hands, she was not entitled to receive any from law. Again, though the appellee, if found guilty, would be out of the reach of the pardon from the Crown, yet the appellant might sell his life to him for any sum he liked to ask. This last mode of estimating a man's life like that of an ox or a sheep, was a remnant of the most barbarous ages, and is still to be found among many tribes of African and Indian savages.

The Scales of Justice

The ordeal of the balance was common in medieval Europe and in India until quite recently. As one writer describes it, the beam is adjusted, and both scales are made perfectly even. After the accused has been bathed in sacred water, and the deities worshiped, he is placed in the scale-pan and carefully weighed. When he is taken out, the Pundits pronounce an incantation, and place round his head a piece of paper setting forth the charge against him. Six minutes later he again enters the scale, and the balance is called upon to show his fault or innocence. If he weighs more than before, he is held guilty; if less, innocent; if exactly the same, he must be weighed a third time, when, according to the Mitacshera, a difference in his weight will be discernible. Should the balance break down, the mishap would be considered as proof of a man's guilt.

An incident is recorded in English history in which Susannah Haynokes of Aylesbury was accused of bewitching her neighbor's spinning-wheel and preventing it from working properly. Susannah loudly protested her innocence and demanded an ordeal to prove it. She was taken to the church, and weighed in a semi-nude condition against the copy of the Bible, and being able to outweigh the Scriptures, was considered innocent of the charge against her.

Going by the Book
Another custom was to tie a key in a Bible opened at Psalm 50, verse 18: "When thou sawest a thief, then thou consentedst with him." One then had to balance the Bible in the belief that the book would turn over in the hands of somebody guilty.

Blood Test
Related to the ordeal was the custom of getting a person accused of murder to approach the bier and to place his hand on the naked breast of the corpse, while declaring his innocence. It was believed that the body would bleed, move, or show some sign if approached by the assassin.

This method of finding out murderers had its origin reputedly in Denmark, where Christian II adopted it to discover the murderer of one of his courtiers. The belief survives even in some English villages, where everyone attending a funeral is expected to touch the body, to show that they bear no ill will toward the dead.

Beyond the Grave
We are used to certain legal concepts, such as the statute of limitations, which states that a person cannot be prosecuted for a crime after (usually) seven years. Even so, there are capital crimes, which have resulted in people being brought to justice many decades later, as for example the few Nazis who have been tried

twenty or even forty years after their acts of genocide. In the Middle Ages, there was no statute of limitation, and time did not run out on a criminal when he died. George Neilson, in an article called Post-Mortem Trials, *wrote at the end of the nineteenth century that the dead continued to have status and even duties:*

Continental laws recognized acts of renounciation in which a widow laid the keys to their house on the husband's corpse, or tapped his grave with the point of a halberd. The body of a murdered person, or it might be just his hand, was sometimes carried before a judge to demand vengeance.

By English law of the thirteenth century legal possession of real estate was thought to remain in a man, not until he died, but until his body was carried out to funeral. The dead might be a very potent witness, as shown by the ordeal of "bier-right," a practice founded on the belief that the murderer's touch would cause the victim's wounds to bleed afresh.

An ancient chronicle recalls the strange scene enacted at the monastery of Caen in 1087, when William the Conqueror lay dead there, and the ceremonials of his interment were interrupted by a weird appeal. Ascelin, the son of Arthur, loudly claimed as his, neither sold nor given, the land on which the church stood, and forbidding the burial, he appealed to the dead to do him justice. The outcome of his plea is not recorded.

Death Is No Excuse

It had been a part of the border code, prevalent on the (frontier) marches of England and Scotland, that an accused should, although dead, be brought to the place of judgment in person. In 1249, the marchmen of both realms had declared the law in that sense. They said that in any plea touching life and limb, if the defendant died his body should be carried to the march on the day and to the place fixed between the parties, because—concludes this remarkable provision—"no man can excuse himself by death."

Sober Justice

Drunkenness has perplexed lawmakers and rulers from ancient times to the present day. At the great Festival of Dionysus in Athens and at the Bacchanalia in Rome it was considered bad form, and an insult to the god of wine, to remain sober. Prizes were awarded to those who could drink most. On the other hand, the punishment was doubled for crimes committed under the influence of alcohol. The Spartans made their slaves drunk one day a year to demonstrate to the owners' children how foolishly human beings behave when intoxicated. Lycurgus of Thrace ordered all vines to be uprooted. The Athenians made it a capital offense for a magistrate to be drunk. Charlemagne went further: he ordered that lawyers and judges should abstain from both food and drink while administering justice.

Simplicity

Lycurgus, the great lawgiver of ninth-century B.C. Sparta, claimed to have obtained his laws directly from the god Apollo. Lycurgus forbade foreign travel, except in the interest of the state, and excluded all foreigners, and foreign commerce as well, from the city. To maintain equality, he perpetuated poverty. Lycurgus reduced his laws to three fundamental prohibitions:

1. Not to resort to written laws.
2. Not to employ in housebuilding any other tools than the axe and saw.
3. Not to undertake military expeditions often against the same enemy.

Lawgiver

Solon, the Greek lawmaker, on being asked how wrongdoing can be avoided in a state, replied: "If those who are not wronged feel the same indignation at it as those who are."

The Twelve Tables

Three hundred years after the foundation of Rome (or around 453 B.C.), the Romans sent three deputies to Greece to make an exact compilation of the laws of Solon, the lawgiver of the Athenians. On their return, the Decemviri were elected, ten of the most distinguished citizens given sovereign authority to dispose these laws under proper heads, and propose them to the people. They were at first summed up in ten tables, but in the following year two more were added. Hence they were called "The Laws of the Twelve Tables"—the foundation of Roman jurisprudence.

That Leaves Only the Muddle in the Middle

The court of the Areopagites, as the supreme court of ancient Athens was called, enacted a law "that the orators who addressed them in criminal cases should neither in the beginning of the speeches, nor in the conclusion of them, use any rhetorical flourishes; because in those parts of their orations they could most easily introduce arguments to delude the understanding, and excite the passions of the audience."

Today We Have Jargon

The mad Roman emperor Caligula wrote his laws in very small letters, and had them hung up high on very tall pillars, in order to deceive his people.

Common Law

Common law dates back in England to the reign of Edward the Confessor. The Saxons, though divided into many kingdoms, were similar in their manners, laws, and languages. The differences that did exist between the Mercian law, the West Saxon law, and the Danish law, were removed by Edward with great facility, and without any dissatisfaction. He made his alteration famous by a new name rather than new matter: when abolishing the three distinctions mentioned above, he called it the Common Law of England.

1066 and All That

William the Conqueror abolished all the laws of England in order to introduce those of his own country: he ordained that lawyers plead in the Norman tongue, and all legislation was transacted in that language until the reign of Edward III. According to the French philosopher Voltaire, "William is falsely accused of affecting tyrannical caprices: they instance the law called *courvrefeu* or curfew. At the sound of a bell, all the fires at every house were extinguished at eight o'clock in the evening. But this law, far from being tyrannical, is no other than an old ecclesiastic regulation, established in almost all the ancient cloisters of the north. The houses were wholly built of wood, and the fear of fire was one of the most important objects of the general police."

Serving Two Masters

Judge George F. Lawton of Massachusetts told a story at the turn of the century about a minister friend of his going to Europe on a sabbatical. Upon arriving in London he made every effort to get an intimate view of the two branches of Parliament. As no strangers were allowed into the House of Lords, except the personal servants of the peers to deliver messages, the American minister was stopped by a doorkeeper, who asked:

"What lord do you serve?"

"What lord?" repeated the astonished clergyman. "Why the Lord Jehovah!"

For a moment the doorkeeper hesitated and then admitted him. And, turning to an assistant standing near, he commented:

"He must mean one of those poor Scotch lairds."

The Process

Justice Oliver Wendell Holmes recounted to Justice Felix Frankfurter his early days on the Supreme Court, and his sharp disagreements with Justice John Harlan. "I did lose my temper at something that Harlan said and sharply remarked, 'That won't wash! That won't wash!' At which point small, gentle, and silver-haired Chief Justice Melville Fuller intervened: 'Well, I'm scrubbing away. I'm scrubbing away.'"

At a later date, when Justice Holmes lost an argument, with Justice Butler carrying the rest of the court, the latter turned to Holmes and said solemnly: "Well, I'm glad we have arrived at a just decision." "Hell is paved with just decisions," replied Holmes, who was sometimes called the Great Dissenter.

Intense Labor

In the middle of the nineteenth century, after many years of debate among the best legal minds, the New York Code of Practice, governing the administration of justice in the state, was born. One of its architects was David Graham, Jr., who had so exhausted himself in the process that he died of it. During his final illness, an advocate who did not like the changes produced by the Code of Practice ran into one of the codifiers in the Supreme Court room in New York City:

Advocate: Do you know how Mr. Graham is?

Codifier: He is very ill—completely broken down. The code has ruined the health of all of us who were engaged upon it, the labor was so intense.

Advocate: I am not surprised, for it has made all the bar sick.

Look Around

The Roman historian Tacitus wrote in the first century A.D.:
Corruptissima republica, plurimae leges ("When the state is the most corrupt, then you have the most laws").

Spending

At the close of a parliamentary session, Queen Elizabeth I of England asked the Speaker of the House of Commons what its members had passed. "If it please Your Majesty," the lawmaker replied, "we have passed two months and a half."

Wise Blood

In 1950 Justice William O. Douglas visited some of the remote tribes of Iran and Iraq, including a village of the Bakhtiari called Oregon:

Morteza Gholi Khan and I sat on an exquisite Bakhtiari rug under the walnuts and talked of Bakhtiari customs and law. These tribes have a hierarchy of chiefs. The Ilkhan is the head chief, the leader of many tribes. Next in order comes the khan, and then the kalantar, kadkhoda and rish-safid. The latter is the elder or white beard of a clan or of a village.

The Kurds and the Lurs divide judicial functions between the khans on the one hand and the mullahs or priests on the other. The Bakhtiari, though very religious and devout Moslems, have no mullahs among them. The khans handle the matters which the mullah customarily administers; and, as among the other tribes, adjudicate all civil and criminal disputes or controversies besides. Their system of rewards and punishments differs in some details from that of the Kurds and Lurs, but in general the concept of justice is similar. There is one important difference. The Bakhtiari, like the Northern tribes, assess damages for manslaughter, the family of the killer being required to pay to the family of the deceased from $2,000 to $2,500 depending on the age and condition of the deceased. But the Bakhtiari do not stop there. They require the family of the killer to give a sister or daughter in marriage to a member of the family of the deceased. This custom goes back to immemorial days. Morteza Gholi Khan explained it this way. "The union of blood works in a mystic way. It washes away all desire for retaliation. The two warring families become peacefully united as one."

The Goat Strikes Back

The nomadic chieftain then told the American jurist about another, higher kind of justice:

He looked up and his eyes were searching me as he asked, "Do you believe in God?"

"Yes, I do."

"Will you believe a story if I tell it to you?" he asked. "I can't tell you unless you promise to believe it."

"I will believe it if you say it is true."

"It is true."

"Then I will believe it." There was a long pause as Morteza Gholi Khan put the pieces of his story together. When it came, the telling had the polish and forcefulness of Walter Hampden.

"It was the fall of the year, perhaps twenty-five years ago, and the tribes had started their migration south. Many groups had gone ahead; I was still at Shalamzar. Word came to me that there was trouble between two tribes. A dispute had arisen over some sheep. Hot words developed into a fight. One man was killed. Since he was killed while a large group of men were milling around, no one could be sure just who the killer was. The khans who were handling the case were troubled and perplexed. They could not decide whether or not the one accused was guilty.

"I sent word ahead to hold twenty men from each tribe including the accused; that I would be there in about a week.

"I reached there by horseback in six days. The khans and the twenty men from each of the two quarreling tribes were waiting for me at a village. Twenty men stood on one side of the road, twenty on the other. They remained standing while the khans and I had a consultation. As we were talking, a herd of goats came down the road. In the lead was a big billy, who led the other goats between the two rows of men.

"When the lead goat got opposite the man who was accused of the killing, he stopped for just a second. Then quick as a flash he put his head down and charged this man. It happened so quickly and unexpectedly that the goat caught the man off guard. He hit him in the stomach with a terrible thump. The man fell to the ground; his eyes rolled; and in just a few minutes he was dead."

Morteza Gholi Khan's voice had been loud as he acted out the drama of the goat and the man showed with gestures what had happened. Now his voice was hushed.

"When the men saw what had happened they fell on each other's necks and started kissing one another."

"Why did they do that?" I interposed.

"Why did they do that?" Morteza Gholi Khan said in a voice expressing surprise that I need to ask. "They did it because all of us who were there knew at once that God had appeared through a goat and done justice."

The Sicilian Caper

My friend John Hogarth, distinguished Canadian law professor and international authority on policing and sentencing, told me the following story to illustrate how the honor system continues to work even in a corrupt society:

I met Giuseppe Falcone at a conference in the mid-1980s in Vienna while researching a book on the laundering of money obtained through drug trafficking. He invited me at once to visit him in Sicily. As investigating magistrate in Palermo, Falcone had been responsible for the arrest and prosecution of three to four hundred of the leading figures in the Sicilian and Calabrian Mafia. His predecessor had been murdered, as had his closest collaborator, Palermo's chief of police. Three attempts had failed on his own life, including one by a hit team armed with bazookas. Falcone traveled everywhere with armed guards and yet nobody would have laid a bet that he'd live out the year.

I decided on a trip to Sicily during Easter holidays, with my teenage son, Adam, and in a brand new export model SAAB that I planned to take back to Canada at the end of my sabbatical. This was to be our first real spin in the car.

Security officers at the Canadian embassy in Rome thought it too dangerous to visit Falcone in Palermo without bodyguards, but none could be spared just then. They advised that we call the embassy every day, use false names on our luggage, and stay out of Palermo until the day of the interview with Giuseppe Falcone. There were other extraordinary security measures. I was given a certain number, upon phoning which I would be told where to go to receive another call, and then be picked up and taken to see him. Following the interview, we were to leave Palermo at once.

After a leisurely drive down and around the main cities of Sicily, we still ended up near Palermo four days ahead of schedule. We decided to take a hydrofoil to a nearby island and spend the next few days there. The one problem was what to do with the car? It seemed sensible to leave it in Palermo. So we made our first mistake by checking into the most expensive hotel in Palermo, which could only be owned by the Mafia.

We arrived at the hotel around two in the afternoon, and explained what we wanted to do with the car. They said they could not put it in the garage until the evening. In the meantime, they told me to park it across the street from the busy, grand circular entrance to the hotel.

We stayed indoors for the rest of the day. Dressing for dinner, I realized that my good shoes were still in the car. I asked Adam to run down and get them. He came back and said, "Dad, the car's gone." I ran outside and sure enough, the shiny new SAAB was nowhere to be seen. We asked people on the street if they had seen anything. No one spoke English.

After about an hour the police arrived. There was a man who could interpret between us. I learned that they didn't know anything and they didn't want to investigate. I was getting frustrated, so finally I said that I wanted to see Giuseppe Falcone. Uttering the name was like setting off a grenade.

My fourteen year-old son and I were arrested and immediately whisked off to the station by a swarm of uniformed and plainclothes police. How did we know Giuseppe Falcone? What were we doing in Palermo? I showed them a letter of introduction in Italian from the Canadian consul, and finally they phoned Falcone, who confirmed our appointment for three days later.

Meanwhile, the police captain explained that there was very little chance of getting the car back. A professional theft ring had probably switched the plates by now; in the morning it would be repainted and then be on its way to a customer perhaps in the Middle East. I was naturally upset both about the theft and our arrest. We were soon released and placed under round-the-clock protection, while I spent more than a day to get a friend in Rome to obtain the SAAB's chassis number from my apartment there. The search for the car continued, without success.

On our third morning in Palermo, a fleet of police cars with flashing blue lights came to pick us up at the hotel. Adam and I got into the back seat and were whisked through the city at high speed, surrounded by machine-gun toting police. Eventually we arrived at the station, and had a cappucino with the captain. I thanked him perfunctorily for his futile efforts. I told him we had a flight booked back to Rome. He kept looking at his watch, and finally said, "Piano, piano," which in Italian means "calm down, calm down." "Piano, piano," he repeated, "you return now to the hotel."

We had the same escort back. And there, in the circular driveway, right in front of a picturesque doorman, stood the SAAB. There wasn't a scratch on it. Opening the hatchback, I saw my dress shoes. But in place of a bag of dirty laundry that had been there, our clothes were now cleaned and neatly folded.

I had been in regular contact with the Canadian embassy in Rome and now called them up with the latest developments. When the security officer heard about the laundry, he said:

"Leave Palermo. At once. Leave immediately."

I didn't react, so he explained:

"You got a message from the Mafia that's one step down from a wrapped, dead fish. In their parlance, 'you messed up, we cleaned up; this is your last chance.'"

Adam and I screeched out of Palermo and did not stop to catch a breath until the Italian mainland.

I found out the details three months later, when I saw Giuseppe Falcone at another conference in Milan. While I was getting nowhere with the police, the magistrate called up the Mafia chief of Palermo, and said:

"A friend of mine is here to visit me. Please find out who took his car. I would like to have it returned."

There is this transcendent idea of courtesy within Sicilian society, even among mortal enemies. Such a request could not be refused. They had no choice but to return my car.

John Hogarth was lucky. In the April 1929 issue of The Bookman *I came across an article about Arthur Train, the famous lawyer and author, who had written a book about the Camorra, a sinister organization with the same aims and methods as the Mafia. In the article, Arthur Bartlett Maurice wrote:*

In 1910 Arthur Train went to Italy to study and write about the Camorra trials that were being held at Viterbo. He carried with him powerful letters of introduction to the Italian authorities. When his motor car reached the open square just outside of the city gates of Viterbo, it stopped, out of gas. Mr. Train left the car, walked across the almost deserted square and into the city to seek for the needed petrol. He returned to find a surging crowd of five thousand surrounding his car, which was in flames. The Camorra had been apprised of his coming and his mission and set fire to the car. In the conflagration went letters of introduction, passports, letter of credit and personal belongings. The only bit of paper salvaged was part of the charred manuscript of the first and unfinished draft of *Honor Among Thieves*.

SILLY LAWS

The Law Is an Ass

In 1897, the State of New York adjudged John Armstrong Chanler a lunatic and had him committed to Bloomingdale Asylum. He escaped and moved to Cobham, Virginia and changed his name to Chaloner. In 1901 he was judicially declared sane in the State of Virginia, which judgment was confirmed in 1908 by the United States Circuit Court of Appeals. This made him insane in New York, but legally competent in every other state of the Union. In 1909 Chaloner had a quarrel with a man named Gillard and killed him. Tried before a jury of Virginia farmers, he was acquitted. Later Chaloner coined the famous phrase: ''Who's looney now?''

Slander and Irony

During the reign of Charles II it was slanderous to call an Englishman a Papist or to say that he went to Mass; but it was held otherwise during the brief reign of his brother, James II, who was Catholic. Writing about libel and slander laws in the early 1930s, two American attorneys found a woman may be called a *hermaphrodite* with impunity in Tennessee but not in Ohio. One must beware where one says that a single woman is *fat*, for if the expression is the colloquial equivalent of *pregnant*, the woman may sue and recover. It is libelous to publish of a man that he is an arch hypocrite or a religious hypocrite, but not that he is a political hypocrite. In the eighteenth century *dunce* denoted a pedant; by the twentieth it became actionable to call a lawyer a dunce. Equally libellous would be to describe an attorney as a pettifogging shyster, or refer to him with irony as an *honest* lawyer.

Are You Blue?

Connecticut's early blue laws prohibited cooking and all housekeeping activities on the Sabbath. The Puritans were forbidden to eat mince pie, to travel, to have a haircut, to shave, to dance, to kiss the children, to cross a river, or to play a musical instrument except the drum, trumpet, or Jew's harp.

Thou Shalt Not

Since ignorance of the law does not grant immunity from penalties for breaking it, citizens need to know about the danger they are in. In a humorous little book called You Can't Eat Peanuts in Church and Other Little Known Laws, *Barbara Seuling cites the following curious prohibitions, many of which presumably may still be on the books. It is (or was at one time) illegal:*

- In Virginia to have a bathtub inside the house.
- In Minneapolis to install a bath tub without legs.

- In Nebraska for a woman to wave her daughter's hair without a state license.
- In Massachusetts for men to go to women's hairdressing salons for tinting or waving their hair.
- In Georgia to kiss in public.
- In Halethorpe, Maryland to kiss for longer than one second.
- In Norton, Virginia to tickle a girl.
- For a girl to phone a man for a date in Dyersburg, Tennessee.
- To sleep in the kitchen, if you are a resident of California.
- To keep oyster shells in your apartment in Boston.
- To wear a mask while shopping in Louisiana.

Louisiana also outlaws appearing drunk at a literary society, which seems to be a way of doing away with literary societies altogether.

The state of Illinois, on the other hand, technically forbids English: the statute was revised in 1919 to make American the official language of the state. This was partly due to the influence of journalist H.L. Mencken, whose work on *The American Language* later became a classic.

Don't Even Think of Breaking These Laws

Here are more silly laws culled from a variety of sources:

- A law in Maryland determined that six visits to a girl's home is the equivalent of a proposal of marriage.
- The city fathers of Santa Barbara used to forbid anyone to advertise for a spouse.
- One of the old laws on the books in Michigan holds that a husband owns his wife's clothes, and if she left his home, he had the right to follow her on the street and remove every stitch of said clothing.
- A Georgia law prescribed that a lifeguard must wear a bathing suit of bright solid red, with a leather harness around his neck, attached to a life line two hundred feet long.
- Another law in the same state declared, "anyone bathing in a stream or pond of water in view of a road or leading to a church on Sunday shall be guilty of a misdemeanor."
- The Mississippi Code (chapter 28, section 1296) stated that "any person shall not keep a stallion or jack nearer than one hundred yards to a church, or in public view in an enclosure bordering on a public highway, or nearer thereto than one hundred yards; nor shall any person stand such animals in open view of any public place, or negligently keep such an animal or suffer it to run at large . . ."

- The Kansas Revised Statutes, 1923, (21-2426) held it unlawful "for any person to exhibit in a public way within the State of Kansas, any sort of exhibition that consists of the eating or pretending to eat of snakes, lizards, scorpions, centipedes, tarantulas, or other reptiles."
- North Dakota (Compiled Laws 1913, Section 9998) declared that "every person who offers to sell any beef and fails to exhibit to the purchaser on demand the hide of the animal to be sold or sold, and does not keep such a hide for ten days after the sale, at his place of residence, or refuses to allow the same to be inspected by any person" to be subject to penalty.
- An Oklahoma law made it illegal to catch a whale in any of the inland waters of the state.
- In contrast, the California State Vehicle Act, (Chapter XVIII, para. 187) held it "a misdemeanor to shoot at any kind of game bird or mammal—except a whale—from an automobile or airplane."
- The same laid-back state of California introduced an act in 1935 "to prohibit marathons, marathon dances, walkathons, skateathons, and other mental or physical endurance contests," prescribing penalties for the violation thereof.
- Also in the 1930s, it was illegal in the movie capital to drive more than two thousand sheep down on Hollywood Boulevard at any one time.
- In the early days of motoring, the city of Tacoma, Washington passed a law that made it mandatory for motorists approaching the city limits to stop, telephone the chief of police and inform him that they were coming into Tacoma.
- The New York Penal Code law (section 2219) for a long time has held the view that "any person who arrests a dead man for debt is guilty of a misdemeanor."

Ah, Politics!

The Kansas legislature, trying to regulate the undesirable side effects of the horseless carriage, passed on March 13, 1903, laws regulating the use of automobiles. Chapter 67 opened thus:

BE IT ENACTED BY THE LEGISLATURE OF THE STATE OF KANSAS:

Section 1: That the term "automobile" and "motor vehicle" as used in this act shall be construed to include all types and grades of motor vehicles propelled by electricity, steam, gasoline, or other source of energy, commonly known as automobiles, motor vehicles, or horseless carriages, using the public highways and not running on rails or tracks. Nothing in this section shall be construed as in any way preventing, obstructing, impeding, embarrassing or in any other manner of form infringing upon the prerogative of any political chauffeur to run an automobilious band-wagon at any rate he sees fit compatible with the safety of the occupants thereof; provided however, that not less than ten nor more than twenty ropes be allowed at all times to trail behind this vehicle when in motion, in order to permit those who have been so fortunate as to escape with their political lives an opportunity to be dragged to death; and provided further, that whenever a mangled and bleeding political corpse implores for mercy, the driver of the vehicle shall, in accordance with the provisions of this bill, "Throw out the lifeline."

And More Politics

· The Kansas Revised Statutes (1923, Nos. 25-1703) declared it unlawful for any candidate for public office to give away cigars on election day.

· The State of Virginia Code of 1930, (section 252) prohibited "corrupt practices or bribery by any person other than candidates." After all, the lawmakers who passed that law were all candidates once.

How to Prevent a Silly Law

In the 1930s the state of Georgia proposed a luxury tax of two hundred fifty dollars per year on bachelors. It did not even have the merit of being a new idea. In The Percy Anecdotes, *published in London in 1820, one finds the following curious item:*

A bill having been brought into the House of Legislature of New York, to lay a tax upon all bachelors above the age of twenty-eight, for the encouragement of literature among females, a meeting of upwards of two hundred old bachelors, and others, approximating to that state, was held, to take the measure into consideration. After a good deal of fine speaking, and many witty observations, the oldest bachelor in the room was called to the chair, when the following recital and resolutions were offered, and passed unanimously.

"WHEREAS it appears by the public papers, that a bill has been introduced into the legislature of this state, to lay a tax upon bachelors, etc. In what manner the funds are to be applied, whether for the endowment of a seminary, in which old maids are to be employed as instructors, or whether to educate old maids in some of the useful and polite branches of literature, that they may be enabled to get a living without an helpmate, is unknown to us, not having seen the said bill, or its provisions; but whatever may be the provisions of the said bill, we conceive it unconstitutional to lay a specific tax upon old bachelors, and calculated to produce much mischief in the community; because it will drive from the state many good citizens who prefer a life of celibacy; it will tend to increase bachelors, inasmuch as when women find they can be maintained in a single state, many will prefer that mode of life, and refuse all offers of matrimony; it will cause many bachelors to conceal their ages, and thereby lead them to tell untruths, which otherwise they never would have thought of; it will cause old maids to be ten times more intolerable than they usually are, by making them independent of husbands for a livelihood: it will have the effect to destroy that exquisite sensibility in men, who having lost their sweethearts by 'hook or crook,' have made pledge to do penance all their lives by living in a single state; it will lead many a man to enter into the holy bands of wedlock, without being guided by that bewitching and electable passion, love (so essentially necessary to connubial felicity), and hurry them to marry merely to save the tax, and consequently produce many unhappy matches; for no marriage can be productive of happiness, without love. For

> Love is a curious thing you know,
> It makes one feel all over so.

"It will excite to a retaliation on the part of bachelors, and cause them to use their influence to get a tax upon old maids, thereby bringing on a civil war between old maids and old bachelors, to the entire destruction of the peace of society, and there will be nothing to attend to but

> Hear the pretty ladies talk,
> Tittle tattle, tittle tattle.

"THEREFORE RESOLVED, that we will use our most earnest exertions to prevent the passing of the above named bill, which we consider unconstitutional, and fraught with the most alarming consequences to the peace and happiness of society.

"RESOLVED, that a committee be appointed to draft a memorial to the legislature, praying that the bill may never be passed, and to obtain the signatures of all persons who are opposed to its passage.

"RESOLVED, that should the said bill be thrown under the table, we pledge ourselves to unite in the holy bands of marriage, as soon as we can find pretty creatures that will have us.

"RESOLVED, that we deeply commiserate the unfortunate situation in which many old maids are placed, though we are sensible that some of them are like

> Jeremiah's figs—the good are very good;
> The bad, too sour to give the pigs.

"RESOLVED, that it be recommended to establish a House of Industry for old maids, and that old bachelors contribute toward their support, by giving them their linen to make, and their stockings to darn.

"RESOLVED, that the thanks of the meeting be given to the landlord for the use of the room.

IT WAS MOVED AND CARRIED, that a committee of five gentlemen be appointed to draft a memorial to the legislature.

"IT WAS ALSO MOVED AND CARRIED, that proceedings of the meeting be published in all the papers that will consent to do it without charge.

A. Wolkere, Chairman.

D.K.T. Smythe, Secretary

The infamous bill was withdrawn.

The Eyes of Texas Are Verboten

Abilene, Texas, passed a law in 1935 which in part read: "It shall be unlawful for any person to idle or loiter on any street or thoroughfare, sidewalk, or alley, or in any store, theater, motor car, motion picture show, business house, or in the entrance or doorway of any place within the corporate limits of the city of Abilene for the purpose of plying the avocation of a flirt or masher.

"It shall further be unlawful for any man to stare at or make googoo eyes at, or in any other manner look at or make remarks to or concerning, or cough or whistle at, or do any other act to attract the attention of any woman upon or travelling along any of the sidewalks, streets, public ways of the city of Abilene with an intent or in a manner calculated to annoy such woman."

The Freedom of the City

According to ordinance 25 (Section 1), in Corning, Iowa, it has been against the law "to speak to anyone passing along the street or sidewalk, and . . . for a man to ask his wife to ride in any motor vehicle."

The city of Columbia in Tennessee outlawed "three or more persons to assemble upon any of the sidewalks, so as to impede the free passage of persons upon the sidewalk."

And throughout Minnesota it used to be a criminal offense for a woman to impersonate Santa Claus on the street.

Stalemate
An old Kansas law mandated that "when two trains approach each other at a crossing, they shall both come to a full stop, and neither shall start up until the other has gone."

Why Communism Works
In the Soviet Union there may still be a law on the books that mandates trains, whenever they come upon a sleeping citizen on the track, to stop and wait until the comrade has finished his rest.

In the old days in Cuba when a person's house burned down, the owner was immediately arrested and jailed for three days.

Splitting Hairs
A Los Angeles ordinance banned the wearing of whiskers, "whether complete or partial."

The town of Waterloo in Nebraska passed an ordinance in 1910 which made it illegal for any barber to eat onions between 7 A.M. and 7 P.M.

An Alabama law declared that "wearing a false moustache in church which causes laughter will support a conviction."

Real Men Don't Shave
An ordinance in Centralia, Washington required every male resident to let his beard grow between June 28 and August 4.

The town of Brainerd, Minnesota compelled its male citizens to grow a beard all year round, the only exception to be made in the case where the citizen was unable to do so.

And the Truth Shall Make You Free
In 1893 the U.S. Supreme Court ruled that the tomato was a vegetable, not a fruit.

No Complaints So Far

Omaha, Nebraska came up with an ordinance (Sections 14-802) which stated that the city clerk must be notified five days before the occurrence of an injury caused by defective public ways or sidewalks or the claimant cannot recover damages from the city.

STRANGE WILLS

Pay Now, Die Later

When Montaigne, the great French essayist, felt he was dying, he rose from his bed in his nightshirt and, throwing round him a dressing gown, opened his secretaire, called all his valets and servants and such other legatees as he had named in his will, and paid to each one of them, then and there, bequests he had left them, thus forestalling any difficulties his executors might raise against satisfying them after his death.

Montaigne died on the 13th September, while Mass was being celebrated in his room, and at the very moment of the elevation of the Host.

A Sense of Fun

Rabelais, the French scatological satirist, included in his will, dated 1553, the famous sentence: "I have no available property; I owe a great deal; the rest I give to the poor."

A certain Smith Willie, a Pennsylvanian gentleman who died in 1880, appointed as executors of his will "a jury of honor consisting of all the householders in his native town, who can prove that they came honestly by their fortunes; each to receive for his trouble the sum of two hundred dollars."

What he wanted executed was no less difficult. Mr. Willie wrote:

"Seeing that I have no direct descendants, and that I am wholly unacquainted with those I may possess collaterally, I bequeath my fortune to any one among them who, in the course of a twelvemonth from the date of my death, may distinguish himself by an act of heroism worthy of ancient times.

"In case none of my collateral descendants should be justified in making this claim, I then leave all I possess to be divided between all women who can prove that they have been my mistresses, be it for ever so brief a period."

Or What You Will

According to John Proffatt, a nineteenth-century authority on wills:

The will of Shakespeare, executed on March 25th, 1616, not quite a month prior to his death, forms a most interesting document for the scholar, as well as the lawyer. It is registered in Doctors' Commons verbatim as it was written, and is prized as a unique and interesting document relating to the poet. It is written in the usual clerical hand of the period, on three sheets of paper, fastened at the top. Each sheet is signed by the poet, the final signature, "By me, William Shakespeare," being the most distinct.

In one item he gives a bequest to his sister Joan:

"I give and bequeath unto my said sister Joan twenty pounds, and all my wearing apparel, to be paid and delivered within one year after my decease; and I do will and devise unto her the house with the appurtenances in Stratford wherein she dwelleth, for her natural life, under the yearly rent of twelve pence."

In another item Shakespeare gives to the poor of Stratford ten pounds; to Mr. Thomas Combe his sword; to his daughter Judith his "broad silver gilt bowl." He left to his daughter, Susanna Hall, his landed property in Stratford, limited to the first or other sons of her body after her life. One clause interlined in the will has occasioned a good deal of marvel and censorious criticism—the bequest to his wife, who has been represented as cut off by him, not indeed with a shilling, but with an old bed:

"I give unto my wife my second best bed with the furniture." It is said the object of the poet in leaving the bulk of his property to Mrs. Hall was evidently to found a family, the darling object of Shakespeare's ambition. But as she was entitled in law to dower out of his real estate, Shakespeare may not have deemed it necessary to make any further bequest to his wife than that of the second-best bed, as a special mark of affection. It must be admitted, however, that making full allowance for her provision by right of law there still remains a feeling of dissatisfaction with the total exclusion of Anne Shakespeare from all parts of her husband's will, with the exception of an interlined clause of a dozen words. It is also a significant fact that, with the exception of the bed, no household furniture is bequeathed to the widow; so that she must have been left dependent on her daughters for lodging and residence.

No Nonsense

Many wills reflect the singular notions, the eccentricities and prejudices of the makers (writes John Proffatt in his 1877 book about *The Curiosities and Law of Wills*). In many cases, the testator speaks his mind so freely that his opinion of others really amounts to a libel; again his antipathies or his affections are as freely exhibited; while the instances are not rare in which he bequeaths to posterity the benefit of his religious opinions.

Testators often give directions as to the place and manner of burial, as well as the expenses of their funeral pageant. In one case cited by the *Illustrated London News* (October 18th, 1873), a testator desired to be buried in a space between the graves of his first and second wives. Mr. Zimmerman, whose will was proved in 1840, in England, accompanied the directions for his funeral with something like a threat in case they were not carried out. In his will he says: "No person is to attend my corpse to the grave, nor is any funeral bell to be rung; and my desire is to be buried plainly and in a decent manner; and if this be not done, I will come again—that is to say, if I can."

The countess dowager of Sandwich, in her will written by herself at the age of eighty, proved in November 1862, expressed her wish to be buried decently and quietly: "no undertakers' frauds, or cheating; no scarfs, hat bands, or nonsense."

Generosity

Pinedo, a Portugese Jewish merchant who lived in Amsterdam and died there in the middle of the eighteenth century, had spent much of his immense wealth on philanthropic causes. His will reflected an ecumenical liberality:

I bequeath to the city of Amsterdam the sum of five tons of gold. [A ton was the equivalent of 100,000 florins, and much more than that in dollars.]

I lend to the said city for ten years, and without interest, the sum of a million and a half florins.

I give to every Christian church at Amsterdam and at The Hague the sum of ten thousand florins each, and to the church in the southern quarter of Amsterdam twenty thousand florins.

I give to each Christian orphanage in the two towns the sum of ten thousand crowns.

I give to the poor of Amsterdam forty shiploads of peat.

I give to the orphan who shall first quit the orphanage one thousand florins, and to the one who shall succeed him six hundred florins.

I give to the synagogue at Amsterdam two and a half tons of gold.

I give to the Portuguese orphanage thirty thousand crowns.

I lend to the Government at three per cent interest, ten tons of gold on condition that the interest shall be paid to Jews domiciled at Jerusalem: the capital to belong to the Government in perpetuity.

I give to the German synagogue five thousand florins.

I give to my nephew Ovis thirty-one tons of gold, with all my houses and appurtenances.

I give to my widow ten tons of gold.

I give to my other relations in equal portions ten thousand crowns.

I give to each of my neighbors who shall assist at my funeral one hundred ducats.

I give to every unmarried person of either sex who shall be present at my burial one hundred florins, and to every Christian priest in Amsterdam and at The Hague one hundred crowns, and to every sacristan fifty crowns.

Bitterness

William Pym, an English gentleman of Woolavington, Somerset, made out his will on January 10th, 1608. After various charitable bequests, he proceeds:

> I give to Agnes, which I did a long time take for my wife—till she denied me to be her husband, although we were married with my friends' consent, her father, mother, and uncle at it; and now she sweareth she will neither love me nor ever be persuaded to by preachers, nor by any other, which hath happened within these few years. And Toby Andrews, the beginner, which I did see with my own eyes when he did more than was fitting, and this by means of others their abettors. I have lived a miserable life this six or seven years, and now I leave the revenge of God—and ten pounds to buy her a great horse, for I could not this many years please her with one great enough.

Two years after writing this bitter record of his wrongs, William Pym, gent., gave up the ghost, and his last wishes were faithfully carried out by his two executors.

When There's a Will

Senator Sam Ervin told one of his many stories set in his native North Carolina. Marshall Bell, a lawyer practicing at Murphy, the county seat of Cherokee County, was retained to effect the sale of a lot that a parishioner had left to his church. When he examined the title deed, Bell discovered to his consternation that instead of transferring the lot to the church or its trustees, it conveyed it to "God Almighty, his heirs and assigns in fee simple."

Shortly after this discovery Bell encountered Judge Stacy on

Fayetteville Street in Raleigh and confessed his inability to fathom the legal steps necessary to consummate the sale.

With a grin on his face and a twinkle in his eye, Judge Stacy assured him, "Brother Bell, you have a simple legal remedy for your problem. All you've got to do is to bring a suit against God Almighty in the superior court of Cherokee County to quit title to the lot, show by affidavit to the satisfaction of the court that God Almighty cannot be found in Cherokee County, and serve Him with summons by publication."

Last Will—Not Quite

A well-known Budapest lawyer at the turn of the century, Károly Eötvös, was taken to court by a client of long standing. The case was eventually settled amicably, but this is how it started. A wealthy widow fell ill and urgently summoned Eötvös to her bedside to make out a new will. The lawyer never made housecalls, but because she had been his client for so long, he drove with a clerk to her elegant villa in the hills of Buda.

The old woman had about forty thousand gold crowns of which to dispose. She started dictating:

"I wish to leave five thousand to my brother."

The clerk's quill pen scratched the sentence on the form.

"I wish to leave a thousand to my faithful maidservant, Mari."

"What else?" asked the lawyer, as his assistant wrote down the bequest.

"I bequeath two thousand crowns to the Church to say Masses for my soul."

"All right," said the clerk, noting it down.

There was silence.

"What else?" asked Eötvös, somewhat impatiently. But the old matron looked at him surprised:

"What d'you mean, what else? That's it."

"I don't think these bequests amount to one quarter even of forty thousand. That's why I'm asking who else you wish to leave the rest of your money."

"You don't think I'm going to let them rob me of everything?" The client's vital signs were growing stronger with her indignation. But the lawyer's rage also grew:

"What are you talking about? Who's going to rob you? What's going to happen to the rest of the money—that's what I want to know!"

"What?" the old lady burst out bitterly: "And am I not going to have anything left for myself . . .?"

· 9 ·

THE WEIGHT OF TRADITION

THE DRESS CODE

Deep Pockets

The gown of an English barrister has traditionally a fold in the back, in memory of the original pocket into which his fees were dropped. The counsel was not supposed to be able to see it. He could not sue for his fee in an English court, as it was an honorarium for his services and was usually placed into his gown pocket before he undertook the pleading. If the barrister chose to retain the fee, but not carry out his obligation, no power could bring him to book for such an offense.

Wig and Gown

Evidence of the clerical origin of lawyers still survives in the circular orifice in the center of the British judge's wig, all that remains of the monastic and clerical tonsure. Serjeants-at-law derive their name (via the French *frères serjens*) from the Latin *fratres servientes* of the Knights Templars. The coif on a serjeant's wig was originally introduced to hide the tonsure of such renegade clergy as were still tempted to remain in the secular courts, after the Church prohibited them from practicing there. It was designed to cover the tonsure, sometimes called the *corona clericalis*; because the crown of the head was close shaved, and a border of hair left round the lower part, which made it look like a crown.

Antiquarian George Williamson explained in 1925 that, as part of the same ecclesiastical heritage, the full ceremonial robes of the courts were worn on the great saints' days:

"When a judge wears red, he sits representing the sovereign power, but when he wears black, in the *nisi prius* courts, he is only an official settling disputes. The cap which the judge assumes when he passes sentence of death is just part of his ordinary full-dress costume, and is placed on his head in order that when he is executing the most serious part of his duties, he may be shown in his full robes. The judges wear their black caps also on the occasion when they receive the Lord Mayor. The sign of covering the head when condemnation is being carried out is also a very ancient sign of mourning, and takes us back to remote antiquity, because Demosthenes speaks of covering his head when he was insulted by the populace, and in scripture we frequently hear of the head being covered on such occasions. King David had his head covered, Haman covered his head, and Jews still cover their heads in the synagogue, or taking the oath in a court of justice and as a sign of reverence."

A Matter of Interpretation

South Carolina kept many of the old rules of the English courts to the end of the nineteenth century. Just before they were changed, James L. Pettigrue, one of the leading members of the bar, challenged the tradition that required attorneys to wear "a black gown and coat" in court. As soon as he stood to speak, the judge interrupted him:

"Mr. Pettigrue, you have on a light coat. You cannot speak, sir."

"May it please the court, Your Honor," Pettigrue replied, "I conform to the law."

"No, Mr. Pettigrue, you have on a light coat. The court cannot hear you."

"But, Your Honor," the lawyer insisted, "you misinterpret. The law says that a barrister must wear 'a black gown and coat,' does it not?"

"It certainly does," said the judge.

"And does Your Honor hold that both the gown and the coat must be black?"

"Certainly, Mr. Pettigrue, certainly, sir."

"And yet it is also provided by law," Pettigrue continued, "that the sheriff must wear 'a cocked hat and sword,' is it not?"

"Yes, yes," the judge replied impatiently.

"And does the court hold," Pettigrue went on calmly, "that the sword must be cocked as well as the hat?"

"Eh—er—h'm," mused His Honor, "you—er—may continue your speech, Mr. Pettigrue."

A Scottish Tale

Robbie Johnson was Provost of Dundee in 1769. His services being required on a certain occasion, a messenger was dispatched to his house, where he was told by the Provost's good wife that her husband was "awa to the whin hill for a pockfu' o' whins." The messenger went off to the whin hill, and soon the Provost appeared. Throwing down his load, he pulled off his bonnet, and wiping his bald pate, said:

"Janet, where's ma wig? I'm tae sit in judgment the day."

"Your wig! Did I ever hear sic a man! Your wig! Hoo can ye hae your wig? D'ye no ken the hen's layin' in it?"

His Own Petard

Samuel Rogers, the banker-poet, tells the story of Lord Ellenborough when he was about to go on the circuit and Lady Ellenborough said that she should like to accompany him. He replied that he had no objections, provided she did not encumber the carriage with bandboxes, which were his utter abhorrence. They set off. During the first day's journey, Lord Ellenborough, happening to stretch his legs, struck his feet against something below the seat. He discovered that it was a bandbox. His indignation is not to be described. Up went the window, and out went the bandbox. The coachman stopped, and the footmen, thinking that the bandbox had tumbled out of the window by some extraordinary chance, were going to pick it up, when Lord Ellenborough furiously called out, "Drive on!" The bandbox accordingly was left by a ditch-side.

Having reached the county town where he was to officiate as judge, Lord Ellenborough proceeded to array himself for his appearance in the courthouse. "Now," said he, "where's my wig—where *is* my wig?"

"My lord," replied the attendant, "it was thrown out of the carriage window."

Something Was Awry

A judge's wig was somewhat awry, causing titters in court. "Curran," asked the judge of the famous barrister, "do you see anything ridiculous in this wig?"

"Nothing but the head, my lord," Curran replied.

Stinginess

Chief Justice Kenyon was curiously economical about the adornment of his head. It was observed for a number of years before he died that he had two hats and two wigs—of the hats and the wigs one was dreadfully old and shabby, the other comparatively spruce. He always carried into court with him the very old hat and the comparatively spruce wig, he shoved his hat under the bench, and displayed his wig; but on the days of the very old wig and the comparatively spruce hat, he always continued covered. He might often be seen sitting with his hat over his wig, but the Rule of Court by which he was governed on this point is doubtful.

Lord Kenyon's shoes were patched to such an extent that little of their original material could be seen, and once when trying a case he was sitting on the bench in a way to expose them to all in court. It was an action for a breach of contract to deliver shoes soundly made, and to clinch a witness for the prosecution, the judge suddenly asked: "Were the shoes anything like these?" pointing to his own. "No, my lord," the witness replied, "they were a good deal better and more genteeler."

The Ultimate Secret

Lord Erskine used to say that when the hour came that all secrets should be revealed, we should know the reason why shoes are always made too tight.

Defeat Snatched from the Jaws of Victory

John Marshall presented the appearance of a plain countryman, rather than a chief justice of the United States. He had a farm in Fauquier County, Virginia and another near Richmond, and he would often return from the latter to take his seat on the bench with burrs sticking to his clothes. A bet was once made that the judge could not dress himself without exhibiting some mark of carelessness. He good-humoredly accepted the wager. A supper was to be given him; if his dress was found to be faultlessly neat upon that occasion, the parties offering the wager were to pay for the entertainment. But if they detected any carelessness in his attire, the expense was to fall upon him.

The guests and the judge met at the time and place agreed upon, and to the surprise of all, the judge's dress seemed faultless. The supper followed, Judge Marshall being in high spirits over his victory. Near the close of the repast, however, one of the guests who sat next to him chanced to drop his napkin. Stooping down to pick it up, he discovered that the judge had put on one of his stockings with the wrong side out. Of course the condition of affairs was immediately changed, and amidst the uproarious laughter of his companions, the chief justice acknowledged his defeat.

Dressed for Success

One morning at the beginning of his practice as a lawyer found John Marshall strolling through the streets of Richmond, Virginia, dressed in a plain linen suit and a straw hat. The hat was held under his arm, and was filled with cherries, from which he ate as he walked. In passing the Eagle Hotel he stopped to exchange salutations with the landlord, and then continued his walk.

Sitting near the landlord, on the hotel porch, was a Mr. P., an elderly gentleman from the country, who had come to the city to engage counsel in an important case that was to be tried in a day or two. The landlord referred him to Marshall as the best lawyer in the city, but the old gentleman was so much prejudiced against the young advocate, on account of his careless appearance, that he refused to hire him. On entering court, Mr. P. was a second time referred to Marshall by the clerk of the court, and a second time he refused the recommendation. At this moment entered Mr. V., a venerable-looking legal gentleman, in a powdered wig and black coat, whose dignified appearance produced such an impression on Mr. P. that he engaged him at once.

In the first case that came on, Marshall and Mr. V. each addressed the court. The vast inferiority of the well-dressed advocate was so apparent that at the close of the other case Mr. P. introduced himself to young Marshall and frankly stated the prejudice that had caused him, in opposition to advice, to employ Mr. V. He extremely regretted the error, he said, but did not know how to remedy it. He had come to the city with one hundred dollars as his lawyer's fee, which he had paid, and had but five left, which, if Marshall chose, he would cheerfully give him for assisting in the case. Marshall, pleased with the incident, accepted the offer, not however without passing a sly reference to the omnipotence of a powdered wig and black coat.

Dressed to Kill

Even though most lawyers dress conservatively, some trial lawyers especially carefully consider their costume as part of their courtroom performance. William Howe, the senior partner of the famed and feared New York firm of Howe and Hummel a hundred years ago, wore clothes that matched other Broadway personalities of the era, such as "Diamond Jim" Brady. In his New Yorker *profile Richard H. Rovere paints this portrait:*

"Old Bill" Howe was a stocky man weighing nearly three hundred pounds, with closely cropped white hair and moustache—pompous, gruff and with immense self-assurance. But apart from his versatility in the tricks of the legal trade, his face was not so much his fortune as his costume. He wore it, I suppose, in part to advertise himself and in part because it was his idea of elegance. Did not Mark Twain habitually wear a white Panama suit even in London?

Howe's personal application of the famous maxim of Polonius resulted in an appearance like nothing else on earth—a cross between Coney Island barker and costermonger. In imitation, it was said of Commodore Perry, he always wore a blue yachting cap, sometimes a navigator's blue coat and white trousers, but more often a loudly checked brown suit, with low-cut vest, displaying the starched bosom of a bright pink shirt, and a pink collar innocent of tie, in place of which he sported a gigantic diamond stud, with others of equal size adorning his chest. These he changed on occasion to pearls in the afternoon. Diamonds glittered upon his fingers; on his feet were either yachting shoes or dinky patent leathers with cloth uppers; in his lapel a rose or carnation; in his breast pocket a huge silk handkerchief into which he shed, with enormous effect, showers of crocodile tears while defending his clients.

The Nude Judge
E. S. P. Haynes (1877-1949), the English solicitor who published anonymously The Lawyer's Notebook *and other delightful collections, recalls a strange encounter:*

I have particularly pleasant memories of Judge Bacon, with whom for many years I conversed every Monday evening in the hottest room of a Turkish bath in the Harrow Road. In this congenial climate his always pungent remarks on human affairs and litigation in Whitechapel and elsewhere and excellent anecdotes about his beloved father (the famous Vice-Chancellor) beguiled many an hour of intensive perspiration.

One day I passed in the street an old gentleman who stared hard at me and then indignantly asked why I pretended not to know him. I timidly confessed that I did *not* know him and he announced that he was no less a person than Judge Bacon! I had to excuse my ignorance by pointing out that I had never before seen him in his clothes, for I had never appeared in his Court or seen him anywhere except in the nude!

Headgear
On October 31st, 1946 the London Evening News *reported that a man calling himself*

"His Majesty Wladyslaw, fifth King of Hungary and Poland and other territories," wearing long purple robes, was ordered by Judge Earengey,

K.C., at Clerkenwell County Court to remove his crown. He declined to do so and was told he would not be heard.

Under the name of G.V. Potocki he had been sued for arrears of rent by the landlords of premises at Peter-street, Islington.

He was applying for amendment of the particulars so as to describe him as "Count Geoffrey Wladyslaw Varle Potocki of Monteith," in conformity with his rent-book, national identity card, and former British passport.

"Count Potocki" wore a purple beret when he came into court, but just before the judge took a seat he removed the beret and disclosed a crown.

"We appear in person," announced Count Potocki.

Judge Earengey: "I cannot allow headgear of this sort. In this court every man has to appear uncovered—a soldier or anyone else."

Count Potocki then left the court.

QUAINT AND CURIOUS

Ancient Rites

On one occasion of his being in London, eighteenth-century Scottish judge Lord Monboddo attended a trial in the Court of King's Bench. A cry was heard that the roof of the courtroom was giving way, upon which judges, lawyers, and people made a rush to get to the door. Lord Monboddo viewed the scene from his corner with much composure. Being deaf and shortsighted, he knew nothing of the cause of the tumult. The alarm proved a false one; and on being asked why he had not bestirred himself to escape like the rest, he coolly answered that he supposed it was an annual ceremony with which, as an alien to the English laws, he had no concern, but he considered it interesting to witness as a remnant of antiquity.

Of Bar and Bench

Certain courts of law are still known as the Courts of King's Bench (wrote George Williamson in his fascinating book *Curious Survivals*), although the judges are given a more convenient seat than the wooden bench upon which they were wont to sit, but the word "bench" is still applied to magistrates sitting in session, because originally they all sat on one long narrow bench. In front of it, some little distance down the court, was a wooden barrier, called a bar, which separated the superior from the lower pleaders; the more important barristers sat within the bar, and were termed Inner Barristers, and those who were less important were without the barrier, and were termed Outer Barristers, a phrase that still continues in the local word *utter*, and certain proceedings in the Law Courts are still declared to be "in banco," the phrase referring to the bench on which the judges sat. When the courts sat "in banco" the judges occupied their respective benches.

The Lord Keep 'Er—Both of 'Em

The Great Seal of England (according to various antiquarian sources) is the signet of the Lord Chancellor, also known as the Lord Keeper. He is the head of both the judicial and the legislative system in the kingdom, being also president of the House of Lords. Although English monarchs have usually had but one seal at a time, it has been the custom since time immemorial to speak of the Lord Chancellor as "holding the seals." Ambitious lawyers were spoken of as candidates "for the seals," and those who realized their ambition, as having "won the seals."

Voltaire, in his *Philosophical Dictionary*, mentions as public knowledge that Chancellor Cowper married two wives, "who lived together in his house in such singular harmony that did credit to all three of them. Many of the curious still possess the little book that the Lord Chancellor had composed in defense of polygamy." Commenting on this, one wag asserts that "it appears that Frenchmen maintain that the custodian of the Great Seal of England was called the 'Lord Keeper,' because by English law he was permitted to keep as many wives as he pleased."

Adventures of the Great Seal

The history of the Great Seal is indelibly stamped with the fortunes of England, as chronicled by John Cordy Jeaffreson in A Book About Lawyers *(1867):*

Kings who had occasion to travel in foreign lands not infrequently had two great seals, one to be used by the king on his travels, the other for the use of the chancellor entrusted with the conduct of affairs at home. When Richard I started for Palestine on the Crusades, he left the government of his realm to Chancellor Longchamp, and took with him the Great Seal, under the custody of Vice-Chancellor, or Keeper, Malchien. Proud of his office, and obeying the usage of the time, Keeper Malchien always bore the Seal round his neck, to the great admiration of the vagrant and chivalric courtiers. Off Cyprus the good man had the ill luck to topple overboard into the sea and to be drowned, together with the bauble under his charge. Whether Malchien could swim, or whether the weight of the Seal and its chain rendered vain his efforts for self-preservation, the record is silent.

Charles I's first Great Seal also found a watery grave, in the Severn, where it was thrown to prevent it from falling into the hands of Cromwell's soldiers. James II made away with his Great Seal in 1688. When the foolish, fallen king, disguised and full of fears, stole from Whitehall on the night of December 10 and entered a hackney coach, the Great Seal was in his pocket. Clattering over uneven ways, the humble carriage passed through dark and dangerous streets to the horse-ferry at Westminster. At that point the fugitive dismissed the driver and made the transit of the river in a boat rowed by a single sculler. Half the passage was accomplished when the sovereign drew forth the seal and dropped it beneath the gloomy surface of the water. But the grave surrendered its victim. William of Orange used this same seal in the first business of his reign. The exact day of its recovery is unknown; but a fortunate fisherman caught it in his net, and, after his surprise had subsided, bore it in triumph to the lords of the council, who in due course placed it in the hands of the Deliverer. It was used until 1690, when a new Great Seal, adorned with the likenesses of William and Mary was substituted for the late king's device.

A strange accident befell George III's third Great Seal at Encombe, in the autumn of 1812. Eldon was then Lord Chancellor, and was staying at his country seat when part of the house was destroyed by a nighttime fire. The fire engine was at work, and Lady Eldon's maidservants were help-ing to supply it with water. "It was," wrote Lord Eldon, "really a very pretty sight; for all the maids turned out of their beds, and they formed a line from the water to the fire engine, handing the buckets; they looked very pretty, all in their shifts." (From which it is evident that Eldon, with all his stupidity and gruffness, had an eye for beauty.) But before the Chancellor found time to survey the maidservants with approval, he had provided for the safety of the Great Seal, which he was accustomed to keep in his bedchamber. At the first alarm of fire the Chancellor hastened out of doors with the Great Seal, and burying it in a flower bed, confided it to the care of mother earth. That prudent act accomplished, he ran to the aid of his maidservants. But when morning came, and the sun looked down on the damaged mansion, it occurred to Eldon that it was time for him to recover the seal from its undignified concealment. He bustled off to the long terrace where he had buried the treasure; but on arriving there, to his chagrin and alarm, he found that he omitted to mark the exact spot of the interment. He sought counsel of Lady Eldon, and by her advice the same maidservants who had figured so picturesquely by firelight, together with the entire staff of gardeners, were provided with spades, shovels, trowels, pokers, tongs, curling-irons, old umbrellas, and other suitable implements, and were ordered to probe old mother earth in the region of the long terrace, until she delivered up the "pestiferous metal" that had been committed to her in trust. "You never saw anything so ridiculous," observed his lordship, "as seeing the whole family down that walk probing and digging till we found it."

Recognition Scene

The Great Seal also became a semi-humorous name for the holder of the office. Sir Richard Bethell, the attorney general, ran into Lord Campbell, then chief justice, in Westminster Hall at about the time that rumors were rampant about Lord Campbell's elevation to the chancellorship (1859). The day was unusually cold for the time of year, and Lord Campbell had gone down to the House of Lords in a fur coat. Bethell saw him and pretended not to recognize him, whereupon Campbell came up to him and asked:

"Mr. Attorney, don't you know me?"

"I beg your pardon, my lord," was Bethell's reply, "I mistook you for the Great Seal."

Invitation

And not long after Thomas Erskine became Lord Chancellor and Keeper of the Seal, he was invited to the traditional Whitebait Dinner at Greenwich. Erskine wrote back: "To be sure I will attend. What would your fish dinner be without the Great Seal?"

Woolly Thinking

Traditionally the Lord Chancellor of England, when presiding over the House of Lords, is said to "sit on the woolsack." Similarly, a new Chancellor is "appointed to the woolsack." This is more than a metaphor. The woolsack actually refers to a large square bag of wool, covered with a red cloth and resembling a cushioned ottoman, which stands in the center of the hall of the Upper House in front of the canopied thrones of the monarch and his or her consort. The tradition dates back to the reign of the first Elizabeth, when Parliament passed an act forbidding the export of wool, and to remind legislators of the importance of this national treasure, the House of Peers was provided with sacks of wool for the judges to sit upon.

Horseshoes and Nails

It may have been during the reign of Alfred the Great (871-901), that the Port-Reeve became firmly established. *Port* in this case meant *city*. Just as the Shires had their courts of law, so did the City of London have its courts. The County Court of the Shire appeared as the Court of Husting in the City, while the Hundred Court of the Shire found its counterpart in the Wardmoot of the City. Wardmoots are still held once a year in the various Wards of the City, when the occupants and the taxpayers can elect their representatives on the Court of Common Council for the coming year.

Although the City sheriffs are elected by the liverymen, their appointment has to be approved by the Crown, and there is a very picturesque ceremony in connection with official procedure on these occasions. The ceremony (as described by Bernard O'Donnell in 1951) is connected with an old tenure custom originating in 1237 when the sheriffs of the City were granted a piece of land from one Walter de Bruin, a farrier who had bought it from the king for the purpose of building a forge. The land was situated in the County of Salop, and Walter made payment of six horseshoes and sixty-one nails. The forge no longer exists, of course, and the land has long since passed from the possession of the Corporation of London, but the ceremony still goes on.

In olden days it was performed on the occasion when the sheriffs of London and Middlesex attended the Court of Exchequer, and the Crier of the Court made the ancient proclamations. These days it is carried out by the City Solicitor before the King's Remembrancer at his office in the Royal Courts of Justice in the Strand. (The King's Remembrancer, who is also the senior master of the Supreme Court, is the official keeper of records of important papers and documents on behalf of the sovereign.)

After formal approval of the elected sheriffs has been given by the king, the City Solicitor attends upon the King's Remembrancer, and the quaint ceremony begins. First comes a proclamation by the City Solicitor.

"Oyez! Oyez! Oyez!" he cries, "Tenants and occupiers of a piece of waste ground called 'The Moore' in the County of Salop, come forth and do your service, upon pain and peril that shall fall thereon."

He then takes a hatchet and cuts a faggot (a bunch of small twigs) and with a billhook cuts a second faggot.

Next, he makes a similar proclamation calling upon the "tenants and occupiers of a certain tenement called 'The Forge' in the parish of St. Clement Danes in the County of Middlesex," bidding them come forward to do service, as before, and then tenders the horse-shoes and nails specially kept for that occasion.

"How many have you?" asks the King's Remembrancer, to which the City Solicitor replies, "Six shoes."

"Good number," remarks Mr. Remembrancer, and then asks, "How many nails have you?"

"Sixty-one," is the solemn reply, and again Mr. Remembrancer replies, "Good number." And the seven-and-half-century-old ceremony is over for another twelve months.

Sheriffs

The office of the sheriff is the oldest in England, and the Sheriff's Court is a survival of the most ancient court of law. Under various titles, sheriffs have presided over courts from Anglo-Saxon days. According to legal antiquarian Bernard O'Donnell, traces of the office are found as far back as the seventh century. In a document of Athelstan's reign (924-940), there is reference to *reeves* being appointed to carry out certain duties in connection with districts called *scirs*, although the first real mention of the *shire-reeve* (from which our word *sheriff* was corrupted) does not appear until about 1018 in the reign of King Canute. *Shire-reeve* was derived from the Old English *scir-gerefa*, meaning bailiff or manager, but Canute invested his *shire-reeves* with powers of jurisdiction very similar to those exercised by the Anglo-Norman sheriffs that came after the Conquest.

Reeves existed in the seventh century, and were the headmen of the *vils* and townships. In the reign of King Eadric of Kent (673-688), if a Kentish citizen went to London to buy cattle, he could only do so lawfully if he was accompanied by a Kentian reeve, who was responsible for keeping the peace in his jurisdiction. The *shire-reeve* wielded greater powers. He took over the duties of the *ealdorman*, or alderman, who had previously presided over the *shire-moot*, as the County Court was called in those days. As a representative of the king in his county, the sheriff was responsible for collecting all the royal revenue, keeping the king's peace, and administering local government. He had to ensure that all free men between the ages of fifteen and sixty would be available for military service. If the occasion arose, he was supposed to take the field at the head of all the military forces of his county. It was his duty to suppress riots of any kind, and a relic of this power survives in that it is the sheriff or his appointed officer who is called upon to read the Riot Act in the event of a disturbance.

The sheriff traveled through his county and held twice a year what was called a Hundred Court (a hundred was originally a community consisting of a hundred households). He asked about the crimes that had been committed since his previous visit and presented a set of questions to the local reeve, who had to provide a jury of twelve men. This was not a jury in the modern sense, but a body of men who decided whether or not there was prima facie case that called for the attention of the sheriff.

These twice-yearly visits became known as the Sheriff's Turn. On these journeys through his shire, not unlike the circuit visits of latter days, the sheriff imposed his august presence upon local landowners for hospitality. As he invariably traveled with a large retinue, entertaining the sheriff became an expensive burden. After several complaints from those who suffered the honor of the sheriff's company, Edward I introduced an act that laid down that sheriffs should not stay too oft at one place.

Rings

Rings have been associated with legal transactions for thousands of years. According to Juvenal, Roman lawyers exhibited their rings while pleading their case. The use of a seal, or signet-ring, for the purchase of property is mentioned in the Old Testament: "And I bought the field of Hanameel, and weighed him the money, even seventeen shekels of silver. And I subscribed the evidence, and sealed it, and took witnesses, and weighed him the money in the balances." (Jeremiah 32:9-10.)

The royal signet-ring in Anglo-Saxon times served as the final authority in settling lawsuits about land. At a meeting of the Archaeological Institute in March 1850, Mr. W. Foulkes exhibited a gold signet ring, preserved by the family of J. Jones, Esq. of Llanerchrwgog Hall, impressions of which are appended to deeds concerning that property from the middle of the thirteenth century. It has been supposed to be the ring of Madoc, one of the last princes of Powis, and to have descended as an heirloom, with lands granted by them to the ancestors of Mr. Jones. In 1504, Anne Barrett, of Bury, willed her "marrying ring with all things thereon." And, among the numerous kinds of evidence allowed in courts of law to establish a pedigree, engravings on rings are admitted, on the assumption that a person would not wear a ring with an error on it.

Serjeants

Serjeants-at-law (in Latin: *serviens ad legem*), until they were abolished in the late nineteenth century, were the highest ranking barristers in English law, who at one point managed to secure a monopoly of pleading cases in the Court of Common Pleas. Until 1876 they had their own Serjeants' Inn and their medieval origin surrounded the position with a wealth of tradition and lore. As monks they were originally required to shave their heads, but gradually they were allowed "for decency and comeliness"—and also perhaps for warmth—to cover their baldness with a coif. This was at first a thin linen cover, gathered together in the form of a skull, or helmet; the material was afterward changed to white silk. By the eighteenth century, the coif was a black patch at the top of the wig, which distinguished them from other lawyers, and after their investiture, they were often called Serjeants of the Coif.

Lords of the Rings

The custom of serjeants presenting rings on taking the coif had great antiquity, going back at least to the reign of Henry VI in the fifteenth century. It was an impressive ceremony, and it was expensive for the new serjeants. All the important people in the legal establishment turned out to receive their rings, as William Jones, in his fascinating book of Finger-Ring Lore *(1877) describes the ceremony:*

On June 8, 1705, fifteen serjeants-at-law took the customary oaths at the Chancery Bar, and delivered to the Lord Keeper a ring for the Queen, and another to H.R.H. Prince George of Denmark, each ring being worth £6. 13s. 4d. The Lord Keeper, and the Lord Treasurer, Lord Steward, Lord Privy Seal, Lord High Chamberlain, Master of the Household, Lord Chamberlain, and the two Chief Justices, each received a ring of the value of 18s.; the Lord Chief Baron, the Master of the Rolls, the Justices of either Bench, and two Chief Secretaries, each, one worth 16s.; the Chief Steward and Comptroller, each ring valued at £1.; the Marshall, Warden of the Fleet, every Serjeant-at-law, the Attorney-General and Solicitor-General, each a ring worth 12s.; the three Barons of Exchequer, one each of 10s.; the two Clerks of the Crown, the three Prothonotaries, the Clerks of the Warrants, the Prothonotary of Queen's Bench, and the Chirographer, each a ring worth 5s.; each Filazer and Exigenter, the Clerk of the Council, and the Custom Brevium, each a ring that cost 2s. 6d. The motto on the rings was 'Moribus, armis, legibus' [By force of custom, by force of arms, by force of law].

On the admission of fourteen serjeants in 1737, 1,409 rings were given away, at a cost of £773, and besides this number, others were made for each serjeant's own account, to be given to friends at the bar, which came to more than all the rest of the expense.

The weight of each ring was carefully prescribed by precedent, and there is at least one instance of a crop of new serjeants getting into trouble for failing to render everything that was due their lordships:

Seventeen serjeants being made the 14th day of November [1669], a day or two after, Serjeant Powis, the junior of them all, coming to the King's Bench Bar, Lord Chief Justice Kelynge told him that "he had something to say to him, viz., that the rings which he and the rest of the serjeants had given weighed but eighteen shillings apiece; whereas Fortescue, in his book *De Laudibus Legum Angliae* says 'the rings given to the Chief Justices and to the Chief Baron ought to weigh twenty shillings apiece,' and that he spoke not this expecting a recompense, but that it might not be drawn into a precedent, and that the young gentlemen there might take notice of it."

As time went on, the expense of presenting so many rings proved simply too onerous, though the ceremonies were kept, rather like the Potlatch of Indian tribes of the Pacific Northwest. Jones tells in 1877 of

some quaint old customs still adhering to the making of a serjeant. He is presented to the Lord Chancellor by some brother barrister (styled his 'colt'), and he kneels while the Chancellor attaches to the top of his wig the little round black patch that now does duty for the 'coif,' which is the special badge of the Serjeant. The new Serjeant presents a massive gold ring to the Chancellor, another to his 'colt,' one to the Sovereign, and each of the Masters of the Court of Common Pleas. These rings used also to be given to all the Judges, but of late years the Judges have refused to receive them, thus diminishing a somewhat heavy tax.

Motto

Mottoes on serjeants' rings are traced by Serjeant Wynne (in his observations touching the antiquity and dignity of serjeants-at-law, published in 1765), to the nineteenth and twentieth year of Queen Elizabeth's reign (1576-7), when the inscription on the ring was *Lex regis praesidium* [The law presides above the king]. Lord Brougham, who detested all lawyers except himself, once suggested that the appropriate motto for some of the barristers who wished to be made serjeants would be the old legal term 'scilicet,' which is most often translated 'to wit.'

Pricking on a Roll

A picturesque and ancient ceremony marks the election of the county sheriffs whose names are put forward by their corporations on November 9 of each year. Then, on the morrow of St. Martin, November 12, these names, three in number from each of the various counties, are listed by the Chancellor of the Exchequer and the judges of the King's Bench Division; the first name is usually "pricked" by the sovereign in council at Buckingham Palace, in the following February or March.

This "pricking" is done with a "heavy, gold-headed bodkin" on the parchment roll that bears the names submitted; the custom goes back to 1461, while the earliest complete sheriff's roll dates from the reign of Henry VIII.

At one time the selected name used to be marked with a dot or tick, and the origin of the "pricking" ceremony is said to have begun with Queen Elizabeth I, who happened to be walking in the gardens at Windsor one day when the historic roll was presented to her for selecting the names. She was carrying a bodkin, and with an impetuous gesture, she used this instrument to indicate her will. This custom of pricking has been followed by every British monarch since.

Legal Prickers

And speaking of pricking, in a less harmless context, the word pricker was applied in Scotland to those who made a trade out of informing against witches. According to Pitcairn's *Records of Justiciary*, "these common prickers became at last so numerous that they were considered nuisances. The judges actually refused to take their evidence, and in 1678 the Privy Council of Scotland condescended to hear the complaint of an honest woman who had been indecently exposed by one of them, and expressed an opinion that common prickers were common cheats."

Getting Organized

The new Supreme Court of the United States got off to a less than auspicious start on February 1, 1790. The scene was at the Royal Exchange in New York, which failed to provide that symbol of judicial authority—a bench. Three of the six justices were missing and there were no cases to try. The court adjourned to dine with President Washington.

The next day, Justice Cushing from Massachusetts was jeered and hooted by a mob of youngsters when he tried to proceed down Broadway in his legal wig looking as dignified as he could. Later the Court decided to abandon the tradition of wearing wigs, adopting Thomas Jefferson's advice: "For heaven's sake, discard the monstrous wig which makes the English judges look like rats peeping through bunches of oakum."

Snuff

The United States Supreme Court borrowed many of its traditions from England. Ben Perley Poore, the old Washington observer, recalling the 1820s, mentions it as

. . . rich in traditions of hair-powder, queues, ruffled shirts, knee-breeches and buckles. Up to that time no Justice had ever sat upon the bench in trousers, nor had any lawyer ventured to plead in boots or wearing whiskers. Their Honors, the Chief Justice and the Associate Justices, wearing silk judicial robes, were treated with the most profound respect. When Mr. Henry Clay stopped, one day, in an argument, and advancing to the bench, took a pinch of snuff from Judge Washington's box, saying, "I perceive that your Honor sticks to the Scotch," and then proceeded with his case, it excited astonishment and admiration. "Sir," said Mr. Justice Story, in relating the circumstance to a friend, "I do not believe there is a man in the United States who could have done that but Mr. Clay."

WOMEN AND THE LAW

Women Sheriffs

Because sheriffs exercised vast local power in England, the elite in each county vied to keep this plum job in their family. Some offices, such as the shrievalty of Westmoreland, became hereditary, and this is how women came to wield great judicial power in the administration of justice. Nicolaa de la Haye was born in the year 1150 in Lincoln Castle, where her father, Richard de la Haye, was the constable. Nicolaa married twice, each time retaining the use of her maiden name. Her first husband, Fitz Erneis, left her in possession of vast lands when he died. Two years later she married Gerard de Camville, who paid a great deal of money for the

Sheriffdom of Lincoln. He was a close friend of Earl John, later King John of Magna Carta fame. In the rebellions against Richard the Lionheart, both Gerard and Nicolaa performed valuable services to John; for example, she conducted the defense of Lincoln Castle against a large force of the barons loyal to King Richard. When her second husband died, King John showed his gratitude by appointing only a nominal sheriff and granting Nicolaa the real shrieval powers of the county as a conjoint sheriff.

Another romantic story from the same period concerns Ela, Countess of Salisbury, who succeeded to her father's lands in 1196, when she was eight years old. Her mother took her to a castle in Normandy, where she was discovered by a traveling troubadour, William Talbot. He brought her back to England, and as a Royal Ward she was betrothed by King Richard the Lionheart to William Longespee, a bastard son of Henry I and the Fair Rosamund. The king created him Earl of Salisbury, and Ela became the Sheriff of Wiltshire, an office she held until she retired from the world and became the abbess of Lacock, an abbey she had built.

Male Logic

Sir Robert Megarry, in his 1969 edition of Arabiniana *(the rulings of William St. Julian Arabin (1775-1841) at the Old Bailey), points out the inconsistent and sometimes silly attitudes towards women in early nineteenth-century English courts:*

When a witness, who was a shoemaker, did not speak out, claiming to have a cold, the judge remarked:

"A man with a cold is not fit to try a lady's shoes on." But to a female witness who did not speak out:

"You come here with your heads in false wigs. If you can't speak out, I'll take off your bonnet; if that won't do, you shall take your cap off; and if you don't speak out then, I'll take your hair off."

To another female witness, the judge said:

"If you don't speak out, I'll take off your bonnet; and you'll never get a husband."

On another occasion, the Court asked a witness:

"Woman, how can you be so stupid? You're tall enough, to be wise enough."

The Long Road

In 1875 a Miss Levina Goodell petitioned to be admitted to the Wisconsin Bar. After conceding that there was nothing objectionable to Miss Goodell's character, and arguing that the statute governing admission employed only the masculine pronoun, Chief Justice Ryan rendered the following notorious opinion, reproduced here in part:

So we find no statutory authority for the admission of females to the bar of any court of this state. And, with all the respect and sympathy for this lady which all men owe to all good women, we cannot regret that we do not. We cannot but think the common law wise in excluding women from the profession of the law. The profession enters largely into the well-being of society; and, to be honorably filled and safely to society, exacts the devotion of life. The law of nature destines and qualifies the female sex for the bearing and nurture of the children of our race and for the custody of the homes of the world and their maintenance in love and honor. And all life-long callings of women, inconsistent with these radical and sacred duties of their sex, as is the profession of the law, are departures from the order of nature; and when voluntary, treason against it.

The cruel chances of life sometimes baffle both sexes, and may leave women free from the peculiar duties of their sex. These may need employment and should be welcome to any not derogatory to their sex and its proprieties, or inconsistent with the good order of society. But it is public policy to provide for the sex, not for its superfluous members; and not to tempt women from the proper duties of their sex by opening to them duties peculiar to ours. There are many employments in life not unfit for female character. The profession of the law is surely not one of these. The peculiar qualities of womanhood, its gentle graces, its quick sensibility, its tender susceptibility, its purity, its delicacy, its emotional impulses, its subordination of hard reason to sympathetic feeling, are surely not qualifications for forensic strife. Nature has tempered woman as little for the juridical conflicts of the court room, as for the physical conflicts of the battle field.

Womanhood is moulded for gentler and better things. And it is not the saints of the world who chiefly give employment to our profession. It has essentially and habitually to do with all that is selfish and malicious, knavish and criminal, coarse and brutal, repulsive and obscene, in human life. It would be revolting to all female sense of the innocence and sanctity of their sex, shocking to man's reverence for womanhood and faith in woman, on which hinge all the better affections and humanities of life, that woman would be permitted to mix professionally in all the nastiness of the world which finds its way into courts of justice; all the unclean issues, all the collateral questions of sodomy, incest, rape, seduction, fornication, adultery, pregnancy, bastardy, legitimacy, prostitution, lascivious cohabitation, abortion, infanticide, obscene publications, libel and slander of sex, impotence, divorce: all the nameless catalogue of indecencies, *la chronique scandaleuse* of all the vices and all the infirmities of all society, with which the profession has to deal, and which go towards filling judicial reports which must be read for accurate knowledge of the law.

This is bad enough for men. Reverence for all womanhood would suffer in the public spectacle of woman so instructed and engaged. This motion gives appropriate evidence of this truth. No modest woman could read without pain and self-abasement, no woman could so overcome the instincts of sex as publicly to discuss, the case which we had occasion to cite, *King v. Wiseman* [a prosecution for the crime of sodomy]. And when counsel was arguing for this lady that the word 'person' necessarily includes females, her presence made it impossible to suggest to him as *reductio ad absurdum* of his position that the same construction of the same word would subject woman to prosecution for the paternity of a bastard, and to prosecution for rape. Discussions are habitually necessary in courts of justice which are unfit for female ears. The habitual presence of women at these would tend to relax the public sense of decency and propriety. If, as counsel threatened, these things are to come, we will take no voluntary part in bringing them about.

BY THE COURT—the motion is denied.

Breakthroughs

One of the earliest women lawyers in the United States was Phebe W. Couzins, Esquire (as a contemporary account describes her), who was admitted to the Law School of Washington University of St. Louis in 1869:

Her application was received without a dissenting voice from either the Law Faculty, or Board of Directors; they taking the noble stand that the university was open to both sexes alike, and if a woman desired to become acquainted with the laws which govern her, or to enter the profession of the law, the university extended the same helping hand to her as to a man.

Miss Couzins graduated in 1871 from the university. Coming from the conservative element of a pro-slavery state, much interest has been manifested as to the influences which caused her to take such a radical step. She considers the war, and its attendant circumstances, as the one great motor which awakened her thought and aroused her interest in behalf of humanity.

The work of her mother on the steamers and in the hospitals, the many harrowing, sad histories which came to her through that source, first awakened her mind to the cause which lay back of all these results, and aroused the thought, whether or no woman's enlightened thought and action might not prevent in the same ratio as she ameliorated the horrors of war and its attendant evils. These ideas were slowly taking root; and in 1869 they received a new impulse from the Woman's Franchise Organization, composed of some of the best and most intelligent women of St. Louis. She then began to think of a profession, and at the earnest solicitation of Judge John M. Krum, a warm personal friend and member of the law faculty, she determined on a legal profession, and applied for admission to the Law School. Since her graduation she has been admitted to all the courts of the State of Missouri, the United District Court, the courts of Arkansas and of the Territory of Utah.

Struggle

More typical of the fights women had to go through to become lawyers was the case of Alta Q. Hulett, of Rockford, Illinois. Here is a stirring account in typical (and sexist) style of the times:

Alta entered the Rockford High School, and graduated on her sixteenth birthday, when she at once began the study of law, although at that time [circa 1870] the door to the profession seemed hopelessly closed against women. But the desire to become a lawyer had been an inspiration from earliest childhood, and being possessed of an indomitable will, which is a kind of genius, our heroine saw no alternative but to fullfil her destiny, which the ripening years seemed also to favor.

She entered, as a student, the law-office of Mr. Lathrop of Rockford, at that time one of the most eminent practitioners at the Bar of the State. Here Miss Hulett made good use of her opportunities: after a few months' study she passed the required examination, and sent her credentials to the Supreme Court, which, instead, of granting or refusing her plea for admission, ignored it altogether. [This followed on the heels of refusing Mrs. Myra Bradwell, the prominent editor of *Legal News*, admission on the grounds that she was a married woman; the case was appealed to the U.S. Supreme Court, which sustained the lower courts.] Miss Hulett had reason to expect that, since she was unmarried, this decision would not prejudice her own case.

Grievously disappointed, but not disheartened, the pressing necessities of the family claimed her immediate attention. She taught at a country school for four months, and bravely went to work again. She prepared a lecture, Justice vs. the Supreme Court, in which she vigorously and eloquently stated her case. This lecture was delivered in Rockford, Freeport, and many other of the larger towns in northern Illinois, enlisting everywhere sympathy and admiration on her behalf, and the family purse was also replenished. After taking counsel with Lieutenant-Governor Early, a friend of the family, and other prominent members of the Legislature, she drew up a bill, the provisions of which read:

> Be it enacted by the people of the State of Illinois represented in the General Assembly, that no person shall be precluded or debarred from any occupation, profession, or employment (except military), on account of sex. Provided that this act shall not be construed to affect the eligibility of any person to an elective office.
>
> Nothing in this act shall be construed as requiring any female to work on streets or roads, or serve on juries.
>
> All laws inconsistent with this act are hereby repealed.

Friends obtained for this bill a favorable introduction into the Legislature, which passed it, and the governor gave it his signature. Miss Hulett was passing up the steps to her home one rainy day, when the telegram announcing that her bill had become a law was placed in her hands. Trembling in every limb, she read the despatch; when her woman's nature asserted itself, and she sank upon the steps, regardless of the fast falling rain, and wept tears of joy. Relating this incident, she said: "I shall never again know a moment of such supreme happiness."

Immediately, upon the advice of trusted friends, she removed to Chicago, a city the peer of Boston in its supreme scorn for old-time prejudices. Here she presented herself for admission. After a most vigorous examination, she stood at the head of a class of twenty-eight; all of the others being gentlemen and her seniors. This time the Supreme Court made the *amende honorable*, and courteously and cordially welcomed her into the ranks of the profession. At the age of nineteen Miss Hulett began the practice of law on an equal footing with her brother lawyers; having been admitted not only into all of the state courts, but also into the Circuit Court of the United States. To say that Chicago is proud of its first lady lawyer is only a mild form of stating the case. Like its famous water-crib, grain elevators, etc., she is regarded as one of its distinctive institutions.

But Can She Type?

Also from the 1870s there is a newspaper notice that,

In the city of Washington, where a few years ago colored women were bought and sold under sanction of law, a woman of African descent has been admitted to practise at the bar of the Supreme Court of the District of Columbia. Miss Charlotte E. Ray, who has the honor of being the first lady lawyer in Washington, is a graduate of the Law College of Howard University, and is said to be a dusky mulatto, possesses quite an intelligent countenance.

The Naked Facts

As women lawyers became more common in the early decades of this century there were still many male colleagues who did not know how to deal with them. F. W. Lehmann of St. Louis, when he was U.S. solicitor general, related during the course of an after-dinner speech the correspondence between a young, rising female lawyer and a well-known attorney, whose names unfortunately he failed to pass on:

Madam:

We agree to compromise as proposed, in your favor of this date, not because your client has a just right to such settlement, but from the fact that we do not care to open a contest with a woman lawyer.

The young lady attorney immediately despatched a reply:

Sir:

I note yours agreeing to a settlement, although I cannot congratulate you on your gallantry in begging the question. Like the original Adam, you seem inclined to hide behind a woman's petticoat.

Not to be outdone, the male chauvinist attorney had the last word in quoting references:

Madam:

If you will turn to the early pages of Genesis you will discover that Eve did not wear a petticoat.

The Same Law for the Gander

In 1947, Soia Mentschikoff was the first woman ever hired to teach at the Harvard Law School, three years before female students were admitted. When she was first invited to lunch at the faculty dining hall, an exclusively male bastion, the headwaiter refused to serve her, until one of the professors had a quiet word with him. After that, the dining room became desegregated.

But Mentschikoff, first to make breakthroughs in so many areas of the legal world, is not a vociferous feminist. When told by a partner at a prominent Wall Street law firm that he was looking to hire "lady lawyers—I repeat—not women lawyers, lady lawyers, lawyers who are ladies," Soia Mentschikoff found nothing wrong with it. "Women should be ladies," she replied, "in the same way men should be gentlemen. Who wants to work alongside a loudmouth?"

Having Come a Long Way

In 1981 President Reagan fulfilled a campaign promise to place the first woman on the Supreme Court. As Betsy Covington Smith, in her book Breakthrough: Women in Law, *recounts how Sandra Day O'Connor was selected, it is clear that whom you know is still as important as what you have done:*

During the spring of 1981, while Sandra was working quietly on the appeals bench in Arizona, there was a flurry of behind-the-scenes activity in the offices of several important figures in Washington. Associate Justice Potter Stewart had announced his intention to resign from the Supreme Court at the end of the term. Attorney General William French Smith began immediately to compile names of lawyers who might replace him. White House counsel Fred Fielding had a similar list. Sandra's name turned up on both. It seemed she had some well-placed connections. Not only had she come to know Chief Justice Warren Burger, but she and Associate Justice William Rehnquist were longtime friends and fellow Arizonans. They had been in the same law school class at Stanford where they'd edited the *Law Review* together. In June, a Justice Department lawyer was sent to Phoenix to gather additional information on O'Connor. Four days later two other Justice lawyers flew to Phoenix and had lunch at her home in Paradise Valley, just outside the city. Charmed by her graciousness, they were equally impressed by her intelligence and her qualities as a lawyer.

Meanwhile, support for her was building. Both Burger and Rehnquist came in with glowing endorsements, as did former Arizona senator

Barry Goldwater, a leading voice of conservatism. Sandra flew to Washington, meeting first with Attorney General Smith, then with several members of the White House staff. According to one participant: "We were testing her psychological and intellectual stamina, the lack of which has caused some justices to desert their conservative base." Finally, Sandra met with President Reagan. After talking to her, he knew that she was everything he wanted—a Republican, a conservative, and, above all, a woman.

· 10 ·

PRIVATE LIVES

HOME AND HEARTH

Lawyer at Home

On Friday, February 17, 1826 Josiah Quincy was invited to a very small dinner party at Daniel Webster's house:

Webster carved the beef and was in charming humor. He told some good lawyer's stories, and gave us a graphic account of the burning of his house in Portsmouth, in the winter of 1813.

"Though I was in Washington at the time," he said, "I believe I know more about the fire than many who were actively at work on the spot. Besides, here is Mrs. Webster, who was burned out. She will correct me if I am wrong."

He told us that all he possessed in the world was lost, there being no insurance upon house or furniture; but as more than two hundred buildings were consumed in the fire, some of them belonged to those less able to make a living than himself, he felt he had no right to murmur. He was, nevertheless, troubled about the loss of his library. His books were full of notes and associations, and could not be replaced.

"I think there was something in the house which Mr. Webster regretted more than his books," said his wife, with an amused expression, which showed her remark was not to be taken quite seriously. "There was a pipe of wine in the cellar, and I am sure that Mr. Webster's philosophy has not yet reconciled him to its loss. You see we were young housekeepers in those days. It was the first pipe of wine we ever had, and the getting of it was a great event."

"Let us be accurate, my dear," said Mr. Webster, with one of those pleasant smiles of his which fairly lit up the room. "Undoubtedly it was a pipe of wine when we bought it; but then it had been on tap for some time, and our table was not without guests. If I had you upon the witness stand, I think I should make you confess that your pipe of wine could scarcely have been more than half a pipe at the time of the fire."

I supposed that there was nothing said at that dinner so little worth preserving as this trifling family jest; yet the sweet and playful manner of Webster has fixed it indelibly upon my memory. That manner I cannot give, and it was everything. It somehow carried one of those aside confessions of the absolute affection and confidence existing between this married pair which were so evident to those admitted beneath their roof.

Imaginary Troubles

Justice Holmes once could not find an old book at home and he made an uproar about it, making the whole household miserable. Mrs. Holmes did not say a word; she just looked at her husband with quiet disapproval. The judge went off to the court and when he returned, the book was in its place on the shelf. There was an American flag hanging above, and beneath there was a sign, in Mrs. Holmes's neat handwriting. It read: "I am a very old man. I have had many troubles, most of which never happened." According to Mary Donellan, the parlor maid, "the judge laughed until he cried."

The Wisdom of Ancestors

Sir William Grant, Master of the Rolls, was a man of simple habits and somewhat remarkable for his taciturnity. As a politician he was more narrow-minded than even several other distinguished lawyers, and with him originated the phrase of "the wisdom of our ancestors." In his time the Rolls Court sat in the evening, from six to ten, and Sir William dined after the court rose. His servant, it is said, when he went to bed, left two bottles of wine on the table, which he always found empty in the morning. Sir William occupied two or three rooms on the ground floor of the Rolls House; and when showing them to his successor in the Rolls, he said, "Here are two or three good rooms: this is my dining room, my library and bedroom are beyond; and I am told," he added, "there are some good rooms upstairs, but I was never there."

Lent

Lord Kenyon occupied a large gloomy house in Lincoln's-inn-fields, where, it was said, "all the year through it is Lent in the kitchen and Passion-week in the parlour." Someone having mentioned that although the fire was very dull in the kitchen-grate, the spits were always bright. "It is quite irrelevant," said Joseph Jekyll, the eighteenth-century English wit, "to talk about the spits, for nothing 'turns' upon them."

Austerity

Before he went on the bench, Louis Brandeis was worth around two million dollars. He gave away most of it to causes. After he became associate justice, Brandeis lived so modestly with his wife that he continued to give away a large part of his $20,000 salary. He once told a young friend: "Man should live austerely. The greatest menace to freedom is an inert people. And, son, there are no degrees of austerity. Either you are austere or you are not austere."

Economy

During the Depression, when the Hoover Economy Act cut the pensions for Supreme Court justices to $10,000, Justice Oliver Wendell Holmes, ninety years old at the time, remarked: "I have always been a prudent man, so this pay cut will not hurt me. But I am distressed that I cannot continue to lay aside for my old age."

(When he died a few years later, Justice Holmes bequeathed to the government $250,000.)

Gone with Miss Scarlett

A case was called on in the Court of King's Bench, but Mr. (later Lord) Campbell was nowhere to be seen; he had taken a matrimonial trip with a former Miss Scarlett.

"I thought, Mr. Brougham," observed Mr. Justice Abbott to the substituting counsel (later Lord Brougham), "that Mr. Campbell was on the case."

"Yes, my lord," replied Brougham, with that sarcastic look peculiarly his own; "he was, my lord, but I understand he is ill."

"I am sorry to hear that," said the judge, taking snuff.

"My lord," replied Mr. Brougham, "it is whispered that the cause of my learned friend's absence is the scarlet fever."

Gallantry

Soon after the Civil War, in the era known as Reconstruction, an Alabama beauty was introduced to Chief Justice Salmon P. Chase.

"I must warn you," she said provokingly, "that I am a rebel who has not been reconstructed."

"Madam," the justice is reputed to have replied, "reconstruction in your case—even in the slightest degree—would be nothing short of sacrilege."

Little Decorum

Lord Chief Justice John Willes (1685-1761) was a man of so little personal decorum that he was perpetually offending against the respect due his office. He would play cards at the public rooms at watering places; and one night when so engaged, he was extremely annoyed by a young barrister who, pretending to be intoxicated, stood by the table, looked over his cards, and was so troublesome, that at last Willes spoke sharply to him:

"Sir," said he, staggering, "I . . . beg pardon; but I wanted to improve in playing whist; so I came to look over . . . you; for if . . . if I . . . I . . . I am not mistaken, sir . . . you are a judge."

Horace Walpole mentions in his memoirs that his lordship never tried to disguise his passions and vices, which for gaming was notorious, for women unbounded. One day a grave person came to visit him to tell him that the world talked of one of his maidservants being with child. Willes said:

"What is that to me?"

"Oh, but they say it is by your lordship," said the man.

"And what is that to you?" was the chief justice's reply.

Precedence

The Cockburn Family Records *contain the following story of Lord Chief Justice Cockburn's extracurricular activities in the Victorian era:*

At a certain trial an extremely pretty girl was called as a witness. The Lord Chief Justice was very particular about her giving her full name and address. Of course he took note. So did the sheriff's officer. That evening they both arrived at the young lady's door simultaneously, whereupon Cockburn tapped the officer on the shoulder, remarking: "No, no, no, Mr. Sheriff's officer, judgment first, execution afterwards!"

Pincher

Lord Eldon's attachment to his dog was extraordinary. His lordship remembered Pincher in his will in 1838, bequeathing him to Lady

Frances Bankes, with an annuity of eight pounds for his maintenance during the term of his natural life. Lord Eldon used to say while he caressed the animal:

"Poor Pincher belonged to poor William Henry [his son], and after I took the Sacrament with him when he was dying, he called me back as I was leaving the room and said: 'Father, you will take care of poor Pincher.'"

Another story Lord Campbell relates in his *Lives of the Lord Chancellors*, concerns Pincher being decoyed by a dog-stealer:

"On receiving a letter signed, 'An Amateur Dog-fancier,' a negotiation was opened which led to Lord Eldon sending a servant with a five-pound note to a house in Cow Cross Street, where Pincher was found. The man being dealt with 'on honour,' freely disclosed the secrets of his trade, and in answer to a gentle reproach, replied: 'Why, what can we do? Now that Parliament has stopped our trade in procuring bodies for the surgeons, we are obliged to turn to this to get an honest livelihood.'"

Pincher was painted in several portraits of the Lord Chancellor, who said:

"Poor fellow! he has a right to be painted with me, for when my man Smith took him the other day to a law bookseller's, where there happened to be several lawyers, they all received him with great respect, and the master of the shop exclaimed, 'How very like he is to old Eldon, particularly when he wore a wig!—but, indeed, many people say he is the handsomer chap of the two.'"

Judge Catches One

When Chief Justice Melville Fuller was a struggling dispenser of the law in Maine, he was universally known as "Judge." One day he discovered to his distress that several hams had been stolen from his smokehouse, and although he was distressed, he did not tell anybody about it. A few days later a neighbor dropped by his house and said,

"Say, Judge, I heard yew had some hams stole t'other night?"

"Yes," Judge Fuller replied in a very confidential tone, "but don't tell anyone. You and I are the only ones who know it."

Bad Fences Make Bad Neighbors

Justice Oliver Wendell Holmes liked to tell the story of an Indiana justice of the peace who owned a farm, one fence side of which ran along the boundary line of Indiana and Ohio. Like others in rural districts who hold that office, this man had an abnormal appreciation of its responsibility, and never lost an opportunity to exercise his prerogative of demanding that the peace be preserved.

One day his son and his hired man got to fighting on a stretch of the farm near the boundary fence. The justice of the peace heard them, rushed out and climbed up the fence, from which commanding position, with head cocked high, he pompously shouted: "In the name of the State of Indiana I demand the preservation of the peace!" Just then the fence gave way under his weight, and as he went down with the fence toppling over to the Ohio side, he shouted to his son: "Give him the devil, Jim; I've lost my jurisdiction!"

I Love New York

After his appointment to the Supreme Court, Justice Benjamin Cardozo never felt comfortable in Washington and missed his beloved New York, especially his summer home in Rye, where he would spend the recess. At a dinner party he overheard a woman mentioning that she had mistakenly exchanged fur coats at a restaurant.

"When I was young, I won a fur-coat case in New York once," Cardozo joined the conversation, happy to bring back memories of New York. "My client, a woman, was so overjoyed after we won that she threw her arms around my neck and kissed me."

Seth Richardson, Assistant Attorney General under the Hoover administration, then remarked:

"Well, Mr. Justice, in view of the type of practice you had, I don't wonder that you want to return to New York."

Fourteen Is Enough

Judge Richard B. Russell, a Georgia politician and justice of the court of appeals in the early part of the century also known as "Plain Dick," was the proud and prolific father of fourteen children. (Being superstitious, he was worried when he got to twelve, but he and Mrs. Russell solved the problem by arranging to have twins for the next round.) On one occasion Judge Russell took all fourteen children to the state fair, where one of the attractions was a two-headed calf inside a tent. The judge cautiously inquired about the price of the tickets.

"Ten cents for whole and five cents for half tickets," explained the showman. Brightening, Plain Dick handed out the money:

"Give me one whole and fourteen halves," he said.

"Have you fourteen children?" the showman eyed him curiously.

"I have that," replied the judge.

"Got 'em all wid yer?"

The judge proudly pointed to the long row of human steps rising in back of him:

"There they are, count for yourself."

The showman counted and then threw up his hand.

"Mister," he said, "keep yer money. Suppose you sell me a ticket, and I'll bring the calf out to see you."

My Son, the Lawyer

In the early part of the century, Justice William Rufus Day had the great satisfaction of hearing his attorney son, W.A. Day, argue a case in front of the Supreme Court. The son was a tall, big man, in contrast to his diminutive father, who was so enchanted with junior's performance that he passed a note to Justice Oliver Wendell Holmes describing him as "a chip off the old block." Holmes passed it back to his fellow justice, with the emendation that it seemed to him that Mr. Day was more like a "block off the old chip."

Sadness

In the winter of 1935 Carl Sandburg, the poet and biographer of Lincoln, asked Texan congressman Maury Maverick to introduce him to Justice Benjamin Cardozo, whom he had admired for years not only as a judge but as a fine writer. Indeed, Cardozo has been widely considered to be one of the greatest literary stylists ever to sit on the American bench. When the justice returned the compliment about Sandburg's writing, the latter asked whether Mr. Cardozo would care to hear his latest poem. Sandburg launched into a recitation of a lengthy prose poem built around the recurring question "What is a judge?" In it the poet contrasted his ideal of a judge with the kind of corrupt men who would sell justice. While Sandburg thundered on, oblivious to his surroundings, Justice Cardozo turned white as a sheet, and Congressman Maverick squirmed in his seat. He knew—and Sandburg did not—that Judge Albert Cardozo, the justice's father, had been the judicial front for Tammany's infamous Tweed Ring, who had fleeced the public coffers of millions of dollars; he was forced from the bench by New York Bar Association preferring charges of malfeasance against him.

When Sandburg concluded with a triumphant flourish, he shouted:

"Judge, what do you think of that?"

"It was a magnificent recitation, Mr. Sandburg. But aren't you somewhat sweeping in your condemnation? I don't think it's fair to denounce the entire judiciary."

"Why not, Judge? They are destroying the country. They are cruel, they are inhuman, they are corrupt."

As these two litterateurs argued and held to their position, according to a contemporary account, "Cardozo never raised his voice, gave no sign of his inner emotions. Sandburg continued to elaborate aggressively on his theory that all judges are infamous, and when finally he rose to leave, the two men parted as cordially as they met. But a certain sadness in Cardozo's tone, unnoticed by Sandburg but clear to Maverick's ear, showed that a secret emotion had been stirred."

Some Enchanted Afternoon

When President Reagan announced his (ultimately failed) nomination of Judge Douglas Ginsburg to the Supreme Court, first hint of the nominee's troubles came when he tried to pick up one of his small daughters and pose for the cameras. The little girl visibly shrank from her father's touch. Mrs. Ginsburg, referring to her husband's long hours of work, explained to the journalists: "Well, wouldn't you, if a perfect stranger tried to pick you up?"

PLEASURES

Federalism and Madeira

When Josiah Quincy accompanied Judge Joseph Story to Washington, the judge was careful not to promise anything after their arrival:

"The fact is," said he, "I can do very little for you there, as we judges take no part in the society of the place. We dine once a year with the President, and that is all. On other days we take our dinner together, and discuss at table the questions which are argued before us. We are great ascetics, and even deny ourselves wine, except in wet weather." Here the judge paused, as if thinking that the act of mortification he had mentioned placed too severe a tax upon human credulity, and presently added: "What I say about the wine, sir, gives you our rule; but it does sometimes happen that the Chief Justice will say to me, when the cloth is removed, 'Brother Story, step to the window and see if it does not look like rain.' And if I tell him that the sun is shining brightly, Judge Marshall will sometimes reply, 'All the better; for our jurisdiction extends over so large a territory that the doctrine of chances makes it certain that it must be raining somewhere.' You know that the Chief was brought up upon Federalism and Madeira, and he is not a man to outgrow his early prejudices."

Charles Henry Butler, in retelling this famous story, adds:

One evening when several Justices were present at a gathering at 1535 Eye Street, in answer to my inquiry as to the authenticity of the story Mr. Justice Brewer said:

"Why, Mr. Reporter, the story is not only true, but you ought to know that the Court sustained the constitutionality of the acquisition of the Philippines so as to be sure of having plenty of rainy seasons."

Ben Perley Poore, a Washington journalist who published his *Reminiscences of Sixty Years* in 1886, wrote that the best Madeira served at dinners in the capital were labeled *"The Supreme Court*, as their Honors, the Justices, used to make a direct importation every year, and sip it as they consulted over the cases before them every day after dinner, when the cloth had been removed."

Home Delivery

It was John Marshall's custom to provide for his table himself when at home, and he might be seen every morning at the Shockoe Hill Market, with his basket on his arm, engaged in making his purchases. Upon one of these occasions he noticed a fashionably dressed young man swearing violently because he could not find anyone willing to carry home for him a turkey which he had just purchased, and which his foolish pride would not permit him to carry home himself. Approaching him quietly, the judge asked him where he lived, and on being told, said:

"I am going that way, and will carry it for you." Taking the turkey, he set out and soon reached the young man's door. Upon receiving his turkey, the young man thanked him for his trouble, and asked:

"How much shall I pay you?"

"Oh, nothing," replied the judge smiling, "you are welcome. It was on my way, and no trouble," and he departed. The young man, with a faint suspicion of the truth, turned to a passerby, and asked in some confusion:

"Who is that polite old gentleman who brought home my turkey for me?"

"That is John Marshall, the chief justice of the United States," came the reply.

"Why then did he bring home my turkey?" stammered the fop.

"To give you a deserved rebuke," said the gentleman, "and to teach you to conquer your silly pride."

Drinking Companions

Lord Chief Justice Cockburn was very fond of describing a circuit scene at Stirling, in his early days at the Bar, under the presidency of Lord Hermand. After the circuit dinner, and when drinking had gone on for some time, young Cockburn observed places becoming vacant in the social circle but no one going out at the door. He found that individuals had dropped down under the table. He took the hint, and by this ruse retired from the scene. He lay quiet till the beams of the morning sun penetrated the apartment. The judge and some of his staunch friends coolly walked upstairs, washed their hands and faces, came down to breakfast, and went into court, quite fresh and fit for work.

With Lord Hermand drinking was a virtue: he had a sincere respect for it, indeed a high moral approbation, and a serious compassion for the poor wretches who could not indulge in it, with due contempt of those who could but did not. No carouse ever injured his health, for he was never ill, nor did it impair his taste for home or quiet, or muddle his head: he slept the sounder for it and rose the earlier and the cooler. It is told that he used very often to go direct from his club to the court on Saturday mornings. When some degenerate youths were once protesting against more wine, he exclaimed mournfully, "What shall we come to at last! I believe I shall be left alone on the face of the earth—drinking claret!"

Hermand, when trying a man at Edinburgh, who had killed a friend in a drunken fray, feeling that discredit had been brought to the cause of drinking, had no sympathy with the tenderness of his temperate brethren, and was vehement for transportation. "We are told," said Hermand, "that there was no malice, and that the prisoner must have been in liquor. In liquor! Why, he was drunk! And yet he murdered the very man who had been drinking with him! They had been carousing the whole night, and yet he stabbed him! After drinking a whole bottle of rum with him! Good God, my laards! If he will do this when he's drunk, what will he no do when he's sober?"

Decline and Fall

Sir John Millicent, a Cambridgeshire judge, was asked how he got on with his brother judges, and replied: "Why, in faith, I have no way but to drink myself down to the capacity of the bench."

Under the Influence

Chauncey M. Depew, one of the prominent statesmen and business leaders in nineteenth-century America, recalled in his memoirs Daniel Webster, the famous drinker:

Hugh J. Hastings, at one time editor and proprietor of the Albany *Knickerbocker*, and subsequently of the New York *Commercial Advertiser*, told me that he worshipped Daniel Webster.

Webster, he said, once stopped over at Albany while passing through the State, and became a guest of one of Albany's leading citizens and its most generous host and entertainer. The gentleman gave in Webster's honor a large dinner at which were present all the notables of the capital.

Hastings organized a procession which grew to enormous proportions by the time it reached the residence where Mr. Webster was dining. When the guests came out, it was evident, according to Hastings, that they had been dining too well. This was not singular, because then no dinner was perfect in Albany unless there were thirteen courses and thirteen different kinds of wine, and the whole closed up with the famous Regency rum, which had been secured by Albany bon-vivants before the insurrection in the West Indies had stopped its manufacture. There was a kick in it which, if there had been no other brands preceding, was fatal to all except the strongest heads. I tested its powers myself when I was in office in Albany fifty-odd years ago.

Hastings said that when Webster began his speech he was as near his idol as possible and stood right in front of him. When the statesman made a gesture to emphasize a sentence he lost his hold on the balustrade and pitched forward. The young Irishman was equal to the occasion, and interposed an athletic arm, which prevented Mr. Webster from falling, and held him until he had finished his address. The fact that he could continue his address under such conditions increased, if that was possible, the admiration of young Hastings. Webster was one of the few men who, when drunk all over, had a sober head.

The speech was very effective, not only to that audience, but, as reported, all over the country. Hastings was sent for and escorted to the dining room where the guests had reassembled. Webster grasped him by the hand, and in his most Jovian way exclaimed: "Young man, you prevented me from disgracing myself. I thank you and will never forget you." Hastings reported his feelings as such that if he had died that night he received of life all it had which was worth living for.

I do not know what were Mr. Webster's drinking habits, but the popular reports in regard to them had a very injurious effect upon young men and especially young lawyers. It was the universal conversation that Webster was unable to do his best work and have his mind at its highest efficiency except under the influence of copious drafts of brandy. Many a young lawyer believing this drank to excess, not because he loved alcohol, but because he believed its use might make him a second Webster.

The Queen and Her Chancellor

Christopher Hatton, one of the Elizabethan Lord Chancellors, was called the "dancing chancellor," and it was of his manor house that Thomas Gray wrote:

> Full oft within the spacious walls
>   When he had fifty summers o'er him,
> The grave Lord Keeper led the brawls,
>   The seal and maces danc'd before him.
>
> His bushy beard and shoestrings green,
>   His high-crowned hat and satin doublet
> Moved the stout heart of England's Queen,
>   Though Pope and Spaniard could not trouble it.

A True Puritan

In the New England colonies Judge Samuel Sewall, later chief justice of Massachusetts, protested the acting of plays in a letter to the authorities:

"To the honorable Isaac Addington Esqr. Secretary. To be communicated to his Excellency the Governour, and to the honorable Council."

BOSTON OF THE MASSACHUSETTS; MARCH 2, 1713-14

There is a rumor, as if some design'd to have a play acted in the Council chamber next Monday, which much surprises me—and as much as in me lies, I do forbid it. The Romans were very fond of their plays, but I never heard they were so far set upon them, as to turn their Senate-House into a Play-House. Our Town-House was built at great cost and charge, for the sake of very serious and important business: the three chambers above and the Exchange below—business of the Province, County and Town. Let it not be abused with dances or other scenical divertisements. It cannot be a honor to the Queen to have the laws of honesty and sobriety broken in upon. Ovid himself offers invincible argument against public plays:

> *Ut tamen hoc fatear: ludi quoque semina praebent*
> *Nequitiae*
> [Yet, I must confess: public spectacles also sow the seeds of evildoing]

Let not Christian Boston go beyond heathen Rome in the practice of shameful vanities.

This is the voice of your most humble and obedient Servant,

Samuel Sewall

Perchance to Dream

Lord Kenyon fell asleep during the first night of Richard Brinsley Sheridan's *Pizarro*. When a friend pointed this out, the dramatist felt at first mortified, but then he quickly recovered his famous wit: "Let the poor man sleep; he thinks he is on the bench."

Might Have Been

Chief Justice Abbott, later Lord Tenderden (1762-1832), once attending services in Canterbury Cathedral, whispered to Judge Richardson:

"Do you see that old man there among the choristers? In him, behold the only being I ever envied. When at school in this town, we were candidates together for a chorister's place. He obtained it, and if I had gained my wish he might have been accompanying you as chief justice, and pointing me out as his old school-fellow, the singing man."

Hobby Horse

Lord Tenterden took up the study of botany late in life as a scientific pursuit and wrote much poetry in Latin, in imitation of Horace and Ovid. Said when doing so: "You see I am now on my hobby, and you must be patient while I take a ride."

Too Much Respect

When John Dunning (1731-1783), later Lord Ashburton, was solicitor general, he diverted himself by making an excursion, in vacation time, to Prussia. From his title of solicitor general, the king supposed him to be a general officer of the British army, so he invited him to a great review of his troops, and mounted him, as an eminent military person, upon one of his finest chargers. The charger carried the solicitor general through all the volutions of the day, the "general" in every movement being in a most dreadful fright, and the horse's duty never allowing him to dismount. He was so terrified and distressed by this great compliment that he said he would never go abroad again as a general of any sort.

Ultra Vires

Justice Cardozo disliked travel by boat because he suffered from motion sickness. Once he was sailing to Europe on the *Aquitania*, when a friend found him leaning far over the rail.

"Can't I do something for you, Judge," he asked with sympathy.

"Yes, you can," the justice replied wanly. "You can overrule this motion."

The late Judge Jacob Braude told about the time Justice Felix Frankfurter was asked and declined to officiate at a friend's wedding. The U.S. Supreme Court justice explained that he did not have jurisdiction over the matter, since marriage was not a federal offense.

Taking His Cue

John Marshall's great passion was the game of quoits, and he was a member of a club that met at Buchanan's Spring, near the city, to play at this game. Here the governor of Virginia, the chief justice, and the most eminent lawyers of the court of appeals were found by a French gentleman, Baron Quinet, with their coats off, gaily pitching quoits, with the ardor of a party of urchins. In these simple amusements passed the hours of leisure that Judge Marshall could steal from his exhausting judicial toil. When upwards of seventy years of age, he still relished the pleasures of the quoit club or the whist table, and to the last his right hand never forgot its cunning with the billiard cue.

Golf

Justice John Harlan of the United States Supreme Court was once playing golf with a very devout clergyman at the turn of the century, when the judge, after making a particularly long drive, turned to his clerical opponent and bade him do better if he could. The man of the cloth teed up his ball with care, swung his club two or three times to limber up for a big drive, and then swung at the ball with all his might. The head of the club fanned the air, leaving the ball tantalizingly on the tee. Without a word, but with a face full of anguish, the clergyman looked at Harlan for fully a minute, and then swung again. "Well," said the judge, "that was the most profane silence I ever heard."

Teed Off

U.S. Solicitor General John W. Davis rarely lost his temper. Once he was playing golf with a government official who prattled on about the books he had been reading. Just at the moment that Davis was about to tee off, his club swinging, the bureaucrat asked if he knew Dante. Without missing his shot, Davis responded:

"Yes, he's been well spoken of."

The Classics

A great lover of the classics, Justice Holmes read Dante in Italian without a knowledge of the language: "I found that with a translation and one's knowledge of Latin, etc., one could read the original very easily." In his late eighties Holmes read the Athenian historian Thucydides in Greek. It required a great deal of effort. When asked what prompted him to do it, Holmes replied: "No gentleman should go to his grave without first having read Thucydides in the original."

Judge's Turf

Justice Henry Hawkins (later Lord Brampton) was a keen sportsman and was frequently seen at the turf. Once in the middle of a murder trial, the prosecutor saw the prisoner say something to the constable and demanded to know what it was. The judge agreed and ordered the constable to disclose what had passed between him and the accused.

"I would rather not," the constable squirmed.

"Never mind what you would rather not," Judge Hawkins insisted, "inform the court what the prisoner said."

"He asked me, your lordship, who that hoary heathen with the sheepskin was, as he had often seen him at the race-course."

Justice Hawkins once found himself sitting at the Lincoln Assize Court on the morning of the Lincoln handicap. After hearing several cases, the hour of the race was approaching, and the judge turned to the jury:

"Gentlemen, it has been brought to my notice that there is an event of some local importance about to take place this afternoon. I should be loathe to stand for a moment between you and your participation in the celebration. Any expression of opinion on your part, therefore, will receive my most serious consideration."

The jury, however, consisting mostly of tradesmen rather than of sportsmen, were only anxious to get their duty and the business of the court over and done with, so that they could get back to their shops. So after a few moments' deliberation, the foreman of the jury informed the bench that they had "no expression of opinion to offer."

"I thank you for your communication, gentlemen," replied Judge Hawkins. "The court is adjourned until eleven o'clock tomorrow morning."

On another occasion, a barrister was prosecuting a man for stealing a teacup before Judge Hawkins when a telegram was delivered in the middle of his summing up to the jury.

"Silvio's won—and I've won!" the attorney exulted, forgetting where he was. His lordship, puzzled by his outburst, insisted on knowing the meaning of it. The barrister explained that he had laid a bet in a bar 'sweep' on a horse called Silvio, and he profusely apologized for his conduct.

"It is most improper," the judge concurred, "and I trust it will never occur again." The barrister promised that it would not, and he was about to resume his argument when the judge interrupted him:

"Oh, by the way, Mr. ——, did the telegram say what placed second and third?"

Workout

Chief Justice Hughes in the 1930s once told a group of Washington ladies about the standing and squatting exercises he had been doing for more than forty years. "Birth control may be your problem," said the judge, "but girth control is mine."

TWILIGHT

Eternal Youth

Justice Oliver Wendell Holmes retained his youth throughout most of his long life. In an oft-told story, he was near ninety and in Washington when they passed a pretty girl. Holmes stopped, glanced back and in self-mocking anguish exclaimed: "Oh, to be seventy again!"

Fertility

After he retired from the Supreme Court at the age of ninety-one, Justice Holmes claimed that he began really to enjoy life. He always had to work too hard while on the Court. Once he was about to set forth to see the famous apple blossoms in Winchester, Virginia, when a messenger arrived with an opinion for him to read. "The goddamned fertility of my colleagues will kill me," cried Holmes and canceled his trip.

Joie de Vivre

Felix Frankfurter, then still at the Harvard Law School, visited the dying Oliver Wendell Holmes in 1935. He found the ninety-four-year-old justice impishly thumbing his nose at him. Dean Acheson (later secretary of state) was a young secretary to Justice Brandeis in 1919 and often delivered draft opinions and messages between him and Justice Holmes, who did not care for the telephone:

I remember very soon after I came to Washington, taking a message from Justice Brandeis to Mr. Justice Holmes. As I was leaving, he took me by the arm, looked at me as though he was seeing me for the first time and said: "How young are you?"

Well, I didn't feel young. I was twenty-six, I was married, I had a daughter, I was a member of the Bar. But suddenly I felt young, because he said so. [Holmes was then seventy-eight.]

And he said, "Isn't life a wonderful thing?"

Well, I hadn't thought about that. Life was just sort of like the air you breathe. He said, "You know, if the ceiling opened now and Le Bon Dieu came down through it and said to me, 'Wendell, you have five minutes to live,' I would say, 'I wish it were ten!'"

Virile Old Bull

In 1841, when John Quincy Adams was in his seventy-fourth year, he argued in front of the Supreme Court a case involving the freedom of certain black men, who while brought into this country illegally by slave traders, had gained mastery of the vessel and murdered the officers. Having been taken together with the vessel into a U.S. port, by a U.S. boat, they were claimed as slaves by their alleged Spanish owners. Justice Story, in a letter to his wife, describes the sixth president:

The old man was full of his accustomed virility and belligerency, and spoke for four hours and twenty minutes. It was extraordinary for its power, for its bitter sarcasm, and its dealing with topics far beyond the record and points of discussion.

In the following year, the seventy-five-year-old Adams was tangling with the Chief Justice, in an incident described by Hugh McCulloch in his Men and Measures of Half Century:

A few days after the unsuccessful effort was made in Congress in 1842, to pass a resolution of censure against Adams, for presenting a petition from citizens of Massachusetts for the dissolution of the Union, in which effort Marshall took a leading part, I happened to be seated with some Southern members of Congress at the dinner table in a Washington hotel, when Marshall came in. It seemed that Mr. Adams had said or done something that day which had irritated these gentlemen, and as Mr. Marshall was taking his seat at the table, one of them exclaimed:

"Well, Marshall, the old devil has been at work again, you must take him in hand."

"Not I," replied Marshall, with a decisive shake of the head; "I have been gored by that d—d old bull, and have had enough of him. If there be any more of this kind of work, it must be undertaken by somebody else. The old devil, as you call him, is match for a score of such fellows as you and me."

Old Codger

The eighteenth-century Irish peer Lord Ligonier was attacked by the newspapers and wanted to prosecute them; his lawyer told him it was impossible—a tradesman might prosecute, as such a report might affect his credit. "Well, then," said the old judge, "I may prosecute, too, for I can prove I have been hurt by this report. I was going to marry a great fortune who thought I was but 74; the newspapers have said I am 80, and she will not have me."

Hounded to Death

The death of Lord Clonmell is said to have originated in a very curious incident. According to Charles Phillips' biography of John Curran:

In the year 1792, Mr. John Magee, the spirited proprietor of the *Dublin Evening Post*, had a fiat issued against him in a case of libel, for a sum which the defendant thought excessive. The bench and the press were directly committed, and in such a case, had a judge tenfold the power he has, he would be comparatively harmless. The subject made a noise—was brought before Parliament—and was at last, at least politically, set at rest by the defeat of the Chief Justice, and the restriction of the judges in such cases, to an inferior and definite sum.

Discomfited and mortified, Lord Clonmell retreated from the contest; but he retreated like a harpooned leviathan—the barb was in his back, and Magee held the cordage. He made the life of his enemy a burden to him. He exposed his errors, denied his merits, magnified his mistakes, ridiculed his pretensions, and, continually edging without overstepping the boundary of libel, poured upon the Chief Justice, from the battery of the press, a perpetual broadside of sarcasm and invective. Wherever Lord Clonmell went, he was lampooned by a ballad-singer or laughed at by the populace.

Nor was Magee's arsenal composed exclusively of paper ammunition. He rented a field bordering his Lordship's highly improved and decorated demesne. He advertised, month after month, that on such a day he would exhibit in this field "a grand Olympic pig hunt," that the people, out of gratitude for their patronage of his newspaper, should be gratuitous spectators of this revised classical amusement; and that he was determined to make so amazing a provision of whisky and porter, that if any man went thirsty it should be his own fault. The plan completely succeeded: hundreds and thousands assembled; every man did justice to his entertainer's hospitality, and his Lordship's magnificent demesne, uprooted and desolate, next day exhibited nothing but the ruins of the Olympic pig-hunt. The Rebellion approached—the popular exasperation was at its height—and the end of it was that Magee went mad with his victory, and Lord Clonmell died, literally broken-hearted with his defeat and his apprehensions.

The Chief Justice, towards the close of his life, was delicate in health, and frequent reports of his death were circulated. On one of these occasions, when he was really very ill, a friend said to Curran, "Well, they say Clonmell is going to die at last. Do you believe it?" "I believe," said Curran, "he is scoundrel enough to live or die, just as it suits his own convenience."

Successful as Lord Clonmell was in his political career, he by no means looked back on it with satisfaction. It is recorded of him that he said on his deathbed, "As to myself, if I were to begin life again, I would rather be a chimney-sweeper than connected with the Irish government."

Decline

Author William Gerhardi met F. E. Smith, Lord Birkenhead, in the 1920s, after hearing him at the Oxford Union:

"This is," said our host, "Lord Birkenhead. You've said something about him in your book. What was it?" Lord Birkenhead put his podgy palm into my hand, leaving it to me to exert the customary pressure. My remark about Birkenhead—"To take the Churchills and the Birkenheads seriously is not to know how to be serious"—was not of a nature to be removed from the context with the advantage to the author, and I confined myself to the statement that it had been airy.

"I have not read your book," said Lord Birkenhead, in suave sonorous periods, more suitable to a court of law than to informal conversation, "but I shall certainly take an early opportunity of perusing it; and if what you say is correct I shall take it to heart, and if it is uninformed I shall despise it." During dinner he said that all Jews were sadists and all Bolsheviks Jews, hence the cruelty in Russia. I was saddened by this indifferent reasoning in a Cabinet Minister; my heart sank and I felt I must render him first aid. When I had finished, Birkenhead looked at me cloudily, as if asking: "Who is this youth who dares heckle me?" When, however, I added that I had spent two-thirds of my life in Russia, he said:

"In that case I shall certainly take an early opportunity of re-examining my facts."

After dinner my mistrust of Lord Birkenhead evaporated completely as he began to address himself more and more to me . . . He told how, when he was an athletic young man at Oxford, Oscar Wilde joined them at lunch and indulged in his famous talk, which on this occasion was all—"I will tell you a fairy tale . . ." while the young man, who was later to assist in placing the story-teller in prison, gathered more and more of the bottles around himself. Lord Birkenhead, who, at a later trial, referred to Wilde as "that unhappy child of genius," endeared himself to me by expressing his admiration for the creative literary gift. With unconvincing humility, he deprecated his own "first-class brains," when, in an endeavor to return the compliment, I drew allusion to them. He had, he said, a "certain facility for dealing with a great mass of legal material," but he was completely devoid of the artistic gift. Music meant nothing to him. As a writer, he said, he was nothing but a journalist. I disputed this warmly. I remembered a flattering reference, in a review of a book of his, to a paper on Kitchener; and though I had not read this paper I now defended it as a piece of writing coming very near to what is known as creative writing.

"How nice of you to say so!" exclaimed Lord Birkenhead, with genuine pleasure. "Michael Arlen said the same thing to me, and indeed I myself think that in that essay I have perhaps come nearer to the kind of imaginative writing which, had I but the gift, I would have so willingly pursued as a vocation." After that Lord Birkenhead suggested that if I "did him the honour" of sending him my book he would be "proud" to send me one of his own. He again placed the palm of his hand in mine, on which, however, I this time declined to exert any pressure, and asked me if he could give me a lift in his car.

Disarmed by his unexpected charm and modesty, I at once sent him a copy of "The Polyglots," with an inscription designed to please him. But by the time, a few days later, I met him again, at a large party at the Savoy Hotel, no book of his had found its way to my flat. He sat there, in a state of extreme lassitude, caressing his dog. I reminded him that I had not had his book. He looked up at me. It was obvious that he did not recognize me. His voice was tired and querulous. "*Which* book?" he kept asking. "I've written many books. D'you see that man over there? He is my secretary. Ask him, he'll send you my book. Any book you like. Send it tomorrow. I can't think of these things. I'm a busy man. I'm a Cabinet Minister. I've got to think of all kinds of things. Can't think of books."

Affairs of state must have exhausted his vitality, his eyes were half closed.

His book had ceased to interest me, and his secretary had not begun to. After a while Lord Birkenhead turned his head and saw that I still stood behind him. There was a pause. "Th . . . thank you," he said, "for your book."

What the Chancellor Would Have Said to the Bishop

When Lord Northington, known also as the "swearing chancellor" for often taking the Lord's name in vain, was in his final illness in 1772, he was recommended to avail himself of the services of a certain prelate. "He will never do," said the Chancellor. "I should have to confess that one of my heaviest sins was in having made him bishop."

Practice Makes Perfect

When John Curran was in his last illness, his doctor remarked that he seemed to cough with great difficulty, "That is strange," said the wit, "for I have been practising all night."

Old Habits Die Hard

Lord Tenterden had been strongly advised, some time before his death, not to attend his court; but he replied, "I have public duties to perform; and while it pleases God to preserve my mental faculties, I will perform those duties—physical suffering I can and will bear." A little more than a week before his death, he was told that were he to continue to set the advice of his medical attendants at defiance, it was impossible that he could live, but a little rest and retirement would restore him to comparative health. "I know better," he replied. "My days are numbered; but I will perform my duty to the last."

On his deathbed not long after, he had been sinking the whole night, but generally retained his faculties. Toward morning he became restless and slightly delirious; all at once he sat up in his bed and with a motion of his hand, as if dipping his pen in the inkstand, as he had been accustomed to do on the bench, he said distinctly, "Gentlemen of the jury, you are discharged." He then fell back on his bed and almost immediately expired.

Choice Epitaphs

Here lieth Lawyer Sparges
  That died to save charges.

★ ★ ★

Here lieth one, believe it if you can,
  Who though an attorney was an honest man,
The gates of heaven shall open wide,
  But will be shut against all the tribe beside.

★ ★ ★

Inscription on the grave of Edward Trelawney, barrister, in Pelynt Church, Cornwall:
  Oh! what a bubble, vapour, puff of breath,
  A nest of worms, a lump of pallid earth,
  Is mud-walled man! Before we mount on high
  We cope with change, we wander after day.
  Here lies an honest lawyer, wot you what
  A thing for all the world to wonder at!

★ ★ ★

On Judge Boat (who died in 1723):
 Here lies Judge Boat within a coffin;
 Pray gentlefolks forbear your scoffing.
 A Boat, a judge! Yes; where's the blunder?
 A wooden judge is no such wonder.
 And in his robes you must agree,
 No boat was better deckt than he.
 'Tis needless to describe him fuller;
 In short, he was an able sculler.

★　★　★

On Mr. Smith, a lawyer:
 Here lies Lawyer Smith, and what is something rarish,
 He was born, bred, and hanged in the selfsame parish.

★　★　★

On Mr. Thomas Heming, attorney:
 Weep, widows, orphans; all your late support,
 Himself is summoned to a higher court;
 Living he pleaeded yours, but with this clause,
 That Christ at death should only plead his cause.

★　★　★

On a magistrate who had formerly been a barber:
 Here lies Justice—be this his finest praise:
 He wore the wig which once he made,
 And learnt to shave both ways.

★　★　★

On a lawyer named Tell:
 He lies all the day like a knave;
   He lies all his night-hours away;
 And when dead he will lie in the grave,
   And tell lies till judgment day.

★　★　★

On Mr. Gripe:
> Here lies old Lawyer Gripe,
>> Who never cried "Jam satis!" [Latin: Enough already!]
> 'Twould wake him did he know
>> You read his tombstone gratis.

A Lawyer's Funeral

William O. Bradley, a Kentucky senator in the early part of the century, told of the death of a well-known Louisville lawyer, who had shocked many of his friends by his liberal views on religion. A friend of the deceased who cut short a hunting trip to hurry back to the city to attend the last rites for his colleague, entered the lawyer's home a few minutes after the ceremonies had begun.

"What part of the service is this?" he asked in a whisper of another legal friend who was standing in the crowded hallway.

"I've just come myself," the other replied, "but I believe they've opened for the defense."

BIBLIOGRAPHY OF BOOKS CITED AND CONSULTED

W. Davenport Adams. *Modern Anecdotes*. London: Hamilton, Adams & Co., 1886.

F.W. Ahrens. *From Bench to Bench*. Pietermaritzburg, South Africa: Shuter & Shooter, 1948.

John A. Alford and Dennis P. Seniff. *Literature and Law in the Middle Ages—A Bibliography of Scholarship*. New York: Garland Publishing, 1984.

Stephen Haley Allen. *The Evolution of Government and Laws*. Princeton: Princeton University Press, 1916.

Norwood F. Allman. *Shanghai Lawyer*. New York: Whittlesey House, 1943.

Mary Clemmer Ames. *Ten Years in Washington: Life and Scenes in the National Capital, As a Woman Sees Them*. Cincinnati: Queen City Publishing, 1874.

William Andrews (ed.). *Legal Lore: Curiosities of Law and Lawyers*. London: Self-published, 1897.

Charles R. Ashman. *The Finest Judges Money Can Buy—And Other Forms of Judicial Pollution*. Los Angeles: Nash Publishing, 1973.

Brandt Aymar and Edward Sagarin. *Laws and Trials That Created History*. New York: Crown Publishers, Inc., 1974.

F. Lee Bailey with John Greeya. *For the Defense*. New York: Atheneum, 1975.

F. Lee Bailey with Harvey Aronson. *The Defense Never Rests*. New York: Stein and Day, 1971.

Ernest Barker (ed.). *The Character of England*. Oxford, England: Oxford University Press, 1947.

Sir D. Plunket Barton, Charles Benham & Francis Watt. *The Story of Our Inns of Court*. Boston: Houghton Mifflin, 1928.

W.H. Beable. *Epitaphs: Graveyard Humour & Eulogy*. London: Simkin, Marshall, Hamilton, Kent & Co., 1925.

James M. Beck. *May It Please the Court*. New York: Macmillan, 1930.

István Békés. *A Világ Anekdotakincse*. Budapest, Hungary: Gondolat, 1975.

————. *A Legújabb Magyar Anekdotakincs*. Budapest, Hungary: Gondolat, 1966.

Griffin B. Bell. *Taking Care of the Law*. New York: William Morrow, 1982.

Melvin M. Belli. *Blood Money*. New York: Grosset & Dunlap, 1956.

Melvin M. Belli with Robert Blair Kaiser. *My Life on Trial*. New York: William Morrow, 1976.

Ambrose Bierce. *The Devil's Dictionary*. New York: Albert and Charles Boni, 1911.

L. J. Bigelow. *Bench and Bar: A Complete Digest of the Wit, Humor, Asperities, and Amenities of the Law*. New York: Harper & Brothers, 1867.

Lord Birkenhead (F.E. Smith). *Famous Trials in History*. New York: George H. Doran Co., 1926.

Lord (Norman) Birkett (ed.). *The New Newgate Calendar*. London: The Folio Society, 1960.

Leslie Blackwell. *Of Judges and Justice*. Cape Town, South Africa: Howard Timmins, 1965.

Louis Blom-Cooper (ed.). *The Law as Literature*. London: The Bodley Head, 1961.

Murray Teigh Bloom. *The Trouble With Lawyers*. New York: Simon & Schuster, 1969.

Catherine Drinker Bowen. *Yankee from Olympus*. Boston: Little, Brown, 1944.

A.E. Bowker. *A Lifetime with the Law*. London: W.H. Allen, 1961.

Jacob M. Braude. *Braude's Treasury of Wit and Humor*. Englewood Cliffs, N.J.: Prentice-Hall, 1964.

Judge Jerry Buchmeyer. *et cetera*. Dallas, Texas: Self-published, 1981.

Evelyn Burnaby. *Memories of Famous Trials*. London: Sisey's Ltd., 1907.

Francis X. Busch. *Guilty Or Not Guilty?*. Indianapolis: Bobbs-Merrill, 1952.

————. *In and Out of Court*. Chicago: DePaul University Press, 1942.

Charles Henry Butler. *A Century at the Bar of the Supreme Court of the United States*. New York: G.P. Putnam's Sons, 1942.

Julia Clara Byrne. *Curiosities of the Search-Room: A Collection of Serious and Whimsical Wills*. London: Chapman and Hall, 1880.

Robert Graham Caldwell. *Red Hannah: Delaware's Whipping Post*. Philadelphia: University of Pennsylvania Press, 1947.

Lord John Campbell. *Lives of the Lord Chancellors and Keepers of the Great Seal of England, from the Earliest Times Till the Reign of King George IV*. London: John Murray, 1845-1869.

————. *Shakespeare's Legal Acquirements*. London: John Murray, 1859.

Bennett Cerf. *Laughing Stock*. New York: Grosset and Dunlap, 1945.

————. *Laughter Incorporated*. Garden City, N.Y.: Garden City Books, 1950.

G.J. Clark. *Great Sayings by Great Lawyers*. Kansas City, Missouri: Vernon Law Book, Co., 1926.

G. Polk Cline. *Polk Cline's Book, By the Old Sage of Arkansaw*. Larned, Kansas: Self-published, 1910.

Alfred Cohn and John Chisholm. *"Take the Witness."* Garden City, New York: Garden City Publishing, 1934.

Concerning Solicitors, By One of Them. London: Chatto & Windus, 1920.

The Court of Session Garland. Edinburgh: Thomas G. Stevenson, 1839.

Charles Cowley. *Famous Divorces of All Ages*. Lowell, Mass., 1878.

Harold R. Danforth and James D. Horan. *The D.A.'s Man*. New York: Crown Publishers, 1957.

Justice Darling. *Scintillae Juris*. London: Stevens & Haynes, 1914.

Clarence Darrow. *The Story of My Life*. New York: Charles Scribner's Sons, 1932.

William H. Davenport (ed.). *Voices in Court: A Treasury of the Bench, the Bar and the Courtroom*. New York: Macmillan, 1958.

John De Morgan. *In Lighter Vein*. San Francisco: Paul Elder, 1907.

Chauncey M. Depew. *My Memories of Eighty Years*. New York: Scribner's, 1922.

Charles S. Desmond. *Sharp Quillets of the Law*. Buffalo, New York: Dennis & Co., 1949.

William Jardine Dobie. *Plain Tales from the Courts*. Edinburgh: Green & Sons, 1957.

William O. Douglas. *Strange Lands and Friendly People*. New York: Harper & Brothers, 1951.

Allison Dunham and Philip B. Kurland (eds.). *Mr. Justice: Biographical Studies of Twelve Supreme Court Justices*. Chicago: University of Chicago Press, 1964.

Alice Morse Earle. *Curious Punishments of Bygone Days.* Chicago: Herbert S. Stone & Co., 1896.

J.P. Eddy. *Scarlet and Ermine: Famous Trials As I Saw Them.* London: William Kimber, 1960.

Charles Edwards. *Pleasantries about Courts and Lawyers of the State of New York.* New York, 1867.

Eldon, Lord [John Scott]. *Lord Eldon's Anecdote Book.* London: Stevens & Sons Limited, 1960.

J.W. Ehrlich. *A Life in My Hands.* New York: G.P. Putnam's Sons, 1965.

John B. Ellis. *The Sights and Secrets of the National Capital.* Chicago: Jones, Junkin, 1869.

Morris L. Ernst. *A Love Affair with the Law.* New York: Macmillan, 1968.

Morris L. Ernst and Alexander Lindey. *Hold Your Tongue! Adventures in Libel and Slander.* New York: William Morrow, 1932.

Sam J. Ervin, Jr. *Humor of a Country Lawyer.* Chapel Hill, N.C.: University of North Carolina Press, 1983.

Henry Edwin Fenn. *Thirty-five Years in the Divorce Court.* Boston: Little, Brown, 1911.

Ross Firestone (ed.). *Getting Busted: Personal Experiences of Arrest, Trial and Prison.* New York: Douglas Book Corp., 1970.

J.A. Foote. *"Pie-Powder"—Being Dust from the Law Courts, Collected and Recollected on the Western Circuit, by a Circuit Tramp.* London: John Murray, 1911.

William Forsyth. *Hortensius The Advocate.* Jersey City, N.J.: Frederick D. Linn & Co., 1881.

Edward Foss. *Biographia Juridica: A Biographical Dictionary of the Judges of England from the Conquest to the Present Time.* London: John Murray, 1870.

Richard Fountain. *The Wit of the Wig.* London: Leslie Frewin, 1968.

Charles Franklin. *World Famous Trials.* New York: Taplinger Publishing Company, 1966.

The French Anas. London, 1805.

Martin Garbus. *Ready for the Defense.* New York: Farrar, Straus & Giroux, 1971.

Charles Garry and Art Goldberg. *Streetfighter in the Courtroom—The People's Advocate.* New York: E.P. Dutton, 1977.

Daniel George. *A Book of Anecdotes.* England: Hulton Press, 1957.

William Gerhardi. *Memoirs of a Polyglot.* New York: Alfred A. Knopf, 1931.

Michael Gilbert (ed.). *The Oxford Book of Legal Anecdotes.* Oxford, England: Oxford University Press, 1986.

Francis Leo Golden. *Laughter is Legal.* New York: Frederick Fell, 1950.

Milton S. Gould. *The Witness Who Spoke with God and Other Tales from the Courthouse.* New York: Viking, 1979.

Joseph C. Goulden. *The Benchwarmers: The Private World of the Powerful Federal Judges.* New York: Weybright & Talley, 1974.

————. *The Million Dollar Lawyers.* New York: G.P. Putnam's Sons, 1978.

Milton D. Green. *It's Legal to Laugh.* New York: Vantage Press, 1984.

Leonard Gribble. *Famous Judges and Their Trials.* London: John Long, 1957.

Arthur Griffiths. *Mysteries of Police and Crime.* London: Cassell & Co., n.d.

John H. Gwathmey. *Legends of Virginia Courthouses.* Richmond, Virginia: The Dietz Printing Company, 1934.

Hans Habe. *Gentlemen of the Jury* (translated by Frances Hogarth-Gaute). London: George G. Harrap, 1967.

Elizabeth Hazelton Haight. *The Roman Use of Anecdotes in Cicero, Livy & the Satirists.* New York: Longmans, Green & Co., 1940.

Albert Halper (ed.). *The Chicago Crime Book.* Cleveland, Ohio: The World Publishing Company, 1967.

Elizabeth Derring Hanscom. *The Friendly Craft: A Collection of American Letters.* New York: Macmillan, 1908.

William H. Harbaugh. *Lawyer's Lawyer: The Life of John W. Davis.* New York: Oxford University Press, 1973.

Mary Ann Harrell. *Equal Justice under the Law: The Supreme Court in American Life.* Washington, D.C.: The Foundation of the Federal Bar Association and the National Geographic Society, 1975.

Margaret Case Harriman. *Take Them Up Tenderly: A Collection of Profiles.* New York: Alfred A. Knopf, 1944.

Arthur M. Harris. *Letters to a Young Lawyer.* St. Paul, Minnesota: West Publishing Company, 1926.

Richard Harris (ed.). *The Reminiscences of Sir Henry Hawkins (Baron Brampton).* London: Thomas Nelson, 1905.

Dennis Hartman. *Jest for Lawyers.* Los Angeles: Mercury Press, n.d.

Peter Harvey. *Reminiscences and Anecdotes of Daniel Webster.* Boston: Little, Brown, 1877.

Margaret Hasluck. *The Unwritten Law in Albania.* Cambridge, England: Cambridge University Press, 1954.

Patrick Hastings. *Cases in Court.* London: William Heinemann, 1949.

E.S.P. Haynes. *A Lawyer's Notebook.* London: Martin Secker, 1933.

————. *The Lawyer: A Conversation Piece.* London: Eyre & Spottiswoode, 1951.

Jerry L. Hayes. *The Benchbook: Anecdotes from the Lighter Side of the Law.* Kent, Ohio: Kent State University Press, 1987.

Franklin Fiske Heard. *Curiosities of the Law Reporters.* Boston: Lee and Shepard, 1871.

———. *Oddities of the Law.* Boston: Soule and Bugbee, 1881.

Joseph Heighton. *Legal Life and Humor.* London: Hodder and Stoughton, n.d.

Robert Hendrickson. *The Facts on File Encyclopedia of Word and Phrase Origin.* New York: Facts On File, 1987.

Emanuel Hertz (ed.). *Lincoln Talks: A Biography in Anecdote.* New York: Viking Press, 1939.

Reginald L. Hine. *Confessions of an Un-Common Attorney.* London: J.M. Dent & Sons, 1945.

Paul Hoffman. *Lions of the Eighties: The Inside Story of the Powerhouse Law Firms.* Garden City, New York: Doubleday, 1982.

Dick Hyman. *It's The Law.* Garden City, N.Y.: Doubleday, Doran and Co., 1936.

———. *Cockeyed Americana.* Brattleboro, Vermont: The Stephen Greene Press, 1972.

Leigh H. Irvine. *The Follies of the Courts.* Los Angeles: The Times Mirror Press, 1925.

Donald Dale Jackson. *Judges: An Inside View of the Agonies and Excesses of an American Elite.* New York: Atheneum, 1974.

Stanley Jackson. *Laughter at Law.* London: Arthur Barker, 1961.

John Cordy Jeaffreson. *A Book About Lawyers.* London: Hurst and Blackett, 1867.

———. *Pleasantries of English Courts and Lawyers.* Jersey City: Frederick D. Linn & Company, n.d.

Rodney R. Jones, Charles M. Sevila and Gerald F. Uelmen. *Disorderly Conduct: Verbatim Excerpts from Actual Court Cases.* New York: W. W. Norton, 1987.

William Jones. *Finger-Ring Lore: Historical, Legendary, Anecdotal.* London: Chatto & Windus, 1877.

Alfred D. Kelly, *Legalaffs.* Philadelphia: Dorrance & Co., 1972.

Robert F. Kennedy, Jr. *Judge Frank M. Johnson, Jr.—A Biography.* New York: Putnam, 1978.

William Kent. *London in the News Through Three Centuries.* London: Staples Press, 1954.

Austin H. Kerin. *Yankee in Court; Humorous Tales from Vermont Courtrooms.* Battleboro, Vermont: Stephen Daye Press, 1937.

Charles Kingston. *Enemies of Society*. London: Stanley Paul, 1927.

William M. Kunstler. *The Case for Courage*. New York: William Morrow, 1962.

Jacob Larwood. *Humour of the Law: Forensic Anecdotes*. London: Chatto & Windus, 1903.

Emanuel H. Lavine. *Stand and Deliver—The Story of "Crooked" New York*. London: Routledge & Sons, 1931.

Thomas Leaming. *A Philadelphia Lawyer in the London Courts*. New York: Henry Holt, 1911.

George P. LeBrun (told to Edward D. Radin.) *It's Time to Tell*. New York: William Morrow, 1962.

Robert Lefcourt (ed.). *Law Against the People*. New York: Random House, 1971.

Robert Leibowitz. *The Defender*. Englewood Cliffs, New Jersey: Prentice-Hall, 1981.

Beryl Harold Levy. *Corporation Lawyer . . . Saint or Sinner*. Philadelphia: Chilton Company, 1961.

Anthony Lewis. *Gideon's Trumpet*. New York: Vintage Books, 1966.

John Livingston (ed.). *Biographical Sketches of Eminent American Lawyers*. New York: The Monthly Law Magazine, 1852.

Sol L. Long. *Recollections of a Country Lawyer*. Winfield, Kansas: Courier Printing Co., 1906.

Everett Lloyd. *Law West of the Pecos: The Story of Judge Roy Bean*. San Antonio, Texas: The Naylor Company, 1936.

Dudley Cammett Lunt. *The Road to the Law*. New York: Whittlesey House, 1932.

Peter V. Macdonald. *Court Jesters*. Toronto: Methuen, 1985.

———. *More Court Jesters*. Toronto: Methuen, 1987.

The Majesty of the Law—A Book of Legal Stories. London: Simpkin, Marshall, Hamilton, Kent & Co., n.d.

Marlene Adler Marks. *The Suing of America*. New York: Seaview Books, 1981.

R.E.L. Masters and Eduard Lea. *Perverse Crimes in History*. New York: The Julian Press, n.d.

John G. May, Jr. *Courtroom Kicktales*. Charlottesville, Virginia: The Michie Company, 1964.

James D. McCabe, Jr. *Great Fortunes and How They Were Made*. Philadelphia: George Maclean, 1871.

Hugh McCulloch. *Men and Measures of Half a Century*. New York, 1881.

Sir Robert E. Megarry, Q.C. *Miscellany-at-Law. A Diversion for Lawyers and Others*. London: Stevens & Sons, 1955.

Oscar A. Mendelsohn. *Liars and Letter Anonymous: The Case Book of an Expert Witness*. Melbourne: Lansdowne Press, 1961.

Cheryl Moch and Vincent Varga. *Deals*. New York: Ballantine Books, 1984.

Robert W. Morgan (ed.). *Twenty-four Dramatic Cases of the International Academy of Trial Lawyers*. Hicksville, N.Y.: Exposition Press, 1975.

Clarence Morris. *How Lawyers Think*. Cambridge, Mass.: Harvard University Press, 1937.

Sir Harold Morris. *The Barrister*. London: Geoffrey Bles, 1930.

Richard B. Morris. *Fair Trial—Fourteen Who Stood Accused*. New York: Alfred A. Knopf, 1952.

Bill Mortlock. *Lawyer, Heal Thyself!*. New York: Macmillan, 1960.

George A. Morton and D. Macleod Malloch. *Law and Laughter*. London & Edinburgh: T.N. Foulis, 1914.

Bruce Allen Murphy. *Brandeis/Frankfurter Connection: The Secret Political Activities of Two Supreme Court Justices*. New York: Oxford University Press, 1982.

James M. Murphy. *Laws, Courts, and Lawyers Through the Years in Arizona*. Tucson, Arizona: University of Arizona Press, 1970.

Ralph Nader and Mark Green (eds.). *Verdicts on Lawyers*. New York: Thomas Y. Crowell, 1976.

Robina Napier (ed.). *Johnsoniana: Anecdotes of the Late Samuel Johnson, LL.D.* London: George Bell, 1892.

Rabbi S.M. Neches. *As It Was Told To Me: A Hundred Little Stories of the Old Rabbis*. Los Angeles: Privately Printed, 1926.

Jack Newfield. *Cruel and Unusual Justice*. New York: Holt, Rinehart and Winston, 1974.

H. Chance Newton. *Crime and the Drama, or Dark Deeds Dramatized*. Port Washington, N.Y.: Kennikat Press, 1970 (reprint of 1927).

Louis Nizer. *My Life in Court*. Garden City, New York: Doubleday, 1961.

———. *Reflections Without Mirrors*. New York: Doubleday, 1978.

John Wesley Noble and Bernard Auerbach. *Never Plead Guilty: The Story of Jake Ehrlich*. New York: Farrar, Straus and Cudahy, 1955.

John T. Noonan, Jr. *Persons & Masks of the Law*. New York: Farrar, Straus and Giroux, 1976.

Obiter Dictum. Concord, N.H.: The Franklin Pierce Law Center, 1975-6.

Richard O'Connor. *Courtroom Warrior: The Combative Career of William Travers Jerome*. Boston: Little, Brown, 1963.

Bernard O'Donnell. *Cavalcade of Justice*. London: Clerke & Cockeran, 1951.

Terrys T. Olender. *My Life in Crime*. Los Angeles: Holloway House, 1966.

F.A. Paley. *Greek Wit*. London: George Bell & Sons, 1881.

Bellamy Partridge. *Country Lawyer*. New York: Grosset & Dunlap, 1939.

Drew Pearson and Robert S. Allen. *The Nine Old Men*. Garden City, New York: Doubleday, Doran & Co., 1936.

Hesketh Pearson. *Lives of the Wits*. New York: Harper & Row, 1962.

A. Laurence Polak. *Legal Fictions*. London: Stevens & Sons, 1945.

————. *Second Thoughts*. London: Stevens & Sons, 1949.

Benjamin Perley Poore. *Perley's Reminiscences of Sixty Years in the National Metropolis*. Philadelphia: Hubbard Brothers, 1886.

Sholto & Reuben Percy. *The Percy Anecdotes*. London: 1820-3.

Archer Polson. *Law and Lawyers; or Sketches and Illustrations of Legal History and Biography*. London, 1840.

John Proffatt. *The Curiosities and Law of Wills*. San Francisco: Sumner Whitney & Co., 1877.

William L. Prosser. *The Judicial Humorist: A Collection of Judicial Opinions and Other Frivolities*. Boston: Little, Brown, 1952.

David Laing Purves. *Law and Lawyers: Curious Facts and Characteristic Sketches*. Philadelphia: J.B. Lippincott, n.d.

Josiah Quincy. *Figures of the Past*. Boston: Little, Brown, 1911.

Frederic Reddall. *The Wit and Humor of the American Bar*. Philadelphia: Jacobs, 1907.

William H. Rehnquist. *The Supreme Court: How It Was, How It Is*. New York: William Morrow, 1987.

John L. Respess, Jr. *Wit and Wisdom of Georgia Law*. Atlanta, Georgia: Self-published, 1952.

Quentin Reynolds. *Courtroom: The Story of Samuel S. Liebowitz*. New York: Farrar, Straus and Young, 1950.

Edward Robey. *The Jester and the Court*. London: William Kimber, 1976.

Richard H. Rovere. *Howe and Hummel: Criminal Lawyers*. New York: Farrar, Straus and Company, 1946.

Maurice Rubin. *Within the Law*. New York: Pegasus Company, n.d.

A.L. Sainer (ed.). *The Judge Chuckles*. New York: Substantive & Adjective Law Publishers, 1935.

Adela Rogers St. Johns. *Final Verdict*. Garden City, New York, Doubleday, 1962.

Salad for the Social. New York: De Witt & Davenport, 1856.

Alexander L. Schlosser. *"Lawyers Must Eat."* New York: The Vanguard Press, 1933.

Philip G. Schrag. *Counsel for the Deceived.* New York: Pantheon, 1972.

Sir Walter Scott. *The Journal of Sir Walter Scott.* New York: Harper & Brothers, 1890.

Judge Ray Scruggs. *Five Hundred Laughs.* Houston, Texas: Self-published, 1927.

William Seagle. *There Ought to be a Law—A Collection of Lunatic Legislation.* New York: The Macaulay Company, 1933.

Joseph Lacy Seawell. *Law Tales for Laymen.* Raleigh, N.C.: Alfred Williams & Co., 1925.

Joel Seligman. *The High Citadel: The Influence of the Harvard Law School.* Boston: Houghton Mifflin, 1978.

Howard T. Senzel. *Cases: A Courthouse Chronicle of Crime and Wit.* New York: The Viking Press, 1982.

Barbara Seuling. *You Can't Eat Peanuts in Church and Other Little-Known Laws.* Garden City, New York: Doubleday, 1976.

Harry C. Shriver. *What Gusto: Stories and Anecdotes About Justice Oliver Wendell Holmes.* Potomac, Maryland: The Fox Hills Press, 1970.

Ralph Slovenko. *Tragicomedy in Court Opinions.* Baton Rouge, Louisiana: Claitor's Publishing Division, 1973.

Betsy Covington Smith: *Breakthrough: Women in Law.* New York: Walker & Company, 1984.

Judge Gerald Sparrow. *The Great Defamers.* London: John Long, 1970.

Gerry Spence and Anthony Polk. *Gerry Spence Gunning for Justice.* Garden City, New York: Doubleday, 1982.

Louis Stark. *A Case That Rocked the World* (from *We Saw It Happen—by Thirteen Correspondents of the New York Times*). Cleveland: World Publishing, 1941.

Aron Steuer. *Aesop in the Courts.* New York: Law-Arts Publishers, 1971.

Janet Stevenson. *The Undiminished Man: A Political Biography of Robert Walker Kenny.* Novato, California: Chandler & Sharp, 1980.

George Stimpson. *A Book About American History.* New York: Harper and Brothers, 1950.

Strictures on the Lives and Characters of the Most Eminent Lawyers of the Present Day. London, 1790.

György Szabó (ed.). *Középkori Anekdoták.* Bukarest, Romania: Kriterion Kiadó, 1976.

C.K. Thompson. *Yes, Your Honour! Sidelights of the Australian Law Courts.* Sidney: Angus and Robertson, 1947.

John Timbs. *A Century of Anecdote; from 1760 to 1860.* London, 1864.

———. *English Eccentrics and Eccentricities.* London: Chatto & Windus, 1877.

————. *The Romance of London*. London: Frederick Warne, n.d.

————. *Things Not Generally Known, Familiarly Explained*. London, 1857.

Arthur Train. *Courts, Criminals and the Camorra*. New York: Charles Scribner's Sons, 1912.

————. *My Day in Court*. New York: Charles Scribner's Sons, 1939.

Robert Traver. *The Jealous Mistress*. Boston: Little, Brown, 1967.

Robertson Trowbridge. *Forty-Eight Years: Anecdotes and other Oddments Collected from Original Sources, 1884-1932*. New York: Privately printed, 1937.

Scott Turow. *One L*. New York: G.P. Putnam's Sons, 1977.

Judge Joseph A. Wapner. *View from the Bench*. New York: Simon & Schuster, 1987.

Arthur Weinberg (ed.). *Attorney for the Damned*. New York: Simon & Schuster, 1957.

Walter White. *Rope & Faggot: A Biography of Judge Lynch*. New York: Alfred A. Knopf. 1929.

Les Whitten. *F. Lee Bailey*. New York: Avon Books, 1971.

Paul B. Wice. *Criminal Lawyers—An Endangered Species*. Beverly Hills, California: Sage Publications, 1978.

George C. Williamson. *Curious Survivals: Habits and Customs of the Past That Still Live in the Present*. London: Herbert Jenkins, 1925.

Judge Minter L. Wilson. *Courtroom Drama: Stories of Exciting Jury Trials*. Philadelphia: Dorrance and Company, 1962.

Seymour Wishman. *Confessions of a Criminal Lawyer*. New York: Times Books, 1981.

Bob Woodward & Scott Armstrong. *The Brethren: Inside the Supreme Court*. New York: Simon & Schuster, 1979.

James Yaffe. *So Sue Me! The Story of a Community Court*. New York: The Saturday Review Press, 1972.

INDEX

PERMISSIONS

Please note that every reasonable effort has been made to secure permission to quote from works not in the public domain. If there has been an oversight, every effort will be made to correct it in subsequent editions of this book. The author and publisher gratefully acknowledge permission to quote excerpts granted by the copyright holders of the following works:

A Lifetime With the Law by A.E. Bowker. Reprinted with permission of W.H. Allen, Publishers; copyright © by A.E. Bowker.

Guilty or Not Guilty by Francis X. Busch. Reprinted with permission of Macmillan Publishing Company; copyright © 1952 by Francis X. Busch. Copyright renewed 1980.

A Century at the Bar of the Supreme Court of the United States by Charles Henry Butler. Copyright © 1942, reprinted by permission of the Putnam Publishing Group.

The Story of My Life by Clarence Darrow. Copyright © 1932 by Charles Scribner's Sons; copyright © 1960 by Mary D. Simonson, Jessie D. Lyon and Blanche D. Chase. Reprinted with permission of Charles Scribner's Sons, an imprint of Macmillan Publishing Company.

Strange Lands and Friendly People by William O. Douglas. Copyright © 1951 by William O. Douglas. Reprinted by permission of Harper & Row, Publishers, Inc.

Humor of a Country Lawyer, by Sam J. Ervin, Jr. © 1983 The University of North Carolina Press. Reprinted by permission.

The Witness Who Spoke With God and Other Tales from the Courthouse by Milton S. Gould. Copyright © 1979 by Milton S. Gould. Reprinted by permission of Viking Penguin, Inc.

It's Legal To Laugh; copyright © 1984 by Milton D. Green and reprinted by his kind permission.

Lawyer's Lawyer: The Life of John W. Davis by William H. Harbaugh. Reprinted by permission of author.

Take Them Up Tenderly by Margaret Case Harriman. Copyright © 1944 by Margaret Case Harriman. Reprinted by permission of Alfred A. Knopf, Inc., a division of Random House, Inc.

Lawyer's Notebook by E.S.P. Haynes. Reprinted by permission of Martin Secker & Warburg Ltd.

Judges: An Inside View of the Agonies and Excesses of an American Elite by Donald Dale Jackson. Reprinted with permission of Atheneum Publishers, an imprint of Macmillan Publishing Company. Copyright © 1974 by Donald Dale Jackson.